The Retreat of Democracy

The Retreat of Democracy
and Other Itinerant Essays
on Globalization, Economics,
and India

KAUSHIK BASU

ANTHEM PRESS
LONDON · NEW YORK · DELHI

Anthem Press
An imprint of Wimbledon Publishing Company
www.anthempress.com

This edition first published in UK and USA 2010
by ANTHEM PRESS
75-76 Blackfriars Road, London SE1 8HA, UK
or PO Box 9779, London SW19 7ZG, UK
and
244 Madison Ave. #116, New York, NY 10016, USA

First published in India by Permanent Black 2007

British Library Cataloguing in Publication Data
A catalogue record for this book is available from the British Library.

Library of Congress Cataloging in Publication Data
A catalog record for this book has been requested.

ISBN-13: 978 1 84331 865 1 (Hbk)
ISBN-10: 1 84331 865 2 (Hbk)

ISBN-13: 978 1 84331 827 9 (Pbk)
ISBN-10: 1 84331 827 X (Pbk)

ISBN-13: 978 1 84331 887 3 (eBook)
ISBN-10: 1 84331 887 3 (eBook)

1 3 5 7 9 10 8 6 4 2

To
AMARTYA SEN

Contents

Introduction

A philosopher I admire greatly is Pyrrho of Elis, *c.* 360–270 BC, arguably the father of scepticism. Can we ever completely trust what we perceive? Since all that we perceive and learn we do through *our* own senses, is it not an act of foolish arrogance to have so much confidence in the senses? A good philosopher must, therefore, always entertain doubt: so argued Pyrrho. And he tried to live by his philosophy. Diogenes Laertius, the third-century writer famous for having written the world's first scissors-and-paste textbook, records how, when a ship in which Pyrrho was travelling was caught in a big storm, only two creatures aboard were completely at peace—a pig and Pyrrho. Presumably, the former saw no reason to expect calamity from the fact of a storm-tossed ship. Indeed, Diogenes Laertius suggests, Pyrrho may even have been a bit envious of the pig, for the pig was not just calm: unlike Pyrrho, it continued to eat.

Given his scepticism, Pyrrho wrote nothing during his ninety long years, for he deemed nothing fit to be immortalized by ink. His philosophy was spread entirely through what he spoke. It is believed that he went to India with Alexander's army and there met some Indian sages who not only believed in writing nothing but had taken a vow against speaking too. Pyrrho came back chastened by the realization that there were others ahead of him in the practice of scepticism.

I begin with Pyrrho because he creates a dilemma for me. My admiration for him and instinctive sympathy for scepticism on the one hand, and on the other my wanton violation of his dictum of not writing (let alone the Indian gymnosophists' dictum of not writing and not speaking and—in some more punishing cases—combining these with not wearing clothes), may seem to be in need of some reconciling. Am I being untrue to myself?

I have now become convinced that I am not. A mistake that Pyrrho made was not to be sceptical about scepticism. Secondly, scepticism does not really lead to any prescription for how one lives one's life. It is as compatible with the vow of silence as with a lifelong commitment to prolixity. Scepticism is simply a propensity to entertain doubt. It also means resisting (if resist you have to) the belief that life has a fundamental meaning and is a journey *towards* something.

Contrary to what some may think, this, far from being a disquieting philosophy of life, is rather a comforting one. My own view is best summed up not by a philosopher or an intellectual but by Richard Avedon, the famous fashion photographer. In a television interview a few years before his death he told his interviewer, Charlie Rose, that he believed life to be ultimately meaningless, a journey towards dust; and, when asked if such a belief did not make him pessimistic, he said, on the contrary, it made him an optimist: it freed him to pursue what his heart desired.

For me, writing has been a form of hedonism. Where scepticism comes in is in the fact that, underlying much of my writing, especially the opinion pieces, there is always a thread of doubt, a nagging awareness that things may not be as I say they are, or as they seem to appear. Often, these doubts have to remain unwritten, for one cannot clutter one's claims with provisos and burden one's reader with the tedium of too many cons. Moreover, I seem to recall Galbraith offering this sage advice somewhere: when a reporter asks you what you think about this year's budget or an editor asks you to write about the month's policy declarations, it is a good idea not to say that you have no opinion because if you do they will not come back next year or next month— when you may have something you desperately want to say. Maybe this fear has made me more diligent as a columnist than I might have been. The advantage of pulling together one's writings is that one can use hindsight to sift through and select what one is willing to stand by, despite the passage of time and the accumulation of knowledge and, even more, cynicism.

This book is a selection of my popular writings from the late 1990s to 2005. What binds it is more than chronology. In the mid 1980s and early 1990s, living and writing in India, a recurring motif in my journalistic output was to urge ordinary citizens and policy-makers to recognize that the market was a critical vehicle for economic progress. I believed then, as I do now, that the ultimate objective of policy-making should be the progress and well being of the poorest and the most disadvantaged in society. But whatever our ultimate objective—whether it be what I recommend, or unfettered capitalism, or totalitarian plunder—to ignore the laws of the market and the role of individual incentives is to court failure. The progressive policy-maker, who may share my ultimate objective, often goes wrong because of an erroneous belief that to recognize the power and relevance of the market is to abandon the objective of helping the poor and the dispossessed. So I argued then.

By the 1990s the focus of my public writing had changed, and for more than one reason. In 1994 I moved to Cornell University, and, though I typically spent a quarter of each year in India, much of my writing over the last seven or eight years has been done from the USA. Also, during this period I was writing mainly for *India Today*, the newspaper *Business Standard* and *BBC News Online* for which I currently write a monthly column. Not surprisingly, much of my interest had shifted to issues of globalization, global democracy, and international economic policies. Hence the preponderance of articles on these subjects in the present collection.

Moreover, by the early 1990s India began a series of much-needed market reforms. So the need to educate the policy-maker about the importance of market-oriented reform had diminished (though it had by no means gone to zero. We must never underestimate the cussedness of politicians). By the late 1990s the risk had moved to the other side— to forgetting that market reforms are important but only as an *instrument*. A good society's ultimate aim must be to improve the living standard of the worst-off people in society. The market has to be used towards this end.

Over the last few years, and before the Indian election of May

2005, when the BJP-led government looked invincible, I wrote a few pieces saying that the time to celebrate 'India Shining' had not yet come, because, while the economy as a whole was growing fast (and the importance of this is not to be dismissed), not enough was trickling down to the poorest sections. Though I would not have predicted the election outcome—victory for the Congress and its allies—I felt vindicated when the government fell and political pundits assured us that the 'India Shining' slogan had backfired for the BJP.

But I make too much of the utilitarian purpose of my popular writing. There are many essays, especially in the last part, of pure description and reportage. Some of my own favourites are the descriptions of bureaucracy. To an economist a useful essay is one that comes loaded with theorems, regressions, and policy prescriptions. But I have learned much about bureaucracies from Kafka's surreal descriptions and intuitive grasp of how an organization can transcend the individuals who comprise it and come to acquire a life and meaning of its own. I like to believe that the purely descriptive essays, even their frivolity, possess an underlying seriousness of purpose and can enhance some of our understandings, or make us realize that to blame the individuals within a faltering system may not be a valid starting point.

In putting together this collection I have drawn from my journalistic works published in *India Today, Business Standard, BBC News Online,* Kolkata's *Telegraph*, and *The Times of India.* But I have also included some of my longer and more academic papers from *Scientific American, Challenge, The Little Magazine, Economic and Political Weekly,* and *Journal of Economic Literature.* A footnote at the start of each essay records the original place of its publication, and I thank the many editors with whom I have worked over the years for the opportunity to make myself heard.

In preparing this manuscript I have tried not to wield the pen or—to sound more contemporary—resort to the keyboard more than absolutely necessary. I have made a few minor corrections and my editor has, off and on, made the sorts of changes that make editors feel gainfully employed. In collating some essays that were written at different times for different outlets into a single chapter I too have made minor alterations, adding and deleting sentences to smoothen the merger. I have resisted the urge to make modifications by using the advantage of hindsight. This has not always been easy, given both the academic's urge to be seen as a person of perspicacity and the ease with which such perspicacity can be planted in such a collection. I have resisted such changes because an important purpose of a book like this is to record the reflections and thoughts of the times, even if they do not do much good for the author's reputation.

The task of putting together this collection began well over four years ago, when I was at Harvard, on leave from Cornell. One of the courses that I taught was on the contemporary Indian economy. This is a sub-ject on which I have worked, written, conferred, and given special lec-tures but never before offered a full course. It was hard work, but the lectures jelled with some of the work that I was doing on this book and essays I was writing for *BBC News Online*. The other course I taught, Social Choice Theory and Welfare Economics, was exciting because I was co-teaching it with Amartya Sen. This is the field of work for which he received the Nobel Prize. I had learned this subject from him in the mid-1970s, when I was a student at the London School of Eco-nomics. Later, I did my PhD under his supervision. It was therefore a surreal and disorienting experience to find myself on the 'wrong side' of the classroom with him. It has been exhilarating for me to be able to interact with Amartya Sen over so many years. I am grateful to him for the mentoring, intellectual stimulus, and generosity of advice on a variety of matters. It is impossible to repay this debt; but I have decided, despite the inadequacy of it, to dedicate this book to him.

While I have worked on this book, with stops and starts, over three semesters, I have in fact written these essays over the last eleven years. My greatest debt is to Cornell University's stimulating research atmosphere and excellent administrative organization which gave me intellectual impetus and freed me from mundane office responsibi-lities—the two essential ingredients for contemplation and writing. I have had the good fortune of having some of the finest students work-ing with me; and talking and exchanging ideas with them have always been a source of inspiration. I should record my thanks, in particular, to my research and teaching assistants over the last two years—Amanda Felkey, Gayatri Koolwal, Hyejin Ku, Patrick Nolen, Young-Ro Yoon, and Homa Zarghamee at Cornell; and Omar Robles and Eyal Dvir at Harvard. I am grateful also to Paulette Carlisle and Rebecca Vliet for excellent secretarial support and for taking a lot of departmental work out of my hands.

These essays, written and published in many different places, would have attracted dust and disintegrated over time had they not been gathered into a book. Eight years ago I met, for the first time, Mr Narayana Murthy in his Infosys office in Bangalore. As a key figure behind India's software take-off, he must be one of the busiest persons in India's booming information technology sector. I was therefore pleas-antly surprised when one of the first things he said was that he regularly read my *India Today* essays, and he urged that I pull these together to make them of some influence among policy-makers and corporate leaders.

Organizing a book of this kind can pose perplexing problems. The choice of the opening essay was easily resolved. The essay, 'Elé Belé', which first appeared in *Business Standard* and was later posted on the website of *Project Syndicate*, generated a huge response. It was translated into a large number of languages—twenty, maybe twenty-five, and reprinted around the world. I like to believe it struck a chord. Most people—from heads of states to distinguished academics to manual workers—have, some time or the other, had the experience of feeling marginalized and inconsequential. 'Elé Belé' is a reminder of how democracy can be subverted by such a process.

In selecting the essays and organizing them I have been lucky to have had exceptionally cerebral advice from Rukun Advani. He helped me not just with linguistic tips but plenty of suggestions on what to merge with what, where to place an essay, and the occasional nudge to leave out a piece that I liked and include something that I may have discarded.

Finally I must record the help that I have received at every stage from the clan—Alaka Basu, Karna Basu, and Diksha Basu. Alaka read the entire manuscript and commented extensively on it. It seems only a few years ago that the best support that I could get from Karna and Diksha was for them not to try to help when I worked. It was a pleasure therefore to see them read parts of the book and mark up the manuscript with suggestions.

As waiters in American restaurants say, having laid the food out on the table and violating the rules of transitivity, 'Enjoy'.

PART I

Democracy
and Globalization

1

Elé Belé: The Subversion of Democracy*

In Calcutta, when as children we played games and some younger kid came along and insisted on joining in, one way of handling the situation was to let the new kid play but only after whispering into one another's ears the words *elé belé*. An *elé belé* is a player who thinks he is participating but who is in truth merely being allowed to go through the motions of participation. Apart from him, everybody playing knows that he is not to be taken seriously. A goal scored by him is not a real goal.

When I was a child growing up in Calcutta, mastering the (admittedly cruel) art of *elé belé* was very important. When that nagging kid arrived, accompanied by a doting mother, we could by a mere glance convey to one another that the new kid would be an *elé belé*. What we do not always realize is how much of the adult world, especially nowadays when 'participatory democracy' is the rage, continues to use this technique of *elé belé*. If we think hard enough, we can all recall collective decision-making situations—a selection committee, a committee for drafting rules—where some committee members were *elé belés*. And though we may not have been aware, there have for sure been situations where we ourselves were the *elé belés*.

International organizations, officially committed to involving all nations in their decision-making, are often run by a small group of

*First published in *Business Standard*, 26 March 2003.

powerful nations, while others merely go through the motions of parti-cipation. It has been pointed out that the WTO, which runs on the principle of 'one country one vote', actually has its agenda fixed behind the stage by a small group of nations, a phenomenon reminiscent of something staged that has come to be known as the 'green room effect'.

It is nowadays the done thing for international organizations pub-lishing a report or a manuscript to involve all the 'stakeholders' and to reflect their opinions. The evolving report is usually put on a website and suggestions are invited from one and all—NGOs, trade unions, and civil society. This develops a sense of participation and has the ad-vantage of placing no additional burden on the international organiza-tion involved. As a friend of mine, seasoned in such matters, tells me, the key to a good report is to finally ignore all the comments received and to write up the report just as you want with no websites and no participation.

Political analysts in India have puzzled over the fact that civil so-ciety, almost across the board, has been critical of the Narendra Modi-led Gujarat government's handling of communal violence, and yet this has had no effect on the government. Likewise the press, especially the English language one, has been vocal about the shameful failure of government to punish the perpetrators of communal carnage. In many other countries, governments resist popular opinion from placing res-traints on them by suppressing the airing of such opinion. In India, fortunately, the freedom of expression is admirably free. The paradox is that such free expression of opinion does not restrain or influence how Indian governments behave.

One witnesses something similar in the United States. People ex-press their opinion freely in newspapers, on television. Take for ins-tance George Bush's war on Iraq. Never before in the US has there been so much opposition to a war *before* it occurred. There have been large student protests in a number of university campuses. The AFL-CIO has taken a position against the war. Ordinary citizens, troubled by the dubious morality of a pre-emptive attack that will kill thousands of civilians, have spoken out everywhere. The respected TV commentator

Bill Moyers, after conducting a regular interview on PBS, faced the camera to forcefully state his opposition to his government's war. We must not do to Baghdad what al Qaeda did to us, he declared.

This aspect of the United States, as also of India, is admirable: there is little effort to muzzle the freedom to criticize government, as in Iraq, China, and scores of dictatorial countries around the world. However, what is not so nice is that these democracies—the US, India, the UK, and others—are becoming increasingly adept at not allowing freely expressed opinion to control and restrain what the governments do. Jimmy Carter has recently written: 'Despite the overwhelming opposition of most people . . . the United States seems determined to carry out military and diplomatic action that is almost unprecedented in the history of civilized nations.' This observation applies equally to Tony Blair's British government.

Keeping aside the immorality of this war—and immoral it is—and the shameful failure (or, more accurately, wilfull neglect) of the Indian government to control the Gujarat killings—and shameful it is—I want to draw attention to this newly-increasing talent of democracies to 'deal' with opinion. This is a manifestation of the same *elé belé* phenomenon—of letting people *believe* that their opinion counts, that they are participating in their nation's decision-making. This is the same strategy as that of posting an emerging 'report' on the web, inviting opinion, and then writing the report while ignoring the opinions received.

As democracies mature, it is only natural that they will learn how to manage opinion, and in many cases, even shape opinion. Every time the UN weapons inspector Hans Blix commented on the UN inspection of Iraq, it was fascinating to listen to members of the Bush administration paraphrase him. The paraphrasing consisted of subtly changing Blix's comments to suit the US government's case for war. The hope was that by repeating the altered comments sufficiently often, mass opinion would favour the war.

It is often pointed out that nascent democracies do not function well because citizens need to learn how to participate in democratic decision-making. It may be hard to overthrow a totalitarian regime and organize an election. But the harder task is to go from there to creating a true democracy. For people who are habituated into living in a totalitarian state, it is not easy to learn what participation entails. Hence, the popular belief that democracies, like wine, improve with maturity. While there may be truth in this, it is vital to remember that there is also a downside to maturity. Just as citizens in a democracy continuously learn to participate, democratic governments also continuously learn how to get their own way despite the participation.

Instead of going into denial, if we recognize this problem we can prevent established democracies from atrophying and help new democracies become more effective. There is so much talk nowadays of the need to 'lean' on nations to establish democracy. This is as it should be. There is much less talk, however, of an even more pressing need, namely, that of minimal global democracy. The quickening pace of globalization has brought people and nations rapidly and unexpectedly close to one another, while institutions of global governance and democracy remain primitive. This is a dangerous brew that could make for political turmoil, instability, and even war.

It is not only morally wrong to leave nations and communities feeling marginalized and without voice: it is a recipe for terrorism and trouble. The way out of this is not unilateral pre-emptive action but the strengthening of global democracy. In doing this, we need to be continuously aware that such a process will have to contend with subversion in the form of powerful nations trying to get away by creating the illusion of democracy and participation. It is in our own long-run interest to avoid being made *elé belés*.

2

The Retreat
of Global Democracy*

One strange and negative fallout of globalization, which seems to have gone unnoticed, not just by the laity but also by professional economists and political scientists, is this. Even if every country becomes more democratic, the world as a whole is firmly on course to becoming less democratic. This paradoxical process is a consequence of globalization, entailing the increasing ease with which countries can exert influence on the society, economy, and polity of one another. This has never been more transparent than in the wake of the East Asian economic crisis, South Asian nuclear tests, and political and military skirmishes and battles around the world, especially the Middle East. What is noteworthy is that the increase in the power of nations to influence one another has not been symmetric. The well being of Cubans, for instance, depends a lot on what the US president does. The US, because of its enormous international power, *can* cut off much of Cuba's trade lines, prevent it from exporting goods, and pursue policies which result in inflationary pressures in Cuba—all without having US personnel step beyond the shores of their country. There is, however, very little that Cubans can do to influence the quality of life in the US. Similar asymmetries can be found all around the world: India and Sri Lanka, Japan and Korea.

*Based on 'Hot Rules for Cold Cash', *India Today*, 12 October 1998 (Section I); and 'One Kind of Global Involvement', *Business Standard*, 23 October 2003 (Section II).

If 'democracy' means people having the power to elect those who have influence over their lives, then, even if one by one each country adopts democratic procedures for choosing its leader, as long as this process happens to be accompanied by increasing globalization, it is entirely possible that the world as a whole will become less democratic. This is because we do not have a system of transnational voting. Thus, a more democratic Iraq may be able to vote in favour of or against Saddam Hussain, but Iraq has no say in the choice of the US president, even though he exerts an enormous influence on their lives. Hence, the current policy in the US and elsewhere to push for greater democracy in every *country* may not be good enough for establishing more democracy in the *world*.

Strictly speaking, for greater global democracy we need to give people in weaker nations a say in the choice of leaders in stronger nations! Now, this is not about to happen. So the trend in global de-democratization is probably going to be with us for some time, along with its concomitant tensions and global instability.

These tensions are most evident in the management of the global economy and finances. Thanks to globalization, the fates of different economies have become intertwined as never before. A bank in Japan can influence the trajectory of the Korean economy. A crisis in Asia can spark trouble in Brazil.

The current system of intervening in these international problems is highly oligarchic, with not even a pretence of democracy. It is not just a linguistic lapse that the standard solution advocated the world over by the IMF used to be called the *Washington* Consensus. The package put together in the late 1990s by the IMF, with backing from the US and Japan, to rescue the South Korean economy was, as was widely recognized, a package meant primarily to help the rescuers. A donor of credit naturally wants to impose conditions to ensure that the borrowing country is able to repay the loan. But when those conditions include virtually unconnected conditions—such as Koreans being required to lift the ban on imports of certain Japanese products or to open up to foreign banks (an item that had long been on America's bilateral agenda)—there is an unavoidable loss of credibility.

Some of the effects of policy choices among the more powerful nations on the weaker ones may be good for the latter; but that is not the issue here. From the point of view of assessing global *democracy* what is relevant is that the people of the weaker nations have no say in who becomes the leader in powerful nations that influence their destinies.

What does one do about this? Since the citizens of Iraq being allowed to vote in the next US presidential election, or the Koreans in the next Japanese hustings, is not quite on the cards right now, one must think of realistic ways to compensate for the retreat in global democracy. This essentially means that the need for *democratically* constituted international organizations is greater today than ever before. This will need a vast reorganization of agencies such as the IMF, the World Bank, and the United Nations, making their leadership structure much more transparently democratic, and more distanced from the wealth of the interested parties—just as we do not allow Mr Ambani or Mr Gates to cast several votes in their respective national elections on the grounds that they have more money and pay more taxes than most other people. Money enables its owner to buy many advantages; that is as it should be. But it is also a precept of democracy that a person's greater financial power should not translate into a louder political voice. It is the failure of this precept in the context of nation states and global decision-making that has seriously handicapped global democracy.

The increasing globalization of capital markets has made it possible for poor countries to grow at rates that were once beyond anyone's expectation, but it has also brought new hazards. The Asian (and, increasingly, global) economic crisis is simply a reminder that we need better international monitors and new rules of the game to take account of the changed conditions of the world economy. But for the global monitoring agency to have credibility it must be recognized as a *democratic* institution and not an instrument of global oligarchy.

II

Rules and customs, once formed, tend to outlive people and even nations. India's caste norms may once have had a rationale, but these norms have long outlived the rationale and the individuals that played a role in their formation in the mists of distant history. We are today living in an age in which the idea of global governance is beginning to take shape. International conventions on climate change, labour standards, the treatment of POWs, and the formation of the International Criminal Court (ICC) in July 2002, are all incipient attempts to bring the world under *some* common norms and laws. The USA has been in the forefront of many of these efforts. During Bill Clinton's presidency it took the initiative for the ICC and signed the 'Rome Statute' that made it possible.

It is unfortunate that the US administration of George Bush, Jr., while on the one hand deeply involved globally, has at the same time become the most vigorous opponent of global governance and democracy. Bewilderingly, it has sought to resist virtually all these conventions. As for the POW convention, the Bush administration does not reject it but insists that it alone has the right to decide who is a prisoner of war, which amounts to pretty much the same thing.[1] Not surprisingly, this unilateralism has met with intense criticism in the media. What has not been pointed out is that, no matter what the advantages are to the US being able to flex its muscles undeterred by global courts and norms (and no doubt there are some), what the US does at this formative stage of globalization will leave its imprint on the future. If, for instance, the rule gets set that the militarily most powerful nation will be above the global laws, then it is likely that this rule will survive changes in the pecking order of powerful nations.

We do not know if the future powers will be benevolent or malicious. But if we, by then, have certain rules of global governance and laws in place, then, no matter who they are, they will be under pressure

---

[1] The abuses at Guantanamo, Abu Ghraib, and elsewhere had not occurred or come to light when I wrote this piece, but clearly they are an outcome of these growing faultlines of global democracy.

to play by those rules, just as, *within* a nation that has a settled tradition of democracy and the rule of law, leaders, no matter how autocratic they are, find it difficult to flout that tradition.

What the Bush administration is asking for is also *morally* flawed. From the time of Immanuel Kant it has been treated as virtually an *axiom* of moral philosophy that laws must be universalizable and 'anonymous', that is, they should apply to all—the name of the person or nation in the dock should be irrelevant. The original objection of the Bush administration to the ICC was that it may be used against Americans. Poor Kant: he must have spun in his grave. Just change the name of the nation and it will be transparent how this demand sounds like a line from the theatre of the absurd: North Korea says it objects to a treaty banning the use of chemical weapons because that can be used against North Korea!

Someone in the Bush administration must have realized this, and so the American argument has been bolstered. It is now being said that the US administration objects to the ICC because, as Mark Grossman, the Under Secretary of State for Political Affairs, puts it, it may be used to bring *politically motivated* charges against American soldiers and bureaucrats. Of course, the law should not be used to settle scores. But again, it is not clear why only Americans should be protected against politically motivated charges. We should try to draft the law such that no one becomes a victim of politically trumped-up charges.

There is talk of nations signing bilateral treaties with the US which exempt the US from the purview of the criminal court. Some nations have already signed up. But to exempt some agents or nations from the purview of a law which is meant to spread justice in the world makes a travesty of the very idea of international justice.

There are other domains where unilateralism is being indulged for even flimsier reasons. Take ILO Convention 138: by signing this a nation vows to do away with child labour. To date 117 nations have ratified it, which include almost all industrialized countries. The surprise is that this number does not include the US.

US laws on child labour are very strict and the incidence of child labour in the US is low. According to the latest estimates available, in any random week there are 148,000 children doing illegal work. Given the size of the US labour force, this is not a large number. The US could easily adopt the ILO convention without, in fact, having to do anything for it. If, despite this, it has resisted the convention, it is to make the point that Jesse Helms often stressed, namely, that the US cannot be subservient to global governance authorities such as the UN or the ILO.

In the first weeks following 9/11, one felt that George Bush Jr was serious in involving and being involved with the whole world. It was almost as if he realized that through military action you can finish a group of terrorists, but not terrorism; he seemed to be saying, we must try to ensure that large masses of people do not feel marginalized and unfairly treated in this rapidly globalizing world. So long as we do not attend to this feeling of marginalization, the resentment of the masses will be the breeding ground of terrorism.

Is it naïve to expect that the US president can play a genuinely international leadership role? I do not think so. There have been American leaders, like Jimmy Carter, who have tried to keep the larger interests of the world in mind when crafting policy. It is true that to do so is to risk losing some popularity at home, among one's electorate (as Jimmy Carter must well know). Hence, it may not be in the self-interest of any politician to think of the world beyond his boundaries. But there is no surprise in the fact that morality does not invariably coincide with self-interest: if it did, there would be no need for a separate concept called morality. When there has been a conflict between the two, some leaders have risen to undertake the moral action rather than the electorally popular one. The leader of the world's most powerful nation has a special duty to serve morality above self-interest.

In this case I am arguing that it is in America's enlightened self-interest to help institute global norms of justice, laws, and courts. These will no doubt restrict some of the freedoms of the world's most powerful nation. But, once instituted, they are likely to outlive the tenure of not just one but of several of the world's powerful nations.

3

Child Labour and International Labour Standards*

Introduction

When promoting his newly invented roller spinning machine in Britain's textile industry, John Wyatt wrote in 1741: 'Adopting the machine, a Clothier formerly employing a hundred spinners might turn off thirty of the best of them but employ an additional ten infirm people or children . . .' The attorney general was won over and, in granting a patent to the invention, noted with awe how 'even Children of five or six Years of age' could operate the machine.

Commending an invention for its ability to facilitate child labour or upholding children's work as an instrument to out-compete other nations in global trade are now matters of distant history. In fact, quite soon after Mr Wyatt's invention began replacing adults with children, Britain started to discuss policy for curbing child labour, which culminated in Robert Peel's Factories Act, 1802. By the end of the nineteenth century child labour was on the decline in most industrialized nations. However, the *global* child labour problem did not come to an end. As data began to emerge from developing countries, it was evident that child labour, especially some of the worst forms found mainly in factories and the manufacturing sector, had simply shifted to the Third World.

Over the last ten years, thanks to serious effort at collecting data, we have come to acquire a fairly good picture of the global map of child labour. According to estimates put out by the ILO, currently there are

*Adapted from *Scientific American*, October 2003, vol. 289, no. 4.

186 million child labourers in the world. Of these, 111 million do hazardous work. These figures have to be treated with caution.* Child labour is notoriously difficult to measure. Moreover, the ILO estimates have problems of both over- and under-counting, in different ways. At times, too little work has a child classified as a 'child labourer', and, on the other hand, the work of the girl child is severely under-counted, since it is often unpaid and home-based. But, even with these corrections, the fact remains that the incidence of child labour is high, with many child labourers working long hours, in dank factory sheds, with lifelong consequences on their health.

This phenomenon, being persistent, does not make headlines. But there are few global phenomena that ought to be cause for as much concern as child labour. What should we do about it? The answer depends critically on our understanding of what gives rise to child labour and why it is so persistent. Fortunately, with a large and growing number of researchers working on this topic, our understanding has deepened considerably in recent times.

Interestingly, this enhanced understanding has diluted some of the support for the zero-tolerance stance on child labour that some politicians and policy-makers in industrialized countries had initially taken. It was common, in the early 1990s, to hear politicians call for an immediate legal ban on child labour, to stop the import of products that had a child labour input, and to use trade sanctions against nations where child labour existed. This call was an unfortunate product of genuine misunderstanding and protectionist politics.

The Causes

It was common in the nineteenth century to think of child labour as a product of parental sloth. This was a convenient assumption for justifying legislative action. But, as we all know today—and as working-class autobiographical writings and large data sets on household

---

*As this book goes to press, ILO has published updates which show that global child labour is now down to 166 million, with 74 million doing hazardous work.

behaviour in developing countries collected over the last decade confirm—the most important cause of child labour is parental poverty. Parents do not want to send their children to work unless forced by circumstances. When child labour occurs as a mass phenomenon, it is a fallacy to equate it with child abuse.

It should be emphasized that to say that child labour is caused by poverty is not to preclude other causes. Just as the cause of the fire that destroys a house can be the spilled kerosene on the floor *and* the discarded cigarette stub, child labour can have many triggering factors. But before turning to those, it is worth mentioning a strange regularity observed in *rural* studies of child labour. Studies using 1991 data from Pakistan, for instance, showed that in some of the poorer areas increased household wealth seemed to result in a higher incidence of child labour. At first sight this seemed to contradict the hypothesis that poverty causes households to send their children to work. However, we know that in backward rural areas labour markets often function poorly. This means that even if a household is very poor and so in need of supplementing its income by making the children work, it may not be able to find work for the children. If, however, this household happens to own some land, then it does not have to rely on the labour *market*; it can employ its children on its own land. Coupling this with the fact that, in rural areas, households that have more land are typically wealthier, it is not surprising to find a positive correlation between wealth and child labour. But this correlation does not mean that it is the greater wealth that causes the children to work; but simply that the greater wealth reflects the fact of the household owning more land, this creating a better opportunity to employ children, and this causing the incidence of child labour to be higher.

My own expectation is that, as a household's landownership continues to increase, the incidence of child labour will fall. This is because once a household becomes *sufficiently* rich, it will have less need to make its children work and will therefore not respond to the greater opportunity to employ children. In the case of Pakistan this is precisely what one finds. If we divide households into three categories:

'marginal'—those owning less than 1 hectare of land, 'small'—those owning between 1 and 3 hectares, and 'large'—those owning more than 3 hectares—we find that the percentage of children who work increases as we go from marginal to small households but declines as we go from there to large households.

The view that child labour declines with increase in *sufficient* prosperity fits well with global time-series statistics. According to ILO data, the percentage of children in the age group 10 to 14 years who work ('participation rates') in China has moved as follows over the years: 1950: 48 per cent; 1960: 43 per cent; 1970: 39 per cent; 1980: 30 per cent; 1990: 15 per cent; 1995: 12 per cent. China's growth rate picked up from the late 1970s and has been perhaps the highest in the world through the 1980s and 1990s. And child labour has dropped sharply and faster in China than in virtually any other country during this period. The same is true for Vietnam, a country for which we have more reliable data. From 1993 to 1998 Vietnam's national income grew at the remarkably high rate of 6.5 per cent per annum; and a study of nearly 5000 households shows that during the same period child labour fell by a total of 26 per cent. India has done moderately well economically and India's child labour participation rate between 1950 and 1995 fell from 35 per cent to 14 per cent. These performances stand in sharp contrast to those in nations whose economic progress has been poor. In such nations the decline in child labour has been much more marginal. Here, for example, are the figures for child labour participation rates in 1950 and 1995 in Afghanistan: 32 per cent and 25 per cent; Cambodia: 29 per cent and 25 per cent; and Myanmar: 33 per cent and 24 per cent.

The other explanations of child labour that have found empirical corroboration are as follows. The availability of schools and improvements in the quality of schools cause child labour to fall. Small incentives, such as providing children with a midday meal in school or giving parents a subsidy for sending their children to school, can sharply reduce child labour. Another major cause of child labour is *fluctuation* in parental income. This can compel parents (during an income downturn) to withdraw children from school; later the children find it difficult to catch up and drop out of school altogether. Accordingly, improvements in credit and insurance markets are believed to help curb child labour.

Economics

If the main cause of child labour is poverty, we have to be careful when we consider imposing a legal ban on child labour. In sufficiently poor regions, a ban can cause children to starve or drive them into underground activities such as prostitution. A study by UNICEF showed, on the basis of evidence collected in the 1990s in Nepal, that in anticipation of the global boycott of hand-knotted carpets made with child labour, entrepreneurs summarily dismissed many children from the labour force; and that between 5000 and 7000 young girls moved to prostitution as a consequence.

Does this mean that there is no scope for using legal action against child labour? The answer is no. There are situations where a legal ban can be extremely helpful in removing child labour and at the same time leaving children and their parents better off. This argument emerges from a slightly non-standard use of the standard concepts of demand and supply curves, which shows that labour markets in poor countries can often be characterized by multiple equilibria. The intuition is easy to spell out.

Consider a poor country where adult wages are very low and all children are (for that very reason) made to work. Now assume, for the sake of argument, that child labour is banned. Then, firms that were using child labour will be forced to seek adults to fill those gaps. Hence, the wage rate of adult labour will rise. Now, it is entirely possible that, if the wage were that high to start with, parents would not have sent their children out to work anyway. Hence, even if the law is now revoked, wages will remain high, children will not work, and this will sustain the high wage. In other words, this economy had multiple equilibria, and hence the law works simply as a mechanism for deflecting the economy from the 'inferior equilibrium', where wages are low and children work, to the 'superior equilibrium', where wages are high and there is no child labour.

Note that the law works in an unusual way here. It is not needed on a continuous basis to sustain a certain kind of behaviour (in this case, to keep children away from work), but as a one-time effort to deflect the equilibrium. Such laws have elsewhere been called '*benign* legislative interventions'; they are to be distinguished from routine legislative interventions which entail continuous surveillance and the sustained threat of punitive action to ensure socially desirable behaviour.

This new research also sheds light on ways in which conventional policy can backfire and explains why child labour has been so difficult to control. In Britain, for instance, child labour continued to rise till around 1860 despite the adoption of new laws and policies to control child labour throughout the first half of the nineteenth century. To understand this, consider the policy of imposing a fine on any firm found employing children below the age of 15. This looks like a reasonable way to control child labour: India's Child Labour Act, 1986, has precisely such a provision.

Consider what this law will do to the hourly child wage rate. It is likely to lower the wage, since, with this law in place, children will be less attractive as inputs (the employer risks being caught and fined). Now, if it is the case that children work primarily to reach a minimal acceptable level of income for their households (as argued above), then a lower hourly wage will induce them to work longer hours. Hence, paradoxically, the incidence of child labour can end up higher as a consequence of such a law.

So it all depends on *why* children work. If they work to achieve a target income, as opposed to working to satisfy an insatiable appetite for more and more income, the impact of this traditional policy gets turned on its head.

Sociology

It turns out that the possibility of multiple equilibria occurs in other ways too. Sociologists have written about stigma and tipping points. It is arguable that a household that sends its children to work has to face some stigma for doing so. However, it seems reasonable to assume that the extent of stigma is negatively related to the amount of child labour that occurs in such a society. That is, if child labour is widespread, people will be used to it and not stigmatize quite so strongly those who send their children to work. To see how this may lead to multiple equilibria, let us start from a society where very few children work. In this society, parents who send their children to work face strong stigma. Therefore, only those parents who have a very great need to send their children to work will do so. Hence, there will be few children who work.

If this same society had instead many children going to work, this would lower the stigma attached to children's work. This stigma cost being low, more parents would be inclined to send their children to work. Hence, if many children work, this fact may reinforce parents' decision to send their children to labour, and thereby constitute an equilibrium.

Another such argument works through dynastic routes. Economists have argued that people who work as children grow up without enough human capital and so are poorer as adults. This compels them to send their children, in turn, to work, thereby trapping the dynasty in a perpetual child-labour cycle.

This theory has recently been tested and validated using a large data set on Brazilian households. Parents who worked as children are more likely to have their own children in the labour force. There is, however, an open question about this causation. Is the cause of this relation mediated entirely through the fact that parents who work as children will be poorer as adults (as was argued above)? An analysis of the Brazilian data shows that parents who worked in their childhood were more likely to send their children to work *even if adult incomes were to be held constant*. This points to causation which goes beyond economics. It suggests that parents who have a history of child labour are likely to have social norms and preferences that make them attach a lower value to their own children's schooling and this affects *directly* the incidence of their own children's labour.

These ideas of multiple equilibria are closely related to the phenomenon of 'tipping', whereby a small change suddenly leads to a sharp movement, just as the jug that is tilted gently will at some point tip over. Consider a society that has multiple equilibria and is caught in the high-child-labour equilibrium. Now, suppose that through some intervention child labour is cut down little by little. Then, typically, at some point, as we move into the zone of attraction of the other equilibrium, child labour will tend to fall off rapidly, without any further intervention.

Direct evidence on this is difficult to get, but we know that in a host of countries child labour did decline rapidly over a very short period. In Italy, for instance, in 1951, 29.11 per cent of children in the age group 10 to 14 years worked. By 1960 this had dropped to 10.91 per cent and by 1970 to 4.12 per cent. Likewise, in the USA child labour was very high till 1900. This was despite the fact that, from 1837, starting with the state of Massachusetts, several states had been trying to bring it down. But when it finally began to decline, the decline was extremely rapid between 1900 and 1920, and child labour was almost gone by 1930.

Politics

A friend of mine once tried to persuade me to take up regular jogging by claiming that every ten minutes of jogging increased one's life expectancy by eight minutes. At first, that seemed incentive enough; but then it struck me that it all depends on what one wants to maximize in life. If it were one's *non-jogging* life that one wished to maximize, then one needed to worry about the fact that every ten minutes of jogging would *decrease* one's non-jogging life by two minutes. Facetious though this example may sound, it points to the important and often overlooked fact that whether a particular policy is desirable or not depends crucially on what one's *ultimate* objectives are.

If controlling child labour is not an end in itself but an instrument for enabling children to grow up into productive and happy individuals, then policies have to be evaluated against this larger yardstick and not just against the immediate aim of halting child labour. This is what brings politics into the complex brew of economics and sociology already discussed. Policy concerning child labour has been mired in political controversy. A number of commentators have sought to involve the WTO in imposing trade sanctions against nations where there is child labour. Others have described such activism as protectionism by stealth or behind a moral façade. Such suspicions have been fuelled by incidents such as the charge brought against the Brazilian company Sucocitrico Cutrale, that it was using 'forced' child labour to pluck oranges in Brazil (the Sanders' Amendment in the US prohibits the import of products made with forced child labour), and the whiff of suspicion that the law was actually being used to settle other scores, in particular Cutrale's decision to cut back the workforce of a juice-making plant in Florida.

Commentators have argued, and I agree, that barring some special cases, legislative action is not the best way to control child labour. We have to think, instead, of interventions where the workers are partners rather than adversaries of the policy-maker. If, for instance, we can improve the conditions and earnings of adult labourers, this can diffuse the incentive to send children to work. In the poorest regions, we may in fact have to permit children to do a few hours of labour each day, since that is often the only way they can finance their own schooling or the schooling of their siblings. This can often ensure the eventual escape from poverty for a labourer's progeny.

That, in very poor regions, *some* child labour can enable some children to go to school seems to be borne out empirically by 1994 household survey data from Peru; and that one child's labour often makes a sibling's schooling possible has been shown by some studies using data from Brazil in 1998. Such findings raise troublesome moral questions but are not facts that we can shy away from when designing policy.

When tackling the problem of child labour it is easy to make two errors—to fall into the trap of complacency, leaving it all to the markets; and to try to remove child labour in one stroke, with no concern for the well being of the alleged beneficiary of such policy, to wit, the child. We have enough information and understanding of the problem now to aim for a time-bound plan to eliminate child labour. But this will require restraint, understanding, and a careful construction of nuanced policy interventions.

4

International Labour Standards: A View from the Tropics*

On the face of it there should be nothing contentious about the International Labour Standards (ILS) movement. It is meant to be a global effort to raise the working conditions and living standards of workers, primarily in developing countries. What is curious is that the biggest opposition to ILS has come from its alleged beneficiaries—to wit, Third World workers, unions, and governments. The fear in the South is that once such a global monitoring scheme is brought into existence, it will get diverted into an instrument of protection for the North. In the name of ILS, arbitrary and inflexible trade sanctions will be imposed on Third World countries. This fear gets heightened if the labour standards are imposed through the World Trade Organization (WTO), via a 'social clause' provision, which would allow the WTO to use trade sanctions against any nation that violates minimal labour standards. The other concern stems from the adjective 'international', which suggests a uniform global standard for all nations.

Recently, Archon Fung, Dara O'Rourke, and Charles Sabel have come up with an ingenious suggestion for international labour standards to get around some of these criticisms. They call their scheme 'Ratcheting Labour Standards' (RLS). They try to bring in flexibility by keeping labour standards away from formal global organizations. Instead, they propose a system of collecting and publicizing information about

*First published in *Boston Review*, February 2001.

the labour practices of firms, and encouraging consumers, journalists, and other ordinary citizens to use social sanctions, such as product boycott and public criticism, against firms that violate minimal standards. In addition, they recommend that the minimal standards that monitors seek and publicize will be different across different nations, depending on their levels of economic development.

I believe that Fung, O'Rourke, and Sabel air the right concerns and steer the debate in the right direction, and there is something attractive in the idea of labour standards that are pegged to the level of the country's development. Nevertheless, as a practical proposal RLS is flawed. It will not attain the objectives that the authors themselves uphold.

One novel and attractive aspect of their scheme, though this is only implicit in their statement, is that they place the burden of responsibility on the firm that violates labour standards rather than on the country where the labour standard is violated. We know from economic analysis in other areas that responsibility, no matter where it is initially placed, can be partly deflected. But holding the firm responsible will have the advantage of the firm not being able to freely play one poor nation against another and driving down standards.

The main weakness of their scheme is rooted in its relying so heavily on social sanctions and citizen action. Such a policy has a nice progressive ring to it, and a certain kind of flexibility—but its shortcomings outweigh these advantages. First, this will handicap small producers. Consider the soccer ball industry in Pakistan. Soccer balls used to be stitched by thousands of small producers working out of their homes, which doubled as residence and factory. Even if such a production unit did not use child labour, there would be no way for it to 'prove' this to outside monitors. A large producer, on the other hand, can easily centralize production in a big factory, stop children from entering the premises, and prove to outside monitors that production is free of child labour. Indeed, Reebok has done just that in Pakistan. Hence, a by-product of this scheme is that it creates a competitive advantage for large firms by making it virtually impossible for small producers to get certification.

Second, once information on firms is collected and publicized and citizens are encouraged to take action, there is no way of ensuring that this system will achieve the right kind of flexibility. In several domains of our civic life social sanctions play a useful role, but social sanctions have also been the basis of witch-hunts and the persecution of harmless behaviour that happens to deviate from the mainstream. Once consumers in a rich country are given the moral responsibility to enforce standards and are told that in Ethiopia workers are paid 90 cents for a day's work, it is easy for consumers to believe that this is not a living wage and begin a boycott of Ethiopian goods, unmindful of the fact that such a boycott could cause unemployment and drive the incomes of many workers down to zero. As Joan Robinson, the eminent British economist known for her radical views, once noted, in some situations what is worse for a worker than being exploited is not being exploited.

Also, in a world of informal control, corporations will soon be competing by deliberately using adverse publicity against firms that sell cheap.

It is not surprising that, while all societies rely on informal mass action for curbing a variety of undesirable actions, there are also domains where we prefer to use more centralized methods for addressing issues of justice—for instance, through the courts. What I am arguing is that labour standards do not belong to the first category—they must not be enforced through informal mass action.

Does this mean that we must take institutional (this includes 'governmental') action for raising labour standards? Before answering this, it is worth remembering that *not* doing so does not mean that labour standards will necessarily be abysmal. As productivity and wages rise, workers can demand higher standards and have many of their demands met, not through government action but by virtue of the standard forces of the market, namely, the implicit threat that the worker will not, otherwise, accept the job. Very few people, however, argue that all labour standards should be left to what workers can achieve through market mechanisms. Most countries have laws against workplace sexual harassment, for example; they do not leave it to workers to ensure that they are not harassed—by threatening to quit if they are. Likewise, there is reason for public action in certain domains of labour standards in developing countries. The question is: How can this be ensured without hurting the very workers that this is meant to help (by causing unemployment or by impoverishing further some already poor nation)?

In the debate on international standards, so much attention has been directed at the alleged (and largely unsubstantiated) conflict of interest between First and Third World workers that the tension among workers in different nations of the Third World is often overlooked. In this age of mobile global capital, it is easy for corporations to move their capital from one nation to another. Hence, each developing country hesitates to take action to raise its labour standards for fear of driving capital away to another developing country. Hence, there is need for collective action on labour standards among Third World nations. If we take this seriously, then we need to allow Third World nations to develop their own agenda—a consensus from the tropics—of what constitutes minimal labour standards.

The trouble with the WTO is that it is viewed by most developing nations—not entirely without reason—as controlled by rich nations. Even though it runs on the principle of 'one country one vote', the 'green room' where the agenda is set is, in practice, controlled by industrialized nations. There is a great need to encourage the reorganization of international organizations so that they represent the interests of all nations democratically, and to provide a forum where poor countries can develop their own agenda for what constitutes labour standards.

Action for international labour standards is desirable, and such action must be carried out through global institutions, not informal mass action. But if the institutions do not have democratic representation, the process can work to the detriment of developing nations.

Hence, while we strive towards this goal of global action, we should also be prepared for the possibility that, given the current structure of global governance, we may for the time being prefer to resist globalization in this one area and leave labour-standards policy and intervention to individual nations. It is sobering to recall that in the United States the attempt to bring all states under a common labour standard code was on the agenda for decades (actively from 1906) before it could finally be implemented in the form of the Fair Labour Standards Act in 1938.

5

Labour vs. Labour: The Politics of Business Outsourcing*

I

Recently, after I gave a lecture in Helsinki on global labour standards, I got into a discussion with some of my audience on what if any should be the common standard for labour markets in the world. A globalized world, with one country's goods, capital, and pollution flowing into another, will inevitably need some common norms and laws. However, the discussion kept veering into questions of free trade and offshoring of work to developing countries. The discussion became animated and it was evident that this is a topic that is as emotionally charged today in industrialized countries as the topic of free trade used to be in developing countries a few decades ago.

The problem of business process outsourcing (BPO) is however a much misunderstood subject. BPO has been a source of hope and progress for many developing nations, such as India, China, and South Africa. With technological breakthroughs in electronic communication and steady increase in bandwidth, it is evident that many jobs that were done in industrialized nations, but did not really need face-to-face interaction, can be shipped out to poorer countries which have cheap labour, an educated workforce, and computer literacy. General Electric (GE) was one of the pioneers that realized the potential in this. In an

*Based on 'Labour versus Labour', *Business Standard*, 10 December 2003 (Section I); and 'Outsourcing: Long-term Gains for All', *BBC News Online*, 29 March 2004 (Section II).

interesting paper on BPO, Rafiq Dossani of Stanford University reports how GE achieved an annual saving of $340 million from the shifting of some of its back-office work to India. According to his calculation, when all costs are taken into account a call centre in Kansas City works out to over three times as much as a call centre in Mumbai. Not surprisingly, India has seen a steady rise in employment in the IT-enabled offshore services sector. In March 2002 the employment in this sector was 106,000; a year later this had climbed to 171,500; and according to the latest projections this will cross the 1 million mark by the year 2008.

Over the last few years Motorola has been laying off workers in the US and moving operations to Brazil, China, and its plant in Chihuahua in Mexico. India has been a major and growing outsourcing location for Microsoft, Hewlett-Packard, British Airways, and other major corporations.

While India and several other poor nations look to these facts and trends with hope, many industrialized countries view them with anxiety and even anger. As one of the persons who talked to me in Helsinki said despondently, he thought poorly of globalization ever since some of his friends lost their jobs through no fault of theirs but because Ericsson decided to shut down some of its European plants and move operations to China.

There are economists who dismiss such concerns out of hand as Northern protectionism. But that is wrong. First, the people being hit by this are not the Northern rich, but, generally, poor workers. Moreover, protectionism or not, these are matters of great emotional significance and, if not dealt with, can engulf politics and policy. If you read some of the websites of the Ku Klux Klan (not that I am recommending you do), you will see that economics now vies for space with their other more traditional—shall we say 'race-related'—concerns. They point out that jobs are being lost to developing nations and they therefore oppose globalization.

There are three counterpoints that we have to make in the face of such opposition. First, all this has nothing to do with the international labour standards problem, which deals with the poorest workers of poor nations and child labourers. The unskilled labourers of poor nations do the kind of work that virtually no one in a developed country would do. So, with the poorest workers of developing nations there is no real conflict of interest because they do not tread common ground.

Second, and this is testimony to the power of propaganda, in the popular perception BPO is viewed as a labour vs. labour problem, that is, a conflict of interest between workers in rich and poor nations. When a corporation outsources operations to a developing country, some of its incumbent workers lose out (at least in the short run), true. But there are many groups who gain. Workers (software technicians and call-centre operators) in the host country gain, of course, but so do the shareholders and owners of the company (whose profits rise) and consumers (who benefit by lower prices). So it is not labour vs. labour alone. There are many others who gain, and therefore there are many others who can compensate the loser. To that extent a large part of the responsibility to provide relocation benefits and social welfare lies with the developed country.

Finally, let me turn to a point that is widely misunderstood by the lay public. If, through such offshore work, and greater trade and capital flows, India, China, Brazil, and South Africa become better off, their demand for goods and services will grow. This will inevitably mean a greater demand from them for goods from other countries and, going by the evidence we have, the larger part of this will be from rich countries. This will in turn create jobs in rich countries. The jobs will not of course be in precisely the sectors that moved to developing countries, but in other sectors. Some standard economic calculation shows that the new jobs created will typically be more in number than the ones lost. Hence, when all the intricate consequences that emanate from the fact of BPO are taken into account, we will find that BPO creates more jobs than it kills. But since the loss of jobs occurs in concentrated, visible sectors, it is easy to take job losses as the net effect of BPO, and it is therefore also easy to lobby certain interests against BPO. But to do so would be to harm the cause of workers in general in developed nations, not help them.

All this is not to deny that workers in industrialized countries may be getting relatively impoverished over time. I believe that there are forces at work that tend to make the total income that accrues to labour relatively small compared to the income that accrues to capital. (The way to counter this is to give workers an increasing stake in the earnings from capital, but that is another subject deserving separate analysis.) But this has nothing to do with the movement of back-office work to poor nations. The fact remains that if the latter were to be stopped, workers as a whole, in industrialized nations, would be worse off than they would be in the absence of back-office outsourcing.

II

I met Paul O'Neill just once. As the US Treasury Secretary, he had invited a small group of economists to hear their views on the Indian economy and the possibility of greater Indo-US economic interaction. I wanted to make myself heard to the person who held, arguably, the most influential economic-policy position in the world; so I went.

But I was apprehensive. I had enough experience to know that when men of power say they want to 'listen', they usually mean 'talk'. Also, if I discussed the Indian economy, I would speak about information technology and the surge of business enterprise, but also of the persistence of poverty and growing inequality. And I wondered if a Republican administrator would have the patience for that end of India.

In the event, it turned out to be one of the most engaging policy meetings I have attended. I was completely taken by O'Neill's interest in India, his ability to listen and his concern for the marginalized. I subsequently wondered if I had been foolish in forming such a favourable opinion of him, based on a single meeting. It was, therefore, good to have my impression confirmed by Ron Suskind's meticulously-researched and gripping book, *The Price of Loyalty*, on O'Neill's tenure in Washington. O'Neill opposed reckless tax-cuts for the rich and the ballooning fiscal deficit, tried to hold CEOs to higher standards of accounting honesty, and (in a more muted way) opposed the Iraq invasion, which, according to the evidence provided by O'Neill, had been decided way before 9/11. These 'un-Republican' positions cost him his job. Suskind's book presents an impressive amount of evidence on O'Neill's effort to battle the intrigues and scripted debates—whereby the innocent are gently led towards agreeing with predetermined decisions—which characterize contemporary politics.

As the momentum for the next election between John Kerry and George Bush Jr picks up in the US, one misses the likes of Paul O'Neill in government.

In terms of economic policy, the focal point of this election is turning out to be trade and outsourcing. The humbug being churned out is impressive. One day Greg Mankiw (Chairman of President Bush's Council of Economic Advisors) makes a statement that outsourcing is a form of free trade, and free trade is good for America. The next day an elaborate political machinery goes into action explaining how that is not what he meant.

The fact is, what Mankiw said is the truth. It is true that outsourcing to India and greater trade with China does cause an *immediate* loss of jobs, but these are more than made up for by the creation of new jobs elsewhere. The textile sector once employed a large number of American workers, and US car manufacturers once dominated the world. If the jobs that were lost in these sectors were protected through trade restrictions, there could be more textile and automobile workers in the US today, but there would be fewer jobs on the whole. This does not mean that government has no responsibility towards workers who lose their jobs, but simply that government must not cut off trade and outsourcing.

In the late 1980s and early 1990s it had seemed that Japan (and maybe even Germany) would overtake America. According to World Bank data, in 1992, US per capita income was $23,200, while Japan (which was rapidly catching up) had reached $20,300. But in 2002 the US economy, with a per capita income of $35,100, had surged ahead of Japan (and also Germany), which had incomes hovering around $26,000.

What caused this? First, this was a period of excellent fiscal management in the US. Second, when an industrialized nation opens itself to economic interaction with a poor country, its scope for gains are the greatest. Freer trade with China and the unprecedented collaboration with India's information technology sector—in the form of admitting computer scientists to Silicon Valley (around half of all American H1B visas, the visa for professionals, were given to Indians) as well as outsourcing work to India—gave the US a competitive edge. It is this openness that the US has used time and again in its history to keep the lead.

Trade and exchange help both sides. A recent McKinsey study estimates that for every dollar of value created by US outsourcing, the US manages to capture 78 cents and 22 cents accrue to the receiving country. Naturally, for India the 1990s have been a period of economic boom.

The changing structure of global politics, which has brought Indian and American interests into alignment, will probably ensure that the two countries will collaborate for some time to come, no matter who is in power in Washington and Delhi; and, despite the rhetoric, trade will remain largely free. The bigger and more latent danger is the large fiscal deficit. With O'Neill not around to hold the line, this can go out of control and crowd out productive investment in the US. If that were to happen, India would feel the strain. The only consolation would be that the rest of the world would too.

6

The Politics of Economics*

Many lay people, aided by the teachings of economists, believe that the major economic processes in life are driven by the inexorable laws of economics. Prices rise and fall responding to demand and supply, which are the aggregation of thousands of atomistic decisions by individuals; trade occurs when there are differences in comparative advantages between nations; wealth accrues to the smart and the hardworking. There is something mildly consoling about this view. When one sees the all-too-visible inequities of economic life, this belief in inexorable laws comes a close second to fate, karma, and religious determinism as a source of comfort.

What most people grossly underestimate is the importance of politics in economics. Transparency not being the hallmark of politics, this is a mistake easy to make. An illuminating illustration of politics behind economics is the recent steel-tariff controversy. President Bush's preaching of free trade and practice of raising steel tariff to nearly 30 per cent caught many by surprise. Bush justified it by referring to the report of the International Trade Commission, which had been asked by him to do a 'global safeguard investigation' into the subject of steel imports and had concluded in December 2001 that increased imports were hurting the nation across the board. But a little research shows that the real reason for the tariff was political. Steel is an important industry for Pennsylvania and West Virginia, and these states have mid-term elections coming up in November 2002. The tariff, no matter how it is justified to the world, is meant to be an instrument to gain favour with the electorate of these states.

*First published in *Business Standard*, 15 May 2002.

This tariff increase is expected to have a major negative fallout outside the US. The impact will be direct on Europe, Japan, and China, which export steel to the US. India has been exempted from the new increases (except for carbon flanges—whatever they are), as have been Canada, Israel, Jordan, and Mexico. But it is expected that these countries, especially India, will be hit by cascading effects, such as India's exports to South East Asian nations becoming harder because of the global glut as well as the possibility of Chinese steel being diverted to India.

What is interesting here is the reaction. The WTO, which is meant to be the main ombudsman in matters like this, is being largely bypassed. Though dispute settlement procedures at the WTO are being launched and the EC is demanding compensation of $2.5 billion—the sum it claims it will lose as a consequence of the US action—the immediate response is to take direct retaliatory action, such as raising tariffs on imports from the US, in particular on textiles and citrus fruit. Why these goods? Someone schooled in textbook economics may think this is guided by direct economic profitability considerations. But reality speaks differently. A tariff on citrus by Europe will hit Florida, which happens to have been the pivotal state in the last presidential election, and so it is expected that this will hurt the Republican government more than anything else. Something similar is also true for textiles, which are very important to North and South Carolina, where again there are mid-term elections later in 2002.

If decisions concerning the economy were guided purely by economic concerns, there would be little scope for lobbying. Yet lobbying is one of the fastest growing sectors of the modern global economy. In 1999 the steel industry spent a large amount lobbying Washington and clearly it must now think it was worth it. And the steel industry's lobbying expenditure was small compared to what was spent on persuasive tactics by the pharmaceutical industry.

The battle to shape opinion is a bigger one than most people realize. The US lobbying economy, with a $1.45 billion expenditure, is larger than the economy of Laos or Lesotho. There are over 12,000 active lobbyists in America. The pharmaceutical industry alone, threatened by the risk that Washington will allow the sale of cheap generic drugs which will cut into their profits, has 625 registered lobbyists in Washington—a larger number than members of Congress. In response to 9/11 and the anthrax scare, drug companies have offered scores of industry scientists, currently employed by drug companies, to work for the government. This seemingly generous gesture is seen by many as a Trojan horse strategy to gain influence in government. A recent study shows that lobbying firms have found 129 former members of Congress willing to lobby on everything from postal rates to defence appropriations.

In India, when Enron was starting work on a new power plant in Dabhol, it had spent a large sum of money under the heading 'to educate the public'. And when the Indian government held back permission to the Tatas and Singapore Airlines from setting up a new airline firm, it was initially believed that this was one more instance of sluggish bureaucracy. But now it is clear that behind the decision was very heavy lobbying by the existing private airlines, eager to stop the entry of new competitors.

Thanks to the US Lobbying Disclosure Act (LDA) of 1995, much of the data on lobbying, including the amount spent by various nations to propagate their interest in Washington, is now easily available to any serious researcher. However, to get around this open disclosure problem many industries, instead of directly lobbying for themselves, are setting up or supporting grassroots 'activists' who will plead their case. Clearly, these industries and firms would not have spent such large sums of money and personnel if they did not hope to tilt opinion and decisions in their interest, such as the decision to raise steel tariffs in the US. That being so, market outcomes are clearly not mere market outcomes but reflect, in addition, a whole world of politics behind the scenes which shapes our opinion and the opinions of politicians.

With globalization, poor countries unused to such sophisticated machinations are being exposed to the rough and tumble of the marketplace. It is hardly surprising that the benefits of globalization are being disproportionately gathered by some, leaving many regions and nations poor and marginalized. Poor countries often react to this by trying to withdraw from the global marketplace and close their borders. This is, however, a wrong reaction.

If we are to help poor nations partake in the benefits of globalization— and I do believe that the potential benefits of globalization outweigh the costs—it is important to explain the risks that come with globalization, to warn them that there are lobbies and big political forces that try to influence the market to their own advantage. To keep such forces at bay we need to make relentless demands for transparency.

In their zeal to promote unfettered globalization, economists have often tried to cover up the downside of free-ranging global capitalism and have promoted the view that exports, imports, and the rise and fall of prices are mere reflections of the inexorable forces of demand and supply, and that everyone will automatically benefit from this. It is therefore heartening to see some prominent industrialists and businesspersons, such as George Soros and Bill Gates—people with the greatest self-interest in unfettered globalization—speak out against such myths and in favour of greater public action as well as more foreign aid to stall the marginalization of some nations and people.

7

Groucho Marx and Global Currency Flows*

The 1997 IMF-led loan package of $55 billion for South Korea was the biggest financial rescue effort to date. When, a few months before that, Thailand's financial crisis spread to the Philippines, Indonesia, and Malaysia, it was nothing but a distant tragedy to much of the industrialized world. Then, suddenly, the contagion jumped the boundaries of South East Asia, touching Brazil, Japan, and, in a very big way, South Korea. The crisis was marked by stock market crashes, currency depreciations, runs on banks, and the actual collapse of several banks—including Hokkaido Takushoku, one of Japan's largest.

In the mayhem, no one really understands what happened, what started the forest fire in South East Asia—there is an actual forest fire in the region, to add to the confusion—and how to douse it without bringing the economies to a halt. As is usual, pundits are cropping up by the day. They claim to have known all along that this was coming. They tell us that these Asian economies had 'weak fundamentals', a safe thing to say since no one knows what that means; their exchange rates were overvalued; their monetary policy was wrong.

Nothing can be further from the truth. On 1 March 1997, *The Economist*, while pointing to several cracks in the Asian economies, noted that 'on most structural issues, these economies have got a large number of big things absolutely right: high savings, prudent monetary and fiscal policies, openness to trade'. Then, after noting that several

*First published in *India Today*, 22 December 1997.

Asian currencies had appreciated a little—the Thai baht having risen 15 per cent over the previous two years—*The Economist* proclaimed that 'in general, though, Asian currencies are not overvalued.' The baht has depreciated over 50 per cent since then.

Now, several months into the crisis, we are better able to see what happened. It is true that Asian banking has been in bad shape for quite a while, with a lot of lending being guided by political interference and cronyism rather than banking norms. Yet it is difficult to say what started the crisis because the origins of financial crises are often innocuous. If some people feel a currency will depreciate, this can infect other people's opinions and soon the depreciation can become a self-fulfilling prophecy.

However, once a crisis starts, its mechanics are familiar and well understood. What has added fuel to the fire this time is that world capital markets are more open than ever before. Thanks to capital accounts being convertible in most major economies, money can rush in and out of nations. This converts into tidal waves what might have been just ripples if the world economy consisted of many small tanks instead of one huge ocean.

If returns are expected to be high in Malaysia, investment today rushes into the Malaysian economy from New York, London, and Tokyo. Likewise, if returns there are expected to be low or if the ringgit is expected to lose value, people convert money out of ringgits all in a rush.

Groucho Marx once noted that to be successful you need to be known as honest and dependable; and so, he went on to add, if you can fake those qualities you have got it made. This is true of banks and currencies. It is important for them to appear strong and dependable. Thus Japan put up a brave face till almost the last moment before the crash of Yamaichi Securities. This is what makes these financial crashes harder: those in charge try to cover up and put on a bold front till the very end.

In the present crisis, one major destabilizing force has comprised currency speculators. Suppose the Malaysian ringgit is expected to depreciate against the dollar. What the currency speculators do is borrow ringgits from Malaysia's banks, convert them into dollars, and wait. After the ringgit loses value they use a part of the dollars to convert enough ringgits to pay back the debt and pocket the remainder as profit.

One way of deterring this is by pushing up domestic interest rates and making borrowing money unattractive. This is why Hong Kong raised its overnight interest rate to 300 per cent in November, when it was anticipating a speculative attack. The trouble with this method is that it deters genuine investors from borrowing money and can thus cause stagnation. Indeed, all the affected economies seem to be entering a period of protracted stagnation. Some countries, such as Thailand, have tried to use dual interest rates—a high one for speculators and a low one for investors. But this too is flawed because it is not always possible to tell one from the other.

Dissenters in Seoul and Jakarta have protested that the loan packages offered them will help the troubled nations too little, that these loans will really guard the interests of lenders and exporters in the 'rescuing nations'. There is truth to this, though it is not clear what the nations in crisis can do to escape the predicament. What the crisis has drawn attention to is that the increasing globalization of the world's economies calls for new rules of the game.

There is a lot to be gained from the flow of capital across national boundaries. It would be foolish for any nation to use the Asian crisis as an alibi to pull down the shutters on international capital. But we need checks and balances on the flow of international money—and a big inter-country effort to frame rules which limit the scope for international speculation.

8

From Cowries to the Euro: Towards a One-Currency World*

The European Union is on track towards a common currency for eleven of its fifteen member nations. The culmination of this currency merger will occur on 1 July 2002, when national currencies cease to be legal tender and all citizens of the participating nations switch over to the use of euro notes and coins. The main motivation behind the euro is, arguably, to boost European trade and challenge the US dollar's primacy as world currency.

Whatever the motivation, this is a more momentous event for the world than most people realize. The reason is that it points to the future. The current international monetary system is increasingly showing up as unviable for the emerging world economy. And my guess is that the euro is the start of a long process that will take us to a single-currency world. This was in fact a recommendation made in 1878 by the English economist Stanley Jevons. In outlining the advantage of an 'international money' he had to, it must be admitted, scrape the barrel's bottom. By the time a similar case was made again in 1984 by Harvard's Richard Cooper (who argued for one currency to be shared by all the industrialized nations of the world), the idea did not seem quite as far-fetched. Since then the structure of the world economy has changed even further; and the repeated crises of the 1990s—Sweden

*First published in *India Today*, 14 December 1998.

1992; Mexico 1994; Thailand, Indonesia, Korea 1997; and Japan currently teetering on the brink—is evidence of this.

The most significant change is the ease with which capital now flows in and out of nations. If the stock market is expected to boom in Bangkok, money pours into the Bangkok stock exchange from all over the world. True, stock markets were always volatile, but in today's interconnected world there is an additional problem. Suppose you have bought shares in Thailand. Unlike a Thai investor, you will be watching two prices, the stock prices in Thailand and the exchange rate of the Thai baht. If you expect the baht to fall, *even if you do not expect the stock price to fall*, you will want to sell your stock because, as an Indian, you'll have to keep in mind that after you sell the stock and collect the bahts you will have to change the bahts to rupees in order to spend the money in India. If the baht loses value, you lose. Now, if all foreigners sell Thai stocks because they expect the baht to fall, this will cause the stock prices to fall. This intertwining of the stock market with the foreign exchange market renders both markets more volatile because a spark in one can ignite the other.

Now, if all countries used the same currency, one half of this twin risk would be gone; there would be no exchange rates to watch. My sense is that, ultimately, for good or for bad, this is the way the world will go.

A common-currency area does amount to reduced elbow room for each country in terms of fiscal and monetary policy. For one, we cannot have one currency with several central banks (one in each country, as now), each possessing the right to create money, because in that scenario each nation's central bank will tend to print money and hand it over to its citizens to increase their buying power. This would fuel inflation. So, a prerequisite for one currency is one central bank shared by all countries. This is difficult enough for homogeneous Europe; in today's fractious world it would be well-nigh impossible globally, since it would entail compromising in national sovereignty.

However, there may be ways of inching towards this goal without going the whole way: clusters of countries can come together under a common currency. Safeguards can ensure that no single country has excessive power over their central bank. All this may not be quite as impossible as it seems today. After all, the institution of money has undergone wild changes in the past. As recently as in the nineteenth century, Mademoiselle Zelie, a Parisian singer, giving a concert in the Pacific Islands, was promised one-third of the collection at the gate. At the end of the concert the islanders kept their promise; she was handed over a pig, twenty-three turkeys, forty-four chickens, plus coconuts, bananas, and lemons. It was handsome payment, even if of little use to her. Indeed, if one thinks of the earlier ubiquitous system of barter, one realizes how much contemporary society owes to the institution of modern money.

Barter societies gradually realized the importance of having one 'good' to serve as the medium of exchange. Corn, cowry shells, and tobacco, all have been tried. In Norway one could even deposit corn in banks. The trouble with most of these 'currencies' was that you could literally grow money in your backyard, and this led to price instability. By the late seventeenth century paper currency had come into existence. In the beginning, and till fairly recent times, banks were allowed to issue their own currency. This resulted in competition and an oversupply of notes. The concept of a single currency for each nation, which only one central bank can legally issue, is fairly recent.

As economies became more complex, many of the older monies got replaced by newer systems. To each generation it must have seemed that money could take no other form than the one they were used to. But history provides ample evidence that the seemingly immutable gets antiquated.

Perhaps the arrival of the euro takes us to the brink of one such stage in monetary history.

9

The WTO and North–South Bargains*

Historically, India's position *vis-à-vis* the WTO has been to argue that the WTO is an instrument of the North and to resist virtually its every move. Thus, before the Ministerial Meeting at Doha, the Indian government's line was to oppose the launching of a new trade round, resist the liberalization of trade in industrial products, and oppose the use of trade sanctions to punish countries that fail to meet minimal labour standards.

The perception that the WTO is largely an instrument of powerful industrialized nations is correct, but India's response to this, namely, opposing it on all fronts, is wrong. We must learn to take a more sophisticated line towards the WTO and the North in general. We can hope to gain much at the fifth ministerial meeting, projected to take place in Mexico in 2003, if we do so.

Spokespersons for the WTO will tell you that it is a democratic organization that runs on the principle of 'one country one vote'. But anybody who has been following the goings-on at the WTO knows that the way the rich countries get around this 'nuisance' is through the 'green room' channel, to wit, the lobbying behind the scenes to fix the agenda in advance.

While all this is true, India's response to it is wrong for several reasons.

*First published in *Business Standard*, 6 March 2002.

First, it is important to recognize that in today's globalized world, with complex trading arrangements and disputes, we cannot do without a centralized ombudsman. It would be like trying to run a modern society without law courts. While law courts are typically more lenient towards the rich and powerful, it is better to have them there than not.

Second, it is a sign of lack of self-confidence when one cannot decide, independently, what is good for oneself, but to instead ask for the opposite of what one's trading partners demand in the belief that if something is considered to be good by them, it must be bad for us. Further, this implies a zero-sum view of the global economy, which is false. In economic transactions there are many instances where all the agents gain or all lose.

We must evaluate items on the agenda independently and from our own perspective. Consider the three Indian demands that I began with. I think it is right for us to have opposed the introduction of international labour standards in the WTO agenda, but it is not at all clear why we were so strongly against a new trade round. And, finally, our opposition to trade liberalization was plain wrong. India's average tariff rate of around 30 per cent, while much lower than it was, is much higher than in most industrialized nations. We have decided to lower it steadily over the next three years. Hence, a global programme to lower tariffs would mean we would be asked to do what we had planned to do anyway; and others would also have to lower their tariffs, thereby increasing our access to other markets.

Third, economic policy is today such a complex matter that it is not always clear what is good for a nation and what is not. Last December, there was furore in India when a dispute settlement panel of the WTO ruled against India's practice of (1) forcing automobile manufacturers in India to buy more than a certain fraction of parts from Indian producers (the indigenization condition), and (2) requiring automotive manufacturers who need to import parts and kits to export goods worth the same value (trade balancing condition). If we reflect on these conditions, it is not at all transparent that these are good for us. The indigenization condition, by forcibly creating a market for Indian automobile parts, eases the pressure on these manufacturers to improve quality. And by forcing Indian cars to use these parts it also handicaps Indian cars from being of fully international quality.

The trade balancing condition seems to me to be premised on a failure to recognize that effective production involves specialization, where you use one good to produce another. Forcing companies to match every use of foreign exchange by the production of foreign exchange is to destroy an essential feature of specialized production. Hence, the WTO ruling, at least in this case, may be a blessing in disguise. At times it is useful to be compelled to do what one may not have done of one's own bidding.

It may not be altogether a coincidence that after Germany and Japan lost the Second World War and were compelled to adopt certain economic policies—such as a draconian antitrust regime—by the victorious Allied powers, it was Germany and Japan that emerged as the big success stories, not Britain and France.

India must engage itself with the WTO actively, while keeping up the pressure on it to give more voice to nations of the South. There are eighteen African countries without any representation in Geneva. What benefit can they expect from the WTO? When there is a legal tussle in the WTO and the big countries bring in the best lawyers to argue their case, what chance do these poor countries stand? As a democratic country with considerable expertise in economics and law, India has a responsibility to fight for better representation of all at the WTO. Once that is achieved, it will be easier to entrust the WTO with many tasks, such as the maintenance of minimal labour standards, which appear contentious today. But the important rule to remember is that even if that is not achieved, we have more to gain by being an active participant in WTO deliberations than by withdrawing or being a habitual naysayer.

Postscript

Fortunately, not all North–South engagements are matters of moment. Some years ago, when I went from Delhi to lecture in another city (which will remain unnamed) in the developing world, I told the director of the institute where I was to lecture that I was planning to explore my host city on foot. With the hospitality that comes so spontaneously to Third Worlders, he said he would have none of it, rang the bell on his desk, and asked the assistant who responded to find out if the 'Fertility car' was available. I was of course intrigued. And so, while the assistant was away on his errand, through some deft questioning I figured out the etymology of 'Fertility car'. The institute had received money from a Northern nation for a project on fertility, and a part of it had been used to buy a car, which had come to be christened accordingly.

After a while the assistant reappeared, panting, to report that the Fertility car was unavailable. But since—and he said this with obvious pride in his ingenuity—I was a guest of the institute, he had gone over to another department and had booked 'Poverty' for me. I vacillated about the ethics of it, but decided it would be too rude to say no. So, the next day, nursing a slight feeling of ambivalence, I explored the beautiful city in 'Poverty', never finding out what the Northern donor would have made of this excursion.

10

Globalization and the Politics of International Finance: The Stiglitz Verdict*

Introduction

Joseph Stiglitz's book, *Globalization and Its Discontents* (2002) defies easy categorization. It is, in part, an academic monograph meant to be read by professional economists and the serious graduate student; but it is also, in part, a diatribe against the injustices of global finance and politics. It is written at times from the ivory tower, contemplating the vast panorama of international economic relations with a researcher's trained but distant vision; but it also reads in places like a rabble-rousing call from an activist who has no time for the niceties of models and regressions. With a title that rhymes with Sigmund Freud's classic monograph, this is also a book where an academic, who has done pioneering work in his field, cuts loose from the binds of his discipline and assesses the world with passion, concern, and also disappointment.

It is the disappointment that makes this such a compelling book. Stiglitz has seen it all. In 1993 he moved out of the groves of academe to join President Clinton's Council of Economic Advisors.[1] From

*This first appeared as a review article on Joseph Stiglitz, *Globalization and Its Discontents*, Norton & Co., New York, 2002, in *Journal of Economic Literature*, September 2003, vol. 41. I am grateful to Mrinal Datta Chaudhuri, John McMillan, Patrick Nolen, Erik Thorbecke, and Henry Wan for comments and discussions.

[1] Initially, as Member, and then, from 1995 to 1997, as Chairman.

there he went to the World Bank as Senior Vice President and Chief Economist. Popular globally for championing the cause of the disadvantaged and dispossessed and for not holding back on criticizing the US Department of Treasury and the IMF, he became unpopular in the bastions of power in Washington for these very reasons. Soon after leaving the World Bank and joining Columbia University he won the Nobel Prize in economics, which he shared with George Akerlof and Michael Spence. He *himself* has little to be disappointed about in the world. And that is exactly what gives poignance and moral force to his disappointment, and strength to his argument.

Moving from the world of theoretical models and the study of market equilibria, he encountered in Washington a world of finance and markets which did not correspond to the theoretical constructs of modern economics. This was true even when one considered the most realistic theoretical models which broke ranks with the orthodoxy of the so-called traditional 'Chicago School' and allowed for imperfect information, multiple equilibria, and Pareto sub-optimality. Moreover, not only was reality less perfect than these models, it was more unfair. Of course, the unfairness works to the advantage of the strong and the powerful and those who side with the establishment. This book is Stiglitz's breaking rank with the establishment.

There are many 'outsiders' who have written critiques of globalization and the global financial system. Insiders typically do not do so; they have too much to lose. It is this recklessness that makes Stiglitz's book effective. This is so in the same way that Soros' (2002) critique of US hegemony and the unfairness of market fundamentalism makes compelling reading—because his recommendations stand at variance with his interests.

Another strength of the book stems from the fact of Stiglitz's command over the length and breadth of economics. So, while he lashes out at market fundamentalism, he is fully aware of and never downplays the importance of markets and incentives. Likewise, while he points to all the negative fallouts of globalization and how it has marginalized so many people, communities, and nations, he shows awareness of the ways in which globalization *can* confer benefits on the poor. In fact, he makes it clear that he is no anti-globalizer. He is fully cognizant of the benefits of trade and global capital flows. This is a book that can be read profitably by the defenders of market fundamentalism as well as the demurrers of globalization.

Despite all these strengths, the book fails to live up to expectations in some important dimensions. Some of these have to do with the minor nuts and bolts of Stiglitz's argument—I shall comment on those as I come upon them. A more major disappointment stems from the fact that, while the book breaks away from so many orthodoxies and builds up expectations of a new and alternative vision, it does not attempt to deliver on these expectations.

Barring a few readers steeped in prejudice, most will agree with the broad contours of Stiglitz's criticism of global politics and orthodox economics. But in the wake of this criticism the natural question that arises is: how, then, should one think of markets and economies, and what should be the paradigm that one carries in one's head when thinking of global political economy? Confronted by the work of a lesser author, it might seem off the mark to even *ask* these questions: it would seem sufficient that the author managed to raise doubts about the orthodoxy. But, given that Joseph Stiglitz has in the past dislodged parts of orthodox economics *and* built new models in their place, one naturally hopes for a little bit of the latter in this book. On that score, one is left disappointed.

Facts, Theories, and Myths

In many dimensions, modern economics has had phenomenal success. On a variety of subject matters there are excellent models—theoretical constructs that help us think through what the consequences of certain actions will be. Thus, if following the Iraq War oil supplies to the world increase, we know that the price of travel will fall. We do not need empirical knowledge of previous experience with the rise and fall of Iraqi oil supplies to make this prediction. We make the prediction using the model of demand and supply, which is founded on a few basic 'truths' (which are admittedly empirical), and then applying a chain of deductive reasoning based on those.

There are other areas where we have little or no theory to go by, but have enough evidence to make intelligent guesses about how one action may affect another.

But despite the much-vaunted success of economics in many areas, economics remains remarkably weak on some of the most important questions that confront nations. What causes an economic crisis, such as the one that affected most of East Asia in 1997? What is the remedy when such a crisis occurs? How does politics intertwine with markets? What kind of political system helps economic growth and what kind hinders?

If we searched through textbooks of economics and the tomes of data at our disposal, we would be forced to admit that we have very little to go by when taking on such questions. But we are, nevertheless, often forced to give answers. An international organization such as the IMF or the World Bank, whose job it is to help nations in economic trouble, cannot keep quiet when such troubling questions are asked. So they give answers, and through a process of herd behaviour, the answers have converged to what seemed like a consensus. Nations must privatize, cut the fiscal deficit, curtail subsidies, remove trade barriers, and allow the free flow of international capital. This broad package came to be known as the 'Washington Consensus'.[2]

It is unwise to think of the Washington Consensus as the product of a conspiracy.[3] The Consensus emerged from serious economists searching for 'best practices' in an uncertain world, from international

---

[2] For a discussion of the Washington Consensus and Stiglitz's position on it, see Chang (2001).

[3] Conspiracy theories are troublesome. Many lay people see more conspiracies than there are, if only because human beings are congenitally prone to believing that someone's volition must be involved whenever they see order. Krugman (1998) is right when he asserts that he is disinclined to believe in conspiracy theories because, from what he has seen of world leaders, 'they seem a lot like the rest of us: Most of the time they haven't got a clue.' On the other hand, we

organizations shirking from having to say 'We do not know', and from various unintentional acts. All the same, the Consensus survives because it fits well with vested interests; it does not upset the apple cart.

The etymology of the term 'Washington Consensus' is interesting. What has come to be known by that term today is a bit of a caricature of the original. The term was probably first used by John Williamson in 1989 to describe a policy agenda *specifically for Latin America*. As he points out in his lucid essay (Williamson, 2003), he was aware even then that the agenda omitted important objectives, such as concern for better income distribution. Williamson's aim, at that stage, was to sketch a minimal agenda that would be acceptable to Washington. It was never meant to be a complete policy manifesto for all countries, not even for all developing countries. But over the years it was seized upon by politicians and bureaucrats wanting to push a particular policy manifesto, and in the popular mind the Washington Consensus came to be associated with this manifesto.

However, given that the Washington Consensus is not a formal document or an agreement, it is right to treat it now as what people take it to be. Hence, Stiglitz is right in directing his critique at this caricatured version of the Consensus rather than at the narrower original.

Stiglitz lived in Washington during the years of the East Asian and Russian crises of the 1990s and through the heyday of transition in the former socialist economies. And he grew disillusioned with the Washington Consensus. As he pushed hard to modify it, he realized that what gradually emerged as the Consensus may have once been a product of serious soul-searching, but interests had developed around it and in it. Much of Stiglitz's book is about the discovery of how myths get etched into institutional consciousness as facts, and are then defended by established interests.

The easy way to defend a disputed idea is to not open it up for debate and to keep one's true findings and doubts in the closet. A natural

---

must not be so naïve as to treat all order as spontaneous order. As Krugman observes in the same article, 'Yet conspiracies do happen.'

concomitant of this is lack of transparency. So Stiglitz is right to argue that, over the years, the IMF has come to possess too little transparency. On some matters he takes too strong a position against the IMF—as we shall see when we come to a discussion of the East Asian crisis.

The East Asian and Russian Crises

The book has a large thesis: globalization can potentially benefit all, but it has not done so. Those who are at the helm of global politics and economics have made sure that their wealth gets amassed and their power stays protected. This has worked to the detriment of the masses of people and regions that have got marginalized. The micro markets for wheat and rice may work entirely according to the laws of demand and supply, but the larger facts of economic life respond as much to politics and power as demand and supply, thereby casting doubt on our textbook theorems of market efficiency and optimality.

Stiglitz treats the East Asian and Russian crises of the late 1990s as case studies in support of his thesis. On 2 July 1997, the Thai baht, after trading for ten years around 25 to a dollar, depreciated overnight by 25 per cent. No one knew at that time that this was the start of one of the greatest economic crises since the Great Depression. The crisis would soon spread to Malaysia, Korea, the Philippines, and Indonesia. Over the next several months these currencies would continue on a free fall, as shown in Table 1.

The start of the crisis may have been inevitable, but for its persist-ence, depth, and consequent human suffering Stiglitz places the blame directly on the IMF—and he does so with no holds barred. The prob-lem, according to Stiglitz, began early, when the 'IMF and the US Treasury seemed to criticize the countries—according to the IMF, the Asian nations' institutions were rotten, their governments corrupt, and wholesale reform was needed'(Stiglitz, 2002, p. 90).

There were many commentators who criticized the IMF for having failed to predict such a major crisis. But in fact there seemed to have been no one who predicted this crisis would happen. Some way into the crisis I researched several old issues of *The Economist* and other

Table 1

Devaluations and Share Price Collapse, 1 July 1997 to
16 February 1998

	% Depreciation of Currency *vis-à-vis* the Dollar	% Change in the Share Price Index
Thailand	87.09	−48.37
Malaysia	55.43	−58.41
Korea	83.04	−63.06
Philippines	51.37	−49.17
Indonesia	231.00	−81.74

SOURCE: Bloomberg Financial Services L.P., and Bank of Mexico. Reproduced in Martinez (1998).

magazines preceding the event. There were, indeed, no forewarnings; the Thai baht's fundamentals were described repeatedly as robust. The only mild criticism of East Asia was in relation to its banking system and burgeoning non-performing assets.

But failure to predict the crisis cannot be reason for criticism. It is, in fact, arguable that there is a logical problem in the very existence of anyone who is known to be able to predict a currency collapse in advance. It is not that no one can know well in advance that a currency will collapse: it is simply that no one can be known to know that.

To understand this: suppose that there is an institution or a person who, through research or intuition, gets to know a month in advance of a currency collapsing. If such a person is known to have this forecasting power, every time he makes such a forecast speculators will immediately sell the currency that he predicts will collapse after a month. That will cause the currency to collapse immediately. So he will never be able to make a public forecast of a collapse well in advance. Ergo, such a person, almost by definition, cannot exist.

Stiglitz is too clear-headed a thinker not to realize this and he never criticizes the IMF for its failure to predict the crisis.[4] His criticism is

---

[4] The IMF's failure to sound a warning on Korea, *after* Thailand, Indonesia, and Malaysia went into crisis was, however, disappointing. Blustein (2001,

directed at IMF's assertion, in retrospect, that it knew this had to happen some time because these East Asian nations were managing their economies so poorly, and at the fact that the IMF then moved rapidly to put in place its standard reform package rooted in the Washington Consensus: these economies would have to raise interest rates, cut deficits, stabilize their economy, and privatize.

This policy prescription, according to Stiglitz, exacerbated the problem. The IMF's big mistake was its failure to realize that the East Asian crisis was different from crises in other parts of the world; and also that the global economic situation had changed quite drastically since the big international debt crisis of Latin America in 1982. Michael Camdessus was right in a sense when he described the East Asian crisis as the first financial crisis of the twenty-first century. But the response of the organization he headed did not reflect a proper understanding of this.

There were, indeed, several important dimensions in which the world economy had changed. The most important of these was economic globalization. It is true that the world has in some ways been globalizing, in the sense of becoming more connected, ever since the dawn of human history. When the first humans moved out of Africa, when Amerigo Vespucci landed in the New World more than 500 years ago, and when Vasco da Gama landed in Cochin around the same time—these were all steps towards globalization. But there can be no denial that after a brief retreat between the two world wars, the pace of globalization gathered pace as never before. This is true in two particular areas: capital movement, and trade. This is captured well in Tables 2A and 2B.

Trade has increased very substantially in all major regions of the world, no matter how one measures this—in absolute terms or as a percentage of GDP. If one goes further back in history one finds that

---

p.118) has quoted from a confidential IMF document, dated as late as 15 October 1997, which observed that Korea's fundamentals were so strong that 'we have confidence in the authorities' ability to prudently manage the situation'. The report was, subsequently, quietly put away in the Fund's files.

Table 2A

Merchandise Export as % of GDP

	1870	1913	1950	1995
Western Europe	8.8	14.1	8.7	35.8
Asia	1.7	3.4	4.2	12.6
Latin America	9.7	9.0	6.0	9.7
Africa	5.8	20.0	15.1	14.8
World	4.6	7.9	5.5	17.2

Table 2B

Value of Foreign Capital Stock in Developing Countries
($ billion and %)

	1870	1914	1950	1998
Total (in 1990 prices)	40.1	235.4	63.2	3,030.7
Stock as % of GDP	8.6	32.4	4.4	21.7

SOURCE: Madison (2001).

between AD 1500 and 1600 there were 770 ships that sailed from Europe to the rest of the world (Madison, 2001, p. 63).[5] Given that, barring a trickle over land, there was in those times no other mode of trade, it is evident that in terms of the sheer flow of goods, services, and electronic material the world has come a very long way.

Regarding capital flows, as a percentage of GDP there has not been a monotonic rise. But the absolute amount of capital flow has risen dramatically. In addition, it has to be kept in mind that, in colonial times, while capital did move from one nation to another, capital flows typically had to be preceded by an army, which would take political control of the colony to which the capital was being directed. The capital of the last two or three decades has been much more footloose, flowing in and out of countries over which the sender of capital may

[5] Actually, this figure that Madison quotes is of ships that sailed from the seven most major European countries. But given that there were no other serious maritime nations at that time, this would be pretty much the bulk of total transcontinental sailing. Interestingly, of these 770 ships, 705 were from Portugal alone.

have no political control. Also important to note in this context is the fact that a lot of the international capital was flowing into the stock markets of East Asia.

Another major difference between the East Asia of the 1990s and other regions, and even the East Asia of some decades ago, is the high savings rate: all the East Asian economies save over 30 per cent of their national income. Under these circumstances there was no need for full capital account liberalization. This, according to Stiglitz, was *'the single most important factor leading to the crisis'* (p. 99). Many economists, such as Jagdish Bhagwati, who on trade matters take a complete free market position, nevertheless take a line on capital account liberalization which is similar to that of Stiglitz.[6] Ironically, even as I write, the Washington administration is once again pushing for the abolition of capital controls,[7] unmindful of the warning by many economists that trade in *goods* must not be equated with *capital* flows (see Bhagwati and Tarullo, 2003; Wan, 2005).[8]

Whatever the precise cause of the crisis, Stiglitz argues that the failure to appreciate the new reality, and the use of the old standard IMF package, backfired in East Asia. It is a theoretically elegant analysis that Stiglitz puts forward in his book.

A standard policy response to crisis that had been used time and again in Latin America consisted of controlling excess demand (by, for instance, cutting government expenditure) and raising the interest

[6] A more disaggregated analysis would emphasize that the problem is not with the overall volume of capital flow but with its composition. A study by Rodrik and Velasco (1999) shows that a country with short-term liability to foreign banks that exceed its foreign reserves is three times as likely to have a sudden outflow of capital.

[7] This is part of the free trade agreements being negotiated by the US with Chile and Singapore. What these countries wanted was not capital controls but the freedom to use capital controls in certain contingencies. But in the end they relented under pressure from US negotiators.

[8] For one, the capital market (unlike the market for goods) seldom takes the form in which an agent can borrow as much as she wishes at the going interest rate. Moreover, a person demanding capital is, typically, asked by the lender to explain why she needs the money. The greengrocer, on the other hand, does not ask you why you want oranges before he agrees to sell you some.

rate. Both these policies, Stiglitz argues, were wrong for East Asia, and were prompted by a crucial misdiagnosis of the crisis. As an aside, it is worth noting that for this same reason, Stiglitz's brief analysis of Argentina is less convincing. It is not clear that the contractionary policy recommended by the IMF to Argentina was wrong. Argentina's government, struggling to compete with Brazil, with its exchange rate policy frozen under a Currency Board, was in a bind. Moreover, in the late 1990s it repeatedly missed its tax revenue targets, which made expenditure cutbacks that much more necessary.

Controlling excess demand is right policy for a nation suffering from inflation or repressed inflation. In East Asia there were no inflationary pressures in 1997 and the economies had reasonable macrobalance, including low fiscal deficits. Under those circumstances, cutting government expenditure was likely to exacerbate a recession instead of aiding its abatement.

The second policy instrument—raising the interest rate—is often used to bring foreign currency into the country—it is lured in by the high interest rate—and thereby stall exchange rate depreciation. In East Asia this policy backfired for an interesting reason. While the governments of these countries had balanced budgets, the corporate sector, including small firms, was heavily indebted. When interest rates were suddenly raised in Thailand (and the same policy pattern would follow elsewhere) this may have temporarily shored up the demand for bahts but it meant that the highly leveraged Thai firms were driven to bankruptcy.[9]

[9] This argument of Stiglitz finds support from a detailed computable general equilibrium model of Indonesia that has been developed by Azis, Azis, and Thorbecke (2001). By running simulations with alternative policy interventions, in particular one where the intervention deviated from the actual IMF one by holding the interest rate at a lower level, the authors found evidence that the IMF policy did exacerbate some of the suffering. It is worth noting here that a recent theoretical exercise by Aghion, Bacchetta, and Banerjee (2001) puts the credit shortages faced by private firms, instead of macro imbalances at the level of government, at the centre of the model in explaining currency crises. In this

Much has been written about 'contagion' and 'infection' when discussing economic crisis and the often mysterious process by which a crisis transmits from one country to another. Another important product of globalization that has not been written about adequately is what may be described as 'market contamination', namely, the process by which a crisis in one market or sector transmits to another. Market contamination is a product of the kind of globalization described above.

To continue with the Thailand example, as companies began to go bankrupt the stock prices, naturally, started to fall. This meant that people began selling off their stocks. In earlier times, when currencies did not flow across borders with alacrity, this crisis could have been contained. But nowadays, with such large capital flows across nations, it is reasonable to expect that a part of the stocks traded on the Bangkok stock exchange is by foreigners. It follows that, with stock prices collapsing, as people sell off stocks, some of those selling the stocks will be foreigners (non-Thailand residents). Since these people would typically have originally converted their currencies (dollars, euros, yens) into Thai bahts in order to buy stocks in Bangkok, when they sell their stocks and collect bahts it would be natural to expect they convert bahts back to their own currency. Hence, a fall in stock prices would now have a direct impact on the foreign exchange market causing the baht to devalue. Once the foreign exchange market gets destabilized, it tends to rapidly contaminate other markets.[10]

To return to the epidemiological analogy and to steal a macabre insight from the SARS epidemic, note that some markets are more

---

sense, it is close to Stiglitz's description of the East Asian crisis. However, they find that, typically, raising the interest rate may be the right policy and one that can stall a crisis.

[10] The contamination of one market by another is illustrated well in Table 1. In each of the East Asian crisis countries, at least in the early stages, the collapse of the currency was matched by the collapse of share prices. In many of these nations, land and property prices also collapsed around the same time.

effective at spreading trouble than others. Just as there was Typhoid Mary in 1907, and just as some people have been identified as 'super-infectors' in the spread of SARS, some markets are better than others at spreading contamination. Clearly, the foreign exchange market is a 'super-infector' since it underlies so many other activities. This is especially so given globalization. To understand this, note that, if the baht is expected to fall, foreigners who bought stocks in Thailand or property in Thailand and measured their profit in dollars, would have some reason to sell off their stocks (even though stock prices are not expected to fall), and then of course they will sell off the bahts thus acquired. Likewise for property. Hence, stock prices and property prices will begin to collapse even though nothing happened in the stock market or the housing market to warrant this.

This is what happened in East Asia. The contamination travelled from one market to another and the echoes returned to worsen the initial crisis. And soon the contagion caught on in other countries.

One problem with Stiglitz's analysis of the East Asian crisis is that he gives too little benefit of the doubt to the IMF. While he is right to be heavily critical of IMF conditionalities, its lack of transparency, and its inadequate concern for poverty,[11] one is left wondering how the IMF could have been so systematically on the wrong side in so many decisions. And Stiglitz is ambiguous on an important question that naturally arises from his analysis: were the IMF's mistakes instances of malfeasance or just plain bungling?

In places Stiglitz suggests that the IMF represented Wall Street's interests mediated through the Treasury, even when it was working ostensibly to help poor nations. 'While Wall Streeters defended the principles of free markets and a limited role of government, they were

---

[11] In fact one of the beneficial by-products of Stiglitz's hard-hitting criticism of the IMF is that it has now instituted programmes to monitor the consequences of IMF stabilization programmes for the poor. I have argued (in Basu, 2001) that international organizations should move towards evaluating nations in terms of the performance of the poorest 20 per cent of their population. Apart from the fact that such a measure has some attractive technical properties, it should over time help tilt our aims in favour of the most disadvantaged.

not above asking help from government to push their agenda for them. And we shall see, the Treasury Department responded with force' (p.102). And the US, with over 17 per cent of the votes in the IMF, worked hard to 'help the *special* interests of Wall Street'.

But there are other times when he seems to say it was not a case of malfeasance, that it was caused by ignorance in the IMF. 'If only they had better economists', he seems to be suggesting. Of course, if the IMF were representing special interests, better economists would not have made it more receptive to the concerns of developing countries; they would simply have made the IMF more effective in serving special interests.[12]

I believe that in subtle ways the big powers do take control of the major international organizations and defend certain policies and ideas that are convenient to them. But they often do this not by directly twisting the agenda. Instead they settle organizations into an ideology and promote ideas compatible with their interests. This is not hard because, as we saw earlier, while economics has had some major successes, it remains woefully inadequate on many of the most important questions that confront policy-makers. In these latter areas, it is easy for myths to develop. By repeating certain propositions sufficiently often, they can be made to sound like facts and, given the credibility of economics in other areas, most people treat these myths as facts. This creates scope for subversion—that is, feeding people with 'facts' which are convenient to those who have cooked them up. The British satirical magazine *Private Eye*, responding to the obsession of some American magazines to repeat-check facts, once asserted that they, on the other hand, ran on the principle that 'some facts are too good to be checked'.[13] The powerful do precisely this. The critical eye is turned

[12] Hence, the question, 'Why did the best and the brightest fail?', does not seem to me to be particularly interesting. They may not have been trying to do what we thought they were trying to do. Also, the best and the brightest can be locked in games like the Prisoner's Dilemma among themselves, and so may end up doing badly even for themselves.

[13] Quoted from Sarah Lyall's essay, 'Recipe for Roasting the Sacred Cow, Tastelessly', *New York Times*, 12 November 2001.

away from myths which are convenient to influential groups and pow-erful nations—Stiglitz's 'Wall Streeters', big corporations, and well-organized lobbies—and by this process they are perpetuated.

The fact that economics has no hard answers to the questions that countries face during a crisis makes it possible for the IMF to behave the way it does. But this also means that the sorts of policies that the IMF propounds are not egregiously or obviously false (see footnote 5). The IMF's fault was not that it recommended what was known to be false, but that it recommended with a tone of certainty on matters about which existing expert opinion is divided.

On balance, I feel persuaded by Stiglitz that the IMF recommend-ations were flawed in East Asia; but the impossibility of doing a coun-ter-factual experiment means that this remains an open question. The IMF has maintained that the East Asian crisis was short-lived because of its policies. On the other hand, Stiglitz and other critics of the IMF argue that the crisis went so deep because of IMF policies. The current state of economics is such that an indubitable answer cannot be pro-vided.

In the case of some of the bigger countries, the IMF has actually, unwittingly, played a useful role. When India had its economic crisis and had to turn to the IMF for support in 1991, the Indian government managed to use the alibi of IMF pressure to push in some essential reforms which, otherwise, may not have been possible because of poli-tical constraints.[14]

Also, the IMF is probably less of a monolith than Stiglitz seems to suggest. His phrasings make the organization seem homogeneous: 'the IMF had feared', 'the IMF felt', 'the IMF opposed'. But there are in-variably many opinions within such a large organization. I witnessed this during my year in the World Bank, 1998–9. On a variety of mat-ters (certainly on child labour) the research going on in the Bank was of high quality and the opinions being expressed in many of the works produced there were at variance with what the higher echelons of the

[14] In fact many of the Indian reforms would be broadly in keeping with what Stiglitz would recommend.

Bank did or said, thereby showing that on many of these matters a phrase such as 'the World Bank's view' would not make much sense.[15]

Stiglitz is on stronger ground with Russia because here he dwells a lot on cases where there were problems of corruption and attempts by the business mafia to twist policy to their own benefit. The crisis that hit Russia in the late 1990s was quite dramatic. During 1940 to 1946 in Soviet Russia, industrial production fell by 24 per cent. Over 1990 to 1999 industrial production fell by 60 per cent and GDP fell by 54 per cent. As Stiglitz notes: 'For the majority of those living in the former Soviet Union, economic life under capitalism has been even worse than the old Communist leaders had said it would be' (p.133).

In Russia the tragedy was that communism gave way to the hands of venal and corrupt profiteers. The new owners of formerly state-owned enterprises looted the companies, literally selling off company assets and stashing away the loot in their private bank accounts. Some of the privatization programmes were run very badly, and surely the IMF knew better. As Stiglitz observes, 'it is easy to privatize quickly if one does not pay any attention to *how* one privatizes: essentially, give away valuable state property to one's friends' (p. 144).

The immediate benefit of privatization is to increase efficiency and there is evidence that this does usually happen.[16] There is however a quandary about *how* firms are privatized, and this has to be kept in mind. If state-owned firms are sold off at cut prices, as happened in Russia, basically the state is making a gift to the buyer. Since such a gift is not always visible to the lay public, this gives rise to corruption, with politicians effecting *quid pro quo* trades with business people. On the

---

[15] This also reveals that smart institutions have a way of dealing with a variety of opinions within the organization without silencing them and, at the same time, not allowing them to interfere with what the institution does. This illusion of participatory democracy could be termed the '*éle béle* syndrome' and is outlined within the opening essay of the present book.

[16] For a survey, see Megginson and Netter (2001). It is however worth mentioning that if the privatization occurs in an environment where there is no appropriate antitrust legislation, then it can aggravate certain kinds of inefficiencies (Bhaskar and Khan, 1995).

other hand, if state-owned firms are sold at their full market price, then this act of privatization does not in itself amount to a transfer of wealth from government. It merely amounts to a re-composition of the government portfolio. In that case, much depends on what is done with the money acquired by government after the sale. If the government uses it to acquire control over some other resource which it is not good at managing, then such privatization is obviously fatuous.

Since the purpose of privatization is to diminish government control over ordinary market activity, an essential feature of successful privatization is the transfer of resources back to the public. The fault with Russian privatization was not that individuals gained by it—they would have to, for the privatization to be considered successful—but the *way* it was done, the disregard for equity and fairness associated with the distribution of spoils. Also, given the institutional setting in which this occurred, the incentive for the new owners was not to run the firm efficiently but to strip it of its assets.

Stiglitz is right to lay a large part of this blame at the doorstep of the international financial community, which with its larger experience and knowledge base could have checked the rampant corruption. His description of the loans-for-share scandal is quite chilling. Government took loans from private banks, with shares of publicly owned firms as collateral. It then went on to default on these loans and the ownership of public firms had been smoothly transferred to friendly bank entrepreneurs.

The finer details of the reform package would not have been so important were it not for the toll it took on ordinary human beings. In 1989, 2 per cent of those living in Russia were below the poverty line, defined by their consumption being less than two dollars a day. By 1999 the figure had risen to 23.8 per cent, and 50 per cent of the children were living in households below the poverty line (Stiglitz, 2002, p. 153).

The story was similar in East Asia. Unemployment rose very sharply within a year—it nearly trebled in Korea; and real wages fell dramatically in Indonesia (by 41 per cent) but also sharply enough in Korea (9.3 per cent) and Thailand (7.4 per cent). This information is summarized in Table 3 below.

We know that in the case of Indonesia this has also led to political instability and violence. In a poor nation, such a sharp downturn is bound to be quite traumatic.

Stiglitz goes on to lament how little the richer nations and power blocs did to assuage the problems, even if we are willing to spare them responsibility for having caused some of the problems. A point he makes poignantly and more than once is how warped global policies are that show willingness to spend billions on bailouts—these were often bailouts more for Western banks than for the nations in trouble—whereas, when it came to the few millions needed to mitigate the degradation and poverty that the crises caused, there was never enough money.[17] This leads to some large questions about global politics and the way globalization has changed the world. The last chapters of the book take Stiglitz into this large terrain. These are extremely valuable chapters which no one can afford to ignore. At the same time, this is

Table 3

Real Wage and Unemployment Changes in East Asia

	% Change in Real Wage During 1998	Unemployment	
		1997	1998
Indonesia	−41.0	4.7	5.4
Korea	−9.3	2.6	6.8
Malaysia	−1.1	2.6	4.0
Philippines	−2.0	8.7	10.1
Thailand	−7.4	2.2	5.2

SOURCE: Betcherman and Islam, 2001.

[17] One concrete plan that he puts forward for this involves the use of Special Drawing Rights (SDRs) to create global public goods and to help the poor. This is somewhat similar to Soros's (2002) suggestion to rich nations to donate their SDR allocations for international assistance to poor nations. But Stiglitz's strategy is really not spelled out enough for us to be able to evaluate it carefully.

where one is left regretting he doesn't take his powers of abstraction and formalization further to give us a more complete paradigm of global political economy.

Take, for instance, Stiglitz's criticism of the IMF. Surely, all the faults that he points to cannot be peculiar to the IMF: were that so, we would have to treat it as an anomaly of nature, as an organization idiosyncratically pernicious. Our prescription would then have to be to excise it, or alter its management totally. But that is not what Stiglitz means. His occasional references to the US Treasury, the World Bank, and Wall Streeters show that the malaise that afflicts the IMF is widespread. Powerful organizations all seem to behave in similar fashion. Hence, the IMF is more likely a product of the 'system', of the 'rules' of the game by which the global economy runs. Even if the IMF were replaced by a JNG, as long as it functioned in the same global ethos, it would, over time, begin to behave in much the same way. My suspicion is that Stiglitz will agree with this analysis.[18]

If that be so, the critique needs to be directed much more at the rules of the global game than at specific players. Policywise, this is a very hard problem. Since we understand so poorly where the fundamental rules of the game of life come from, it is not obvious to anybody how we should go about changing those rules. But given that much of Stiglitz's book builds up to this engaging question, it would have been nice if we could be privy to Stiglitz's thoughts on the matter, however embryonic those thoughts may be. I hope that there is another book by him in the offing.

Globalization, Politics, and Democracy

One reason why our understanding of global political economy is so weak is the way mainstream economics used to be written. Much of it presumed markets to be competitive and information perfect, and

---

[18] As he observes in another paper (Stiglitz, 2003), given the IMF's mandate and its consequent close connection with various finance ministries and financial communities, it would be surprising to find it behaving differently from the way it actually does.

human beings to be fully rational, with there being no room for power politics. Though modern economics has moved far away from that model, especially in terms of recognizing the importance of oligopolies and asymmetries of information,[19] a large number of policy-makers remain under the spell of the traditional model. That model may be a reasonable approximation of some simple intra-country markets; but as soon as we enter the global marketplace, with no overarching system of law and government, we leave the textbook models—even the new ones which, though rich in other ways, are yet to properly characterize the role of power politics in the functioning of economies—behind as inadequate. Hence, as is amply clear from Stiglitz's book, there is a need to go beyond textbook models—even the modern ones—to a deeper critique and a more fundamental reconstruction of an economics that is embedded in sociology and politics.

Let me illustrate this with the far-reaching implication of one assumption that is patently wrong but that most mainstream economics treats as true. This is the assumption of individual rationality.[20]

A major way in which contemporary human beings are better off than humans of an earlier era is that they do not, typically, have to rely on physical strength to guard their own interest.[21] When we walk down a road wearing a nice watch, we do not have to be prepared to fight to keep it. On returning home from an outing we do not expect to have to throw out people who have occupied our homes. This is because of the general recognition that it is wrong for people to grab other people's belongings just because they have the power to, and because of the consequent policing and social norms that have merged around this recognition.

---

[19] Some of these market failures have been written about effectively by Stiglitz himself in his earlier incarnation as an economic theorist. For a comprehensive review of the ways in which market failures occur in developing countries, see Hoff and Stiglitz (2001).

[20] Admittedly the new behavioural economics has at last begun to chip away at this assumption.

[21] This is not to deny that there are regions of the world where the hand of law is so weak that they resemble primitive times.

In primitive times, as in some places even now, those who were physically weak reconciled to the fact that the strong would take away much that was theirs. There may even have been those who argued that that is the way things ought to be. It is a huge achievement towards making the world just and fair that this generally happens no longer.

We do not, however, have an equivalent moral code against one person becoming richer than another by *outwitting* the latter. Outwitting is fair game. When a rural moneylender becomes rich by repeatedly cutting good deals *vis-à-vis* the borrower, when a colonizer buys up valuable property from the colonized, and when a financier extends a home-improvement loan to an old lady living alone in Washington (knowing the odds are that she will not be able to repay the loan and he will foreclose on her property), we consider these deals acceptable as long as no strong-arm tactic is used. If both sides agree freely to a deal, why should anybody else interfere?

What we do not pause to think in these examples is that, maybe, one side is actually miscalculating. Maybe the rural borrower is indulging in hyperbolic discounting and so being dynamically inconsistent, maybe the colonized 'savages' are being irrational and misjudging the future worth of the property, maybe the old lady, in her eagerness to repaint her home, is being overoptimistic about her capacity to repay the loan. One reason why we have so few safeguards against people cutting irrational deals is the economist's assumption that all human beings are rational, an assumption that has seeped into our everyday thinking. If no one is irrational, there is no need to protect the irrational. Deals that look lopsided must merely reflect differences in preferences.

But now that behavioural economics is beginning to open our eyes, we realize that, maybe, some people who are impoverished are so because they cut poor deals over and over again, just as some village lenders are rich because they systematically cut good deals. Likewise, there is now recognition that the lady in Washington who gets lured into that attractive loan may be a victim of 'predatory lending'. It is, in fact, interesting that the Federal Trade Commission in Washington now recognizes predatory lending as a problem that needs to be dealt with.[22]

The failure to recognize that outwitting an intellectually weaker person of her wealth is wrong in roughly the same way as physically unburdening a person of her belongings has had far-reaching consequences, especially in global contexts. First of all, this has meant a lot of unfairness in contracts. Second, being aware of the possibility of being 'duped' into signing complex contracts that they do not fully understand—and knowing too that the law does not protect them well against such happenings—many individuals and nations have taken the precaution of not getting into deals with savvy business people.[23] Hence, the lack of legal or norms-based protection[24] against such possibilities leads to undercontracting, and the consequent inefficiencies.[25]

Moving further, observe that even if people were fully rational and there were no problems with information, the global marketplace would continue to look very different from what textbooks of economics suggest. The reason is the absence of the rule of law and the virtual non-existence of global governance. In much of traditional thinking, especially among those committed to market fundamentalism, governments and markets have been conceptualized as countervailing forces. The

[22] See http://www.ftc.gov/opa/2001/02/predlending.htm

[23] Some years ago in Vietnam I was told by a government official that they hesitate to cut deals with multinationals not because of any inherent aversion to this but for fear that they will not understand complex contracting as well as multinationals do and so they may unwittingly end up signing contracts, that are detrimental to themselves.

[24] In Basu (2000) I argue that the law and social norms can in many situations work as equally effective substitutes.

[25] Before moving on I should emphasize that it is not rejection of the rationality assumption I am arguing for. The assumption has been behind a lot of the success of economics and is very helpful in understanding 'normal' economics. The fault lies in the fact that many economists forget this and take it to domains where its fallibility makes a fundamental difference. This also explains why the new political economy, predicated on the rational actor model, has not met with greater success. I discuss this at length in Basu (2000).

advice has always been that if you want markets to function properly, governments need to withdraw. Here and in his earlier writings, Stiglitz rejects this proposition (see, for instance, Stiglitz, 1989). Good governance, he argues, is a prerequisite of effective markets. As Soros (2002, p.6) observes, 'Markets are designed to facilitate the free exchange of goods and services . . . but they are not capable, on their own, of taking care of collective needs such as law and order or *the maintenance of the market mechanism itself*' (my italics).

Stiglitz argues that on the economic front the world has become interconnected with global markets and money flows, yet global political institutions remain woefully inadequate.[26] This disillusionment with global political economy can easily translate into a blind mistrust of markets and globalization. The protesters in the streets of Seattle during the ministerial meeting of the WTO, and protesters elsewhere at various global meetings since Seattle, while rightly upset about the unfairness of the global marketplace, have been often blinded by emotion and have played into the hands of the very people and groups that they were protesting against.[27]

What is really excellent about this book is that, on this main issue, Stiglitz manages to keep his feet firmly planted on the ground. He makes it amply clear that the potential benefits of globalization are

[26] The same sentiment is echoed by Soros (2002, p. 9): 'While markets have become global, politics remain firmly rooted in the sovereignty of the state.' This idea is elaborated upon in Basu (2002).

[27] A classic example of this is the argument for the use of a 'social clause' by the WTO to uphold international labour standards (see Bhagwati, 1995). Many protectionist lobbies in industrialized nations favour such a clause (as an instrument to block imports from developing nations), and have nicely managed to mingle behind the banners of well-meaning protesters demanding such a provision in the WTO in the genuine interest of workers in developing countries. Exactly what form the international labour standards requirement will take is a matter of detailed legal and political work and can have very different effects depending on how exactly the provisions are drafted. Since the protesters are usually absent in the crafting of the fine print and the lobbies are usually present, the broad agenda agreed with the protesters can be converted into fine print that helps lobbies instead of workers.

large and that markets and incentives are crucial for the effective running of a modern economy. The objective should not be to blunt these instruments but to make them work.

Much of the existing popular literature on globalization is so trite because it is based on a critical misunderstanding: it treats globalization as a detachable part of the economy—as if it is something that we can have or reject. In truth, globalization is a bit like gravity: we may discuss endlessly whether it is good or bad but the question of not having it does not seriously arise. We have to live with it, just as we have to live with gravity (at least in the foreseeable future), no matter what our finer emotions about it. Not being detachable, globalization is very difficult to evaluate since the counter-factual—of a world like the one we have today but without globalization—is difficult to imagine.

If we want to make globalization work in our collective interest without alienating large sections of the world, as has happened, what should we do? True, there are not too many answers in Stiglitz's book, but what he does very well is to remind us not to be lulled into believing that all is fair in the marketplace—a point of view that beneficiaries of the current global economy are eager to promote.

That's not all. Stiglitz makes another suggestion, briefly, but one that can have far-reaching consequences. He argues for a greater democratization of international organizations, so that they become more effective guardians of the interests of poor nations. Similar arguments have been made by others before (see, for instance, Nayyar, 2003), but coming from Stiglitz, who has been involved with the organizations he seeks to reform, this becomes very compelling. He points out how the United States, Europe, and Japan have dominated decisions in the World Bank, the IMF, and the WTO, and how it is time to rethink the structure of voting rights in these organizations.[28]

---

[28] The WTO runs on the principle of 'one country one vote', but the fixing of agenda behind the scenes—the so-called 'green room effect'—has tended to concentrate power in the hands of the industrialized nations with a few developing nations, such as India and now China, having some marginal say (Schott, 2000; Basu, 2002). Some of the poorest nations of the world, such as

At one level, it may seem right that those who contribute more money to these organizations should have the greater say. But given that we do not think along such lines when we talk of intra-national democracy—no one argues that Bill Gates should have more votes than others because he pays more taxes—it shows that our notions of global or international democracy remain quite rudimentary. It is therefore quite radical of Stiglitz to suggest a greater equity in voting rights within international organizations. He, in fact, goes so far as to argue that such rights should not be confined to government ministers but should, presumably, reflect grassroots opinion as well.

One cannot jump to conclusions on this since governance needs expertise, and trying to accommodate too many voices can hurt the quality of decisions. On the other hand, the current structure of decision-making makes it possible for a few powerful interests to hijack everyone's agenda. Moreover, our understanding of the needs of poor nations can itself improve if poor nations are given a greater voice.[29] What one can minimally say is that this is a matter that needs to be debated, and not kept away from the public eye in a conspiracy of silence, as is currently done. Stiglitz's effort at bringing this to public scrutiny is laudable.

Conclusion

Stiglitz's is a hard book to sum up. It cannot be described as a great book, certainly not by the yardstick of Stiglitz's own earlier papers and books. It brings us to the brink of analytically interesting and novel ideas but stops before breaking new ground. As prose it falls short because it is written too much in the form of streams of consciousness. It would have been nice if the material, rich as it is, were better organized.

---

sub-Saharan African countries, surely deserve more say than they currently have.

[29] This is what Sen (1999) refers to as the 'constructive' role of democracy. His discussion is in the context of individual needs in national decision-making. But it clearly carries over to inter-country decision problems.

At the same time, I believe this is an important book, one of the most important that I have read in recent times, and one that must be read by anyone interested in global politics and human well being, whether one is planning a career in international bureaucracy or on taking to the streets. It is a morally courageous book in which the author does not flinch from taking on the powerful and the established. This is a work that could only have been written by an 'embedded academic' who has been involved in global policy-making, who is an acute observer, and who is irreverent enough to write down what he saw.

References

Aghion, Philippe, Philippe Bacchetta, and Abhijit Banerjee (2001), 'Currency Crisis and Monetary Policy in an Economy with Credit Constraints', *European Economic Review*, vol. 45, 1121–50.

Azis, Iwan, Erina Azis, and Erik Thorbecke (2001), 'Modeling the Socio-economic Impact of the Financial Crisis: The Case of Indonesia', mimeo: Cornell University.

Basu, Kaushik (2000), *Prelude to Political Economy: A Study of the Social and Political Foundations of Economics*, Oxford: Oxford University Press.

——— (2001), 'On the Goals of Development', in Gerald Meier, and Joseph Stiglitz, eds, *Frontiers of Economic Development*, New York: Oxford University Press.

——— (2002), 'The Retreat of Global Democracy', *Indicators*, vol. 1, pp. 77-87.

Betcherman, Gordon and Rizwanul Islam (2001), 'East Asian Labour Markets and the Economic Crisis: An Overview', in G. Betcherman, and R. Islam (eds), *East Asian Labour Markets and the Economic Crisis*, The World Bank, Washington.

Bhagwati, Jagdish (1995), 'Trade Liberalization and "Fair Trade" Demands', *World Economy*, vol. 18, pp. 745-59.

——— and D. Tarullo (2003), 'A Ban on Capital Controls is a Bad Trade-Off', *Financial Times*, 17 March.

Bhaskar, V. and Mushtaq Khan (1995), 'Privatization and Employment: A Study of the Jute Industry in Bangladesh', *American Economic Review*, vol. 85, pp. 267-73.

Blustein, Paul (2001), *The Chastening*, New York: Public Affairs.

Chang, Ha Joon (2001), 'Commentary: Joseph Stiglitz vs. the Washington

Consensus', in Ha-Joon Chang, ed., *Joseph Stiglitz and the World Bank: The Rebel Within*, London: Anthem Press.

Hoff, Karla and Joseph Stiglitz (2001), 'Modern Economic Theory and Development', in Gerald Meier, and Joseph Stiglitz, eds., *Frontiers of Development Economics: The Future in Perspective*, New York: Oxford University Press.

Krugman, Paul (1998), 'I Know What the Hedgies did Last Summer', *Fortune*, vol. 138, no. 12.

Madison, Angus (2001), *The World Economy: A Millennial Perspective*, Paris: OECD.

Martinez, Guillermo O. (1998), 'What Lessons Does the Mexican Crisis Hold for Recovering in Asia?', *Finance and Development*, vol. 35, pp. 6-9.

Megginson, William and Jeffrey Netter (2001), 'From State to Market: A Survey on Empirical Studies on Privatization', *Journal of Economic Literature*, vol. 32, pp. 321-89.

Nayyar, Deepak (2003), 'The Existing System and the Missing Institutions', in Deepak Nayyar, ed., *Governing Globalization: Issues and Institutions*, Oxford: Oxford University Press.

Rodrik, Dani and Andres Velasco (1999), 'Short-term Capital Flows', *Annual World Bank Conference on Development Economics, 1999*, Washington, D.C.: The World Bank.

Schott, Jeffrey, ed. (2000), *The WTO after Seattle*, Washington, D.C.: Institute for International Economics.

Sen, Amartya (1999), *Development as Freedom*, New York: Alfred Knopf.

Stiglitz, Joseph (1989), *The Economic Role of the State*, ed. A. Heertje, Oxford: Blackwell Publishers.

———— (2002), *Globalization and Its Discontents*, New York: W.W. Norton & Co.

———— (2003), 'Globalization and the Logic of International Collective Action: Re-examining the Breton Woods Institutions', in Deepak Nayyar, ed., *Governing Globalization: Issues and Institutions*, Oxford: Oxford University Press.

Soros, George (2002), *On Globalization*, New York: Public Affairs.

Wan, Henry (2005), *Economic Development in a Globalized Environment: East Asian Evidence*, New York: Kluwer.

Williamson, John (2003), 'The Washington Consensus and Beyond', *Economic and Political Weekly*, 12 April, vol. 38, pp. 1475-81.

PART II

~

India and the World

11

Jakotra Village, Santalpur Taluka: Debating Globalization*

We have driven for about four hours since leaving Ahmedabad and now the highway meanders into a narrower bumpier road and the landscape is flat and stark, these being the edges of the salt deserts of Kutch. The soil has a parched white texture and the vegetation consists of the ubiquitous *babul*, shrub-like and spreading all the way to the far horizon. The babul, I am told, is not natural to this region. It was plant-ed by some government officials to stop the spread of the desert. It has, ever since, been a losing battle to stop the spread of the babul. This sturdy plant has an ability to dry up the soil and has contributed to the precariously low water table of the region dropping even lower and beyond the reach of dug and tube wells. On the feeble plus side, the babul emits a gum that can be used as binding material, and its branches provide a ready supply of firewood. The gum comes in small quantities and huge amounts of time have to be spent collecting a few rupees worth of gum. For the poor inhabitants of the region this has ensured that survival depends on a life of perennial foraging—for water, firewood, and gum.

During the last half hour of our drive to the village of Jakotra, in Santalpur Taluk, Patan District, no cars cross our path. We see an occa-sional villager trudging into the dusk with some watering instruments in hand. Sairaben tells us that hidden from our view are cumin plant-ations and these need to be watered at night; so the few villagers we see

*First published in *The Little Magazine*, 2004, vol. 5, issue 4.

are heading to a night of hard labour. Saira Balluch, whose first name, as is customary in Gujarat, we suffix with 'ben' (sister), is a young volunteer of SEWA (Self Employed Women's Association). She is from Radhanpur, a small town an hour or so south of Jakotra. She has been assigned to look after us, that is, Jeemol Unni—an economist from the Gujarat Institute of Development Research—and myself, during our stay in Jakotra. Saira turns out to be an amazing person. Cheerful and indefatigable, she seems to know everyone and everything about the villages in this area and is forever gracious with the village folk. Her husband also works for SEWA and she has a small child whom she leaves behind with her mother in Radhanpur on occasions like this when she has to travel.

This lifestyle, which seems natural enough now, did not happen easily to Saira, who was brought up in a traditional Muslim household. When she was finishing school, she heard of SEWA. She was not badly off and so did not need SEWA's support but wanted to work for the organization because of her inclination towards social service. Having started working with the group, she would occasionally need to return home late and would get dropped off by a SEWA car. Neighbours and the leaders of her *samaj* worried this would bring dishonour to the community. So they leaned on her parents to stop her working. But Saira was determined. She worked hard to persuade her parents that SEWA was essentially a sisterhood and so they had nothing to worry about. Her parents were, after a fashion, sympathetic towards her cause, and so to get them on her side was not hard. Saira was lucky that one of her classmates, Mumtaz Balluch, decided around that time to join her in working for SEWA. Some of the SEWA executives also talked directly with the samaj leaders and persuaded them that this was honourable social work that Saira was doing. Eventually, and especially when she married someone understanding and supportive of the SEWA cause, it became smooth sailing for her.

Also travelling with us in the Tata Qualis are Uma Swaminathan and Dohiben. Uma has been working for SEWA for over twenty years and is in charge of organizing our programme and setting up our travel and meeting plans. She does all that but, more importantly, sings classical Carnatic songs like a professional, so that the tedium of the journey melts away. Dohiben is a native of Jakotra, an embroidery artisan. It is to her house that we are headed for the night. I cannot talk to her directly because she speaks only Gujarati, and that too with the accents of a village dialect. Saira does not speak English but speaks Urdu and Gujarati equally fluently and is my translator.

Jakotra is a village like none that I have seen before. It is a poor, desolate hamlet marooned on the edge of India—ten minutes of driving north would take us to the border with Pakistan. The border here has no formal boundary. A stretch of the *rann*, an unfriendly strip of salt desert, acts as a natural deterrent to cross-border migration, though there are occasional transgressions and, even more rarely, transnational romantic liaisons.

The original village of Jakotra was destroyed almost totally on 26 January 2001 in the famous Gujarat earthquake. The new Jakotra was built by the government. As a consequence the homes, made of hollow grey bricks and an asbestos-like roofing, look quite sturdy. The 500 or so homes in the village are arranged along neat perpendicular roads, in the fashion of Manhattan. But the roads are not tarred, and the houses and yards are barren except for the heaps of hay and one or two cows and goats that each household seems to own. That this is a region of extreme poverty is obvious despite the solidity of the houses. And that we are far away from city life became obvious later that evening, when in the middle of our conversation in the courtyard of Dohiben's house, the lights went off and a thousand stars lit up in the sky as if on cue.

When we arrive in Dohiben's house it is already dark. A large number of villagers have gathered to see us. All are women, the menfolk being mostly away working as labourers in other villages. Two coir cots are pulled out for the urban guests and the villagers squat comfortably on the courtyard floor. I need no persuasion to sit on the cot. On the way in I'd asked Saira if there were snakes in the region, regretting my question as soon as it escaped my lips. She had promptly assured me that on that score there was no dearth. In fact, she was confident there were so many that I should be able to see some even on that single day's visit. For the record, I did not; but I did sit on the cot, feet off the ground.

Late into the night we chatter away, Saira being the tireless translator. Religion here is clearly no bar to intimacy and interaction. The people here, including Dohiben, are mostly Aahirs—a cow-herding caste. But among the Aahirs sit some Harijan women and all of them seem to adore Saira, who jokes with them and doubles up with laughter when the villagers in turn return her banter. The Aahirs claim that their ancestors lived in the Mathura region, in Uttar Pradesh, a thousand years ago and, before that, were a part of Krishna's cowherd tribe. Indeed, an anthropological puzzle that must strike even a casual observer is the ornate dress of these poor villagers. They wear skirts heavily embroidered and with inlaid mirror work, blouses equally elaborately crafted, and head-scarves that fall over the back and shoulders all the way down to the waist. The elderly married women wear thick ivory bangles (the young having been dissuaded by SEWA from such a decadent and expensive ritual). These are not the attire you expect in the very poor and suggest an ancestry of opulence. The wealth has vanished over the years but the custom of dress has persisted, that's my guess. Also, ivory is a strange custom in a region devoid of the pachyderm, suggesting that these Aahirs must indeed be immigrants to the region.

The women, without fail, tell us about how their lives have been transformed by SEWA. SEWA helps them market their embroidery and build up small savings, gives them low-interest loans, and has been instrumental in their breaking away from the confines of caste rules and male domination in the household.

Dohiben's own story is typical. She was married to Ajai Aahir and had five children. When the youngest child was five months old her husband died and that is when her travails began. They were always poor, but once the main breadwinner was gone life became a perennial struggle to stave off starvation. She would work long hours collecting gum from the babul, but the earnings were so small that she feared they would perish. So she began to travel all over Gujarat, mainly in Saurashtra, in search of work, and often had to be away several months at a time, leaving her eldest child in charge of the younger ones. Every time she returned after one of those long working trips, she feared she would not see one of the children.

She was literally saved by Reema Nanavatty, one of the senior members of SEWA and a former general secretary. Reema, while working in a nearby village, met Dohiben and persuaded her to return to her traditional work as an embroidery artisan and assured her that SEWA would help market her embroidered fabric in Ahmedabad and elsewhere. Soon Dohiben became a 'member' of SEWA, as the self-employed workers who are part of the SEWA family are called. SEWA now has 700,000 members all over India, with 500,000 in Gujarat. But being a SEWA member meant that she had to, at times, travel to Ahmedabad. This caused eyebrows to be raised. The senior male members of her samaj—I later realized she was referring to the leaders of her caste group and noted that the term used was the same that Saira had used for the Muslim community—met and decided that such travels could not be condoned and so decided to outcaste her. Dohiben who, despite her quiet ways, is a strong personality, tells us that she, in turn, was outraged. These men, who did not say or do a thing when she travelled all over in search of work just to survive and feed her children, had the audacity to outcaste her when she started doing a bit better for herself and interacting with city women.

Senior SEWA officials came and spent long sessions with the men, explaining to them the SEWA philosophy, which at root is Gandhian, and trying to douse the crisis. Gradually the dust settled, and especially when more and more women joined SEWA and more money flowed into the village through the better marketing of its products, the samaj seniors came around. In Jakotra, where now virtually all the women are members of SEWA, the men seem to be a pretty docile bunch, relegated to the background. It was not that way always, I am assured.

As our impromptu meetings disbands, I count there are thirty-eight women and I am the only man (Dohiben's younger sons would join us much later). I do not think I have been in a more gender-imbalanced meeting before.

The Aahir homes are small and cramped but strikingly clean. In fact, late into the night as I lay in bed that night, I heard the clanking of vessels being cleaned and floors swept.

In one room pots, pans, and clothes are pushed to a corner and a part of the floor is swabbed for us to sit down to dinner. The fare is simple— bajra roti, ghee, a hot potato curry, chhas, and gur. Just as I wonder how to tackle rotis as thick as these, Dohiben admonishes her daughter-in-law for not rolling them thinner. The daughter-in-law, who at all times seems to be holding back a smile, smiles at our ineptness.

The home that night is overcrowded. Cots are pulled in from the courtyard for Uma, Jeemol, and myself, and the rest sleep on the floor or on makeshift beds. I insist on mosquito nets (more to keep out snakes than mosquitoes) and the entire village seems to get involved in improvising how to hang the nets that we have carried with us from Ahmedabad, for the walls have no hooks and the beds no stands.

Sleep, as poets have written about and Dali has depicted so disturbingly, is a precarious indulgence. If the mind is weighed down with intense personal problems, one cannot sleep. If the mind is totally idle, waiting for sleep, it does not come. It comes easily and comfortingly if one has a puzzle in one's head which is engrossing and at the same time not personally intense. Some of my best slumbers have occurred when I have gone to bed with a research puzzle in economics and I remain convinced that some of my best papers have been written in my sleep.

I am fortunate today to have a challenging puzzle. Dohiben's house has a single latrine in the far corner of the courtyard and a tiny bathing space attached to it, but there are no taps and this is an area of acute water shortage. The logistics of how one gets through one's bath and the morning essentials constitute a decent intellectual challenge to any city-bred. Should I wake up before everybody else? But that would probably require me to get up while it is still dark and the bathroom, I have checked, has no light and so using it will be a hard balancing act. From where and how will I get water?

These are not matters to be lightly dismissed.

Years ago, visiting an avant-garde commune in a village in Belgium, I wanted to use the bathroom. My host pointed nonchalantly to one of the many open bedrooms. I went in expecting to find a door to the bathroom. There was none, but in one corner of the large bedroom was a commode. Needless to say, I bolted all the bedroom doors before using it. But on the drive back to Brussels the thought struck me, and it still occasionally troubles me, that I may not have looked hard enough and spoilt their dadaist sculpture.

Puzzling over these conundrums and misdeeds, I drift into a cosy, deep slumber.

I wake up early next morning into the most spectacular dawn. As I walk out of Dohiben's house and stroll down a street, a winter mist rolls in and I remember Khosla in my elocution class in Calcutta, reciting with his eyes shut behind thick glasses: 'And the first grey of morning fill'd the east / And the fog rose out of the Oxus stream.' Cows and goats, still lazy from sleep, stir languorously. But all the Aahir homes along the street are—again Khosla's voice—'hushed / and still the men are plunged in sleep.' Only a few womenfolk are out, in their ornate clothes and sets of three progressively smaller pots on their heads.

Much of the day is spent by the women walking to and from the one tank in the centre of the village. The tank is filled by piped water that comes from many miles away. Piped water is a recent innovation. Earlier a tanker would bring in water once a week and villagers would rush to fill up buckets, drums, and pots, causing accidents in the mêlée. Before that, the only source of water was dug wells. Water, tinged with salt, seeped into the wells at a slow pace. Villagers would often sleep next to their wells to guard them and scoop up the little water that would have collected through the night.

Some of these changes, like piped water, are also indirectly the contribution of SEWA. Contact with articulate, urban women has taught the villagers to make their own demands with the government. In fact, the following day, two of the most articulate artisans, Puriben and Gauriben, from the neighbouring villages of Bakhutra and Vauva, tell us how when some essential supplies such as electricity or water, fail badly, they lodge complaints with the relevant government office saying that they are SEWA members; and the response is immediate.

Puriben is quite an incredible woman. She joined SEWA as a member in 1988. Before that she had virtually no contact with city folk. And now, with piercing eyes and a ready smile, she is as much at ease in an Ahmedabad seminar room (though oftentimes I find her squatting on the chair on her haunches) as she is among village artisans. She has attended NGO meetings in Washington and Australia—she does not remember in which city, though. She says she wants to educate herself and become a professional manager in order to market the village products.

We spend a lot of time discussing international trade and globalization. Puriben and Gauriben argue with remarkable lucidity. Their main concern with globalization is that foreign companies will manufacture the stuff they produce using advanced technology, undercut them, and then, when the local production closes down, put the prices back up.

This is, of course, the well-known problem of dumping, where the country with the deeper pocket temporarily lowers prices to destroy the other's industry, and once the decimation is complete, raises prices. Much WTO regulation is devoted to curbing such behaviour. The trouble is that, first, these international regulations have lots of loopholes still to be plugged, and, second, fighting a case in the WTO in Geneva can be prohibitively expensive for poor nations. So the richer countries benefit disproportionately from these international trading rules.

However, this must not be construed as an argument for banishing bodies like the WTO. Law courts in most countries are used disproportionately by the rich and the powerful. Nevertheless, it is arguable that the poor are better off in a nation with functioning courts than one where there are none. Likewise for the WTO. We need to work to reform it and bring it within the reach of all nations. Not to have a central arbiter of international trade is to ensure that poor nations will not have the little recourse to justice that they are now beginning to have.

Globalization is one of the most misunderstood concepts today. First of all, to treat globalization as a matter of choice is a mistake. To say that one is in favour of globalization or against it is, as I said earlier, a bit like saying that one is in favour of gravity or against gravity. Of dubious value even as a conversation starter, it is certainly not useful as a starting point for economic policy or grassroots action. Globalization is the outcome of the individual actions of millions of people. It is doubtful if there is any government, organization, or corporation that can stall it. To pit oneself against a phenomenon where one has no chance is to court failure, as Oscar Wilde did, lying ill and penniless in a drab hotel room in Paris, on 30 November 1900. Ever the aesthete, he is believed, according to one legend, to have looked around the room and said: 'This wallpaper is terrible. One of us will have to go.' Those were his last words.

Given the inevitability of globalization, it is better to try to understand its consequences, good and bad, and to channel our energies to counter the latter.

While it is true that globalization has its pitfalls and can potentially marginalize sections of the population, it can also confer huge benefits. The villagers of Jakotra are much better off today than ten years ago—this they all agree—arguably because of globalization. If they had to sell their products only in the neighbouring villages, the prices that their produce would fetch would be much lower, and the demand for their goods would be tiny. It is because they are now using long-distance trade channels (and there is effort afoot to sell their embroidered clothes abroad) that they are able to earn more.

Historically, one of the more important reasons India remained poor is that our markets were so severely balkanized. Banditry, bad roads, and arbitrary taxes en route meant that one was forced to sell the bulk of one's products in one's neighbourhood. We may nowadays lament the occasional octroi checkpost that the intercity driver has to encounter, but it is sobering to remember that the seventeenth-century

French traveller Jean de Thevenot recorded encountering sixteen customs points during a sixty-mile journey in India.

A macro study of the Indian economy by Maureen Leibl and Tirthankar Roy confirms what one can see at the level of artisans in Gujarat.[1] The economic reforms of 1991, far from hurting handicrafts, have helped this sector. The authors describe the handicrafts sector 'as one of the major success stories in India's globalization' (p.5370). In the last decade the share of handicrafts exports in the overall manu-facturing exports of India has risen from 2 per cent to 5 per cent and employment in this sector has more than doubled. While there is reason to believe that this trend can persist for a while (India's share of the global handicrafts market is still way behind China's), it is fool-hardy to suppose that this will never change. The apprehension among the artisans of Jakotra that they will some day be out-competed by large-scale global producers is probably right. In a small way, similar things are already happening. Indian manufacturers have begun producing 'African-looking' crafts which are then sent to Africa for Western and Japanese tourists to buy from the roadsides of Kenya, Tanzania, and elsewhere.

What is widely misunderstood in India and in the West, where there is mounting opposition to outsourcing, is that the real problem is not globalization but the inexorable march of technology. Technology has brought enormous benefits to mankind. High-tech large-scale manu-facturing and the computer revolution have brought certain comforts and luxuries within the reach of an average person that were once avail-able only to feudal lords and kings. At the same time, this has meant that more and more income is accruing to capital rather than to labour. Hence, many who rely solely on their labour for their livelihood are finding their incomes shrinking. The unbelievable and appalling levels of inequality that we see in the world today are a consequence of this phenomenon. We need to do some innovative thinking to counter this tendency, not only because such inequalities will inevitably give rise to

[1] 'Handmade in India: Preliminary Analysis of Crafts Producers and Crafts Production', *Economic and Political Weekly*, vol. 38, 27 December 2003.

political turmoil, terrorism, and strife, but because they are morally unacceptable.

This trend in inequalities is likely to continue and harden. Over time, labour will become less and less important, and earnings that accrue as labour-income will shrink, especially in comparison to capital income. The solution to this is not to try to stop technological change because, for one, it is unlikely to be within anybody's power to do so; nor to try to resist globalization, but to give workers a share in the earnings that accrue to capital. This is different from giving workers a fixed assured income, as in the standard welfare state. What is being suggested here is that workers be given equity, that is, a share of the profits earned by corporations.

Once such a system is in place, if a company downsizes in the US and goes to India in search of greater profit, workers in the US will have less to complain about because they will get a share of the additional profit. Globalization has led to increasing rancour between First and Third World labour unions. What I am arguing is that this labour vs. labour view of the world is unnecessary and misguided. It is possible and better to go back to the old-fashioned idea of capital vs. labour.

The details of a system that gives equity to workers will need plenty of effort and a lot of creative thinking, and this is not the place for me to outline where such effort should begin. But I have no doubt in my mind that this is the direction in which we will have to go, either through far-sightedness and our own initiative, or perforce after strife, war, and terrorism hit us.

In early January 2004, when I set out from Delhi for my Gujarat travels, the Indian media was euphoric about India's economic take-off. The Indian government's performance in the year 2003 was being hailed as outstanding. Indian entrepreneurs were buying up companies abroad with alacrity. The Sensex had crossed 6000 and India's foreign exchange reserves had breached the $100 billion mark. And to some people the economy looked even better because these statistics somewhere got addled with Tendulkar's 9000 runs.

The celebration seems to me to be mistimed. It is true that the

Indian economy is doing very well overall and, if we stay the course, it will, along with China and maybe Brazil, become a global force. But nothing special really happened *in 2003* other than some round figures being attained. India's take-off started between 1991 and 1993 and the process, fortunately, is continuing. As far as growth rate goes, 2003 is not a record year. Much higher growth occurred in 1988–9, and each of the three years from 1994 to 1997 saw growth rates close to what the growth for 2003–4 is expected to be. Moreover, the monsoon and consequent bountiful agriculture played a major role is this year's good performance.

There is another problem with the euphoria. We must not treat the GDP growth and the build-up of forex reserves as ends in themselves. They are important, no doubt, but only as instruments to improve the conditions of the poorest people in India. As Ela Bhatt, the charismatic Gandhian founder of SEWA, kept reminding us in her soft, characteristic undertone, there is far too much poverty, too much destitution, hunger, and unemployment in India for us to celebrate. It is overcoming these fundamental deprivations that we have to strive for. A country cannot be considered successful as long as it fails to reach out to the marginalized and fails to bring hope to the hopeless.

It is true that in a globalizing world there are severe limits to what a single country can do. We have to be wary that capital can take flight and exchange-rate fluctuations can ruin trade. But even with these limitations there is much that India can do, alongside pushing for a higher growth rate and greater trade, to arrest the growing regional disparities, to bring jobs to the jobless, and in general, to reach out to the dispossessed.

12

India at Fifty and the Road Ahead*

I

To the saying 'Behind every great man there is a woman', Groucho Marx famously added, 'And close behind her is his wife.' Much is to be learnt by looking beyond what meets the eye. In trying to understand India's predicament we often look only for the proximate causes—corruption, squabbling politicians, rhetoric *sans* action. But fifty years of Independence is a good time to go behind these immediate factors to take stock of how we have come to be where we are.

India was born of an astonishing intellectual legacy. It had the good fortune of immense inputs from statesmanship and scholarly intelligence over its formation. This gave us our democratic tradition and commitment to higher education. But it also became the source of economic ambivalence. India's economic system emerged from an uneasy compromise between Mahatma Gandhi's objective of a village-based economy and Jawaharlal Nehru's faith in the welfare state and heavy industry. Nehru confided to his diary in 1933 his growing alienation from Gandhi's ideology: 'I am afraid I am drifting further and further away from him mentally. His continual reference to God irritates me [. . .]. What a tremendous contrast to the dialectics of Lenin & Co.'

*Based on 'Right Marx for the Poor', *India Today*, 16 June 1997 (Section I); 'Fun with Figures', *India Today*, 10 May 1999 (Section II); and 'India's Economy: Can the Boom Last?' *BBC News Online*, 7 January 2004 (Section III).

By the time India became independent in 1947, Nehru was disillusioned by Lenin's method, but he still believed in planning and heavy industry.

Balancing these divergent pulls, the newly independent India began subsidizing small-scale industries and handicrafts and also building large steel plants and dams. The welfare part of Nehru's dream was never implemented and, as a surrogate for socialism, India developed an enormous bureaucracy and an intricate system of controls. Our textile industry, once in the forefront internationally, became a laggard; our automobile industry, which started around the same time as Japan's, showed an unmatched ability to resist innovation; and our illiteracy and poverty rates remained embarrassingly high.

For decades we fooled the world that we were establishing socialism. We must now beware against fooling the world that we are reforming our economy.

To prevent this, we must lay down some clear criteria for progress. In a background paper for UNDP's *Human Development Report* of 1996 I argued that, in evaluating economic well being, we should look at the per capita income of the poorest 20 per cent (quintile income); and that we should assess progress by looking at the growth rate of per capita income of the poorest 20 per cent (quintile growth). The mitigation of inequality is important but should be considered secondary to the aim of improving the lot of the poorest.

This move away from per capita income and growth, to quintile income and quintile growth, changes the ranking of societies quite drastically. In 1993, Switzerland with a per capita income of $35,760 was the richest country, followed by Japan with $31,490; then came Denmark, Norway, and the US. Once we turn to quintile income, Japan with $13,698 ranks first by a wide margin. No other country exceeds $10,000; the US drops to twelfth position.

There used to be a view that growth and equity are inimical to each other. There is now evidence to suggest that this is not true. Between 1984 and 1994, India's per capita income growth rate of 2.8 per cent per annum was faster than almost ever before. Was this a period when the poor got impoverished? No. On the contrary, the quintile growth rate during the same period was a remarkable 5.1 per cent per annum. The advantage of focusing on quintile growth is that it does not matter how the debate between growth and equity is resolved because quintile growth looks directly at how well the poorest are progressing.

This focus on the poorest 20 per cent is the reason why economic liberalization is important for India. It has the greatest potential for the working classes. Globalization has meant that capital from industrialized nations needs labourers from poor countries to produce goods. That is the road Japan initially took. In due course, Japanese labour became expensive and the opportunity was seized by Korea, Singapore, and Taiwan. Wages in these countries are now very high, and so India has tremendous potential for rapid quintile growth.

A great intellectual failing in India has been to presume that trade, investment, and other economic activities are zero-sum games. That is, one country's gain is another's loss. This fallacy, combined with our lack of self-confidence, has meant that whenever an industrialized nation has celebrated an investment deal with India, we have jumped to conclude that we have incurred a loss. But in economics both parties to a deal can be beneficiaries. So we must not look at whether the investor has gained from a deal, but whether our quintile income stands to rise. No one understood the non-zero-sum nature of investment better than the gentleman who wrote in 1853: 'I know that the English millocracy intends to endow India with railways with the exclusive view of extracting at diminished expenses . . . raw materials for their manufacture. But when you have once introduced machinery into the locomotion of a country . . . you are unable to withhold it from fabrication . . . The railway system will therefore become truly the forerunner of modern industry.'

The quotation is from the other Marx—Karl; and *he* was not being funny.

II

As I write this piece, the World Bank has, amid much media hype, published *World Development Indicators* (*WDI*) for 1999. This is arguably the most important publication of the Bank—an enormous compendium of inter-country statistics on the state of the economy, population, and environment. Unlike the better-known *World Development Report*, this is a rather sombre publication, its 399 pages crawling with numbers. What is surprising is that it is fun to browse through, being full of unexpected information.

Let us start at the top end of the table. Of the 148 countries for which detailed income data are listed (this includes pretty much all nations with populations exceeding 1 million), which country do you think is the richest in terms of per capita income? Before reading the answer in the next paragraph, also try your guess at the following. In which country do schoolchildren have the highest mathematical skill? In which country is infant mortality the lowest?

The answer to all three questions is Singapore, though on infant mortality it shares the top berth with Sweden, Norway, Finland, and Japan. The super performer in the *WDI* for 1999 is clearly Singapore.

Where does India stand on income? With a per capita income of $370 per annum, its absolute standing is very disappointing. Where India has done well is in terms of growth. Our national income has maintained an average annual growth rate of 6 per cent through the 1990s. This may not match up to Singapore's 8.5 per cent, but it compares well with the world average of 2.4 per cent.

While it may be interesting to look at per capita income, I believe, as I have argued above, it is morally incumbent upon us to evaluate a society by looking at the condition of its poorest people. Of course, the poor in a developing country will be much worse off than the poor in Switzerland or the US. But if we ask what percentage of the national income goes to the poorest 20 per cent of a nation, India with a figure of 9.2 per cent does much better than most other nations, such as China (5.5 per cent), the US (4.8 per cent), and even Switzerland (7.4 per cent).

The section on the environment has a mass of data, from traffic congestion to air quality. We learn, for instance, that in India there are 7 motor vehicles for every 1000 persons. This is much below the world average of 121 and that of the world's topper, the US, with 773. But do not despair. We may have few vehicles, but they are clearly more active than in most other nations. The number of people injured or killed in 1997 by every 1000 vehicles was 17 in the US, 14 in Japan, and 5 in Norway, whereas India's rickety fleet manages an impressive 61.

Air quality can be measured in many ways. One of them is micrograms of total 'suspended particulates'—scientese for dirt—per cubic metre. Among India's four major cities, Delhi leads with 415, followed by Calcutta 375, Mumbai 240, and Chennai 130. Once we take other cities into account, Delhi loses the lead to Lucknow, which scores 463: at this rate one will not have to enter its Imambara to feel a little lost. And for a sense of how this compares with other nations: Mexico City, so famous for its pollution, has 273 particulates per cubic metre, and Tokyo only 49.

The large amount of statistics provided are not without their controversies and conundrums. Take for example per capita income, the average income earned per person in a nation. Given that an Indian earns in rupees and a Japanese in yen, how do you compare these? The standard practice is to convert all these into dollars by using the going exchange rate. By this conversion, India's per capita income turns out to be $370 and the US's $29,080.

One problem with this is that if the rupee is devalued, India's per capita income will go down even though nothing may have happened to the standard of living of Indians. To correct this, the World Bank tries to make adjustments to a nation's income by taking account of the purchasing power parity (PPP) of the nation's currency. If, for instance, it turns out that with $370 in India you can buy twice as much as you can in the US, then India's per capita income with PPP correction will be $740. As it happens, with PPP correction India's per capita income rises to $1660.

For all their faults, these kinds of statistics can inform us and help us define our policies better. Of course, the numbers do not tell us what causes what. But this does not bother me too much as I do not believe *anything* can inform us about causality. Causality is a construct of the human mind. What the statistics help us with is 'induction', that is, they help us to learn from past regularities. If no nation with literacy below 70 per cent has done well economically, induction would suggest that it would be wrong for India to expect otherwise. The laws of induction can get falsified, but to disregard them systematically is to court trouble.

When my sister's son was a little kid in elementary school in Canada, his class teacher explained: 'The Japanese come from Japan, the English come from England, the Russians come from Russia', and then asked: 'Now, you tell me where do the Chinese come from?' My nephew had to contend with the teacher's displeasure when, disregarding the laws of induction and unwittingly responding to his love of Chinese food, he answered earnestly, 'Restaurants'.

In designing policy in India we have also got our induction wrong far too often, and with consequences rather more momentous than they were for my nephew.

III

For the Indian economy the year 2003 ended on a high, with the foreign exchange reserves breaching the $100 billion mark on 20 December. The year also saw Indian companies breaking into the international corporate market, making thirty-five global acquisitions totalling $450 million. Thinking internationally, Prime Minister Atal Behari Vajpayee floated the idea of a common currency for South Asia. And the industrial sector is booming. Car sales in November were 41 per cent higher than the previous year. Overall, Gross Domestic Product is expected to grow by more than 7 per cent in the financial year ending in March 2004.

But it is easy to overinterpret this news. A sober analysis indicates that India is continuing to do well, as it has done since 1993, with 6 per cent per annum average growth. This robustness, combined with the advantage of its size, means that it is a country that global players cannot ignore. But if India is to go beyond this, to a sustained annual growth rate of over 8 per cent, and with benefits reaching all levels of society, more needs to be done by government than whipping up electoral support by pointing to the headlines.

It is worth remembering that India has seen brief growth spurts before—its growth rate in 1988-9 exceeded 10 per cent. The challenge therefore, is to bring about sustained growth. Consider the $100 billion foreign exchange (forex) news. The large reserve points to good performance by the Reserve Bank—the reserve was $5.83 billion in 1991. But, in itself, this does not mean as much as the screaming newspaper headlines on 21 December suggested. What was more significant was the fact that the news made the headlines. Never before has dry economic news been celebrated so widely in India. The interest of the citizenry in such matters was reminiscent of South Korea in the 1980s.

It augurs well for India as it compels politicians to divert some of their attention from politics to economics. The forex reserve of a government is like an individual's bank balance. The fact that it is high does not indicate economic strength and preparedness to respond to emergencies. Rather, it reflects the person's preference for keeping money in a bank rather than investing it in assets. Indeed, there are economists who argue that India should run down a part of its reserve to increase investment.

The other big news was also one where the symbolic value outstripped the actual. This was the idea, floated by Prime Minister Vajpayee, of a common currency for South Asia. Although this is not about to happen, the suggestion shows a level of maturity that political leaders can think in terms of economic co-operation even while political irritants remain. Moreover, the very effort to build such co-operation could serve to reduce the risk of political conflict.

To guarantee long-run strength, the Indian government needs to raise the level of investment (and that includes investment in people); make a fetish of efficiency; and make it easier for new private firms to start up business. India's investment rate has remained virtually stationary at 24 per cent (with a slight fall in the last three years). A sustained growth rate of over 8 per cent will not be possible unless the investment rate rises to 30 per cent. That, in turn, requires the government to put its fiscal house in order.

On the human side, India has done better than Pakistan but worse than its much poorer eastern neighbour, Bangladesh, in many dimensions. In 1990, under-5 child mortality (that is, the number of deaths before age 5 per 1000 children) was 144 in Bangladesh, 128 in Pakistan, and 123 in India. By 2001 the numbers were Bangladesh 77, India 93, and Pakistan 109. As far as school enrolment of girls as a percentage of boys goes the figure for Bangladesh is an exemplary 103 per cent, whereas for India it is 78, and for Pakistan 61.

India is a potential global economic power. But, for that potential to be realized, its promise must not be treated as an instrument of short-term electoral popularity. Instead, the government must invest more in infrastructure and social improvement. For the Indian government to spend as much as it does—on subsidies and the bureaucracy—and then to wonder why the economy is not growing faster is like my father's youngest sister who, in her old age, lamented to me: 'I don't know why I keep such poor health—I eat only sweets.'

13

The Indian Economy: Take-off and Strategic Policy Issues*

Has India Taken Off?

In recent times India has been getting a better international press than ever before.

When it comes to crafting national economic policy, few political leaders in the world have had the success of Singapore's Lee Kuan Yew. Whatever reservations one may have about his politics, it is remarkable how he steered Singapore from a poor nation to a fully industrialized one in three decades. He has also written on the economic problems of different nations with remarkable prescience. During his term as Prime Minister of Singapore he routinely expressed pessimism on India. 'It was sad to see the gradual rundown of the country', he wrote in his book, *From Third World to First*, and added in his inimitably undiplomatic style that the crockery at a formal government dinner was very bad and 'one knife literally snapped in my hand and nearly bounced into my face.'

It therefore caused a stir when, in early April, on the occasion of the founding of the Lee Kuan Yew School of Public Policy in Singapore, he predicted that India will be propelled into the 'front ranks'. In this speech, crammed with information and analysis, he argued that, over the next decades, 'China and India will shake the world. . . . In some industries, [these countries] have already leapfrogged the rest of Asia.'

*First published in *Hindustan Times*, 4 and 5 May 2005.

Writing about China and India in the *Financial Times* in February, Martin Wolf observed: 'The economic rise of Asia's giants is [. . .] the most important story of our age. It heralds the end, in the not too distant a future, of as much as five centuries of domination by the Europeans.' More importantly, in routine writing in Western newspapers one now finds India being referred to as a 'dynamic economy'.

The question that I want to investigate here is whether this optimism for India is founded in facts.

My brief answer is yes. While India has been doing well for more than a decade, there have been changes over the last three years that are especially significant. I shall dwell on four of these. This does not mean that all is well with the economy; but that is the subject matter of the next part of this essay.

First, Indian companies have come of age. In remarking on what India had to offer to China, Mr Lee mentioned in the same lecture India's 'near world-class companies', good corporate governance, and capital market transparency. This began with software companies like Infosys, Wipro, and Tata Consultancy Services, which set new standards in corporate culture, and spread to other sectors, such as pharmaceuticals, biotechnology, and beyond. And, aided by the sharp rise in foreign exchange reserves, Indian companies have, over the last three years, begun making global acquisitions. In 2003 they bought up thirty-five companies abroad.

Second, there has been a windfall in India's outsourcing business, related, surprisingly, to the US presidential race. Readers will recall that early in his election campaign John Kerry had criticized US companies that outsourced back-office work to developing countries. He later backtracked on this, realizing that it was neither good economics nor commendable ethics to propagate protectionism against poor nations.

But, once this subject made its appearance in the media, it refused to go away. A host of writers and commentators on US television (such as Lou Dobbs on CNN) went out of their way to vilify American companies that outsourced jobs for greed of profit.

A whole lot of small American companies that had the same greed of profit but did not know of this great opportunity suddenly woke up. For the Third World, the repeated attacks on outsourcing in the American media was an unexpected boon, since advertising on US television is so expensive. A large number of countries have gained and India, which already had the organizational infrastructure for back-office work and a ready supply of English-speaking workers, did especially well.

Third, with China joining the WTO, India having removed quantity controls on imports, and the advance of the IT industry, there has been an unprecedented rise in Indo-Chinese trade. The total value of trade between these two nations was $5 billion in 2002, $7.6 billion in 2003, and $13.6 billion in 2004 (the numbers are based on Chinese customs data). Moreover, what is interesting is that it is India that is running a trade surplus. More generally, there seems to be a general rise in India's economic links with Asia.

Finally, these strong economic developments come with a fortuitous political change. No matter what moral position one takes on this, the fact is that, with the rise of global terror, US political interests have come into alignment with India's. As Thomas Simons, ex-US Ambassador to Pakistan, noted, the Soviets left Afghanistan in February 1989 and insurgency in Kashmir rose from the summer of that year. This was no coincidence. Some of the same fundamentalist forces that were engaging the Soviets were clearly settling into a new job.

This is today a common problem for the US and India. And, combined with the fact that India and the US share similar political systems—democracy, a free press, and a constitutional commitment to secularism—this makes India a natural strategic partner for the US. Moreover, especially with Condoleeza Rice as Secretary of State, the US is likely to embark on a policy of trying to use India as a balancing force against China's inevitable rise to world power.

The Straits of Malacca, through which more than 60,000 ships pass each year, is a vital artery for Western trade with Asia and, for that very reason, a potential flash-point in a future US–China conflict. The

Indian navy has been a growing presence in the strait. This is clearly happening with US approval, since the Indian flotilla keeps an eye on terrorist activity and at the same time allays the risk of the region coming under exclusive Chinese control. Even for China, it is better to have a third-country presence in the South China seas than a face-off with the US one on one.

For India to nurture these economic and political advantages will involve a pragmatic assessment of its self-interest but also, I like to believe, a commitment to certain values. It will entail cooperation with China and the US, but also the strength to retain moral independence in matters of global politics and internal economic policy. This may entail giving up some short-term gains, but will command greater respect in the long run.

Despite all these favourable portents for the economy, much remains to be done. The world may judge us by the size of our national income and foreign exchange balance, and by the overall growth rate of our economy. But we must be clear in our minds that these are of no more than instrumental value. India continues to be crushingly poor, and economic growth and trade are valuable only to the extent that they reach the disadvantaged and the poor.

For the next round of policy-making, India will have to craft a package to sustain and step up the momentum in growth that has been gained, and to spread its benefits to all regions and citizens.

Policy Imperatives

Market-fundamentalist economists in India tend to assume that, when it comes to the economy, government's only job is to make itself scarce. This is foolish advice. A modern vibrant market economy cannot function without a powerful government that is willing to invest in its people and provide the infrastructure—physical and institutional—for the market to function.

To sustain the momentum that has been gained by the Indian economy and spread the benefits widely, our government will have to work on many fronts. A comprehensive plan would run into too many pages and lose too many readers. Here are four broad areas that need action.

First, economists typically worry about the big things, like money supply, the balance of trade, and budgetary deficits. These are important of course, but many economies fail not because of these but because of the malfunctioning of small things—the nuts and bolts of the economy. We need to work assiduously on injecting efficiency and cutting down corruption in matters of everyday governance. If this is done, it will make life easier for ordinary people, who will then invest in business and enterprise.

The crucial ingredient of business and trade is the ability to rely on contracts, to start up new enterprises easily and fold them up when the need arises. We now have hard statistics from the World Bank on where India stands on these matters. If you want to start a business in India, it will take you on average 88 days to get the requisite clearance. In China this takes 46 days, in Malaysia 31 days, and in Singapore 8 days. If your business runs into a problem of contract violation, in India it will take you a year to solve the problem, in China 180 days, and in Singapore 50 days. But, even if you can have contracts enforced and start a business, the real catch in India is getting out of business. To resolve an insolvency case and shut down a firm takes 7 months in Singapore, 26 months in Malaysia, and a little over 11 years in India.

These are the crucial ingredients of an economy's success, and they extend not just to matters of business but to the harassment factor— how long a person has to wait in a queue when she goes to lodge a complaint about her electricity bill. If the state provided these functions efficiently, the market would be much more vibrant. And government cannot solve this by making itself scarce. The new World Bank data confirm this. There is very little difference between India and more efficient countries in terms of the *number* of government procedures that one has to go through to start and close a business, and to have a contract enforced. So the problem is not resolved by government removing procedures and regulations. There is no escaping the regulatory tasks; they just have to be done quicker.

One specific facility that government needs to provide urgently is that of patenting inventions. Establishing property rights on one's ideas is not a very generous thing to do, but when the industrial world is doing so, one does not have much choice in the matter. The number of patents filed by Indians in India in 2001 was 234. Of course this is less than in the industrialized nations: what is surprising is how big the gap is. The figure for the US for the same year is 190,907 and for Japan it is 388,390. It is not as if there is not enough scientific work going on in India. By Third World standards India does fairly well on this front. In 1999, the number of scientific and technical journal articles published in India was 9217. The figures for the US and Japan are, respectively, 163,526 and 47,826.

In the US, every university and large institute provides facilities for filing patent protection on ideas. India needs to move towards this.

Second—and moving from nuts and bolts to ports and power—it is time for India to make major infrastructural investments. Poor roads, interruptions in electricity, and inadequate airport facilities are strangling opportunities in many sectors, especially in manufacturing.

To reach New York, starting from a factory in India a garment takes on average thirty-two days. It takes half this time from several East Asian countries. Bureaucracy is a factor; but also, Indian ports are outdated and small. Garments from India have to first travel by feeder vessels to other ports before setting off on larger liners for Europe and America.

This is just one example. We need a big thrust on infrastructure, in several ways. Investment in infrastructure can boost private sector employment and this is the best way to create jobs. But investment requires money. For this we should use a combination of borrowed rupees and some of our foreign-exchange reserves. Some analysts, including certain IMF economists, have cautioned government not to do this for reasons of fiscal prudence. The concern is correct, but the conclusion is wrong. Suppose Mr X earns $100 in New York and, on returning to Delhi, changes it to rupees. India's forex reserves would have risen by 100 dollars. If now government spends this, then, given that X will also be spending his 100 dollars' equivalent in rupees, we will end up spending 200 dollars worth of money as a consequence of having earned 100 dollars. Hence, this will amount to a rise in our fiscal deficit.

But if this money is spent not on consumption but on investment, then the pressure on the deficit is not necessarily bad. In fact, *at this juncture of the Indian economy*, the lid has to be firm on the *revenue* deficit, not the entire deficit. It is like a person who has Rs 1000, but decides to start a new factory by spending Rs 2000. He will run up a deficit; but that is not necessarily bad. It depends on his ability to run the factory.

With all investments there is 'the risk of Gander'. In 1938 the world's largest airport was Gander International. It was an essential re-fuelling stop for planes crossing the Atlantic. Rightly anticipating a growth in transatlantic flights, Gander invested heavily in the airport. But planes became fuel efficient in ways that could not have been anticipated, and Gander is today one of the most under-utilized airports. About this kind of risk there is nothing we can do. The only mistake is to allow fear to paralyse us into doing nothing.

Since India is on the upswing, it is worth the risk to expand our infrastructure. Of course this should be done judiciously. In using some of its dollar reserves, India will be exposing itself to the risk of a liquidity crisis. On the other hand, using dollars has the advantage of not causing an immediate rise in the demand for Indian goods (which could spur inflation). The trick is to use the right combination of borrowed rupees and reserve dollars.

The above policy will also have the desirable byproduct of raising India's investment rate, that is, total investment as a percent of national income. It is time to break the 30 per cent barrier.* Our investment rate has not had any secular rise since the late 1970s, when it crossed 20 per cent.

Third, India needs labour-market reform. A consequence of India's Industrial Disputes Act, 1947, is that it is exceedingly difficult to lay off or retrench workers. This law was enacted in the belief that it would

*As this book goes to press, India's investment rate has crossed the 30 per cent mark.

help employment. But a potential employer who knows that he will not be able to retrench his workers may decide not to employ workers in the first place. Since, in the fashion industry, demand has seasonalities, an obstacle to laying off workers during the lean season could mean that firms will employ, all year round, the number of workers needed during the lean season. Hence, if companies *were* free to lay off workers, they could end up employing more workers *on average*.

While the laws do need reform, much that happens in the labour market depends on more amorphous factors, such as norms and a culture that may have been spawned by the law. So, there will have to be a broad thrust that should begin by educating trade unions that these changes are needed for the welfare of the workers themselves, and that labour reform is such a politically charged subject only because its economics is so misunderstood. Moreover, I would recommend that these changes be complemented with a social security initiative that will protect workers who are temporarily out of work.

Fourth, the country needs to plan a variety of more imaginative direct interventions to improve the standard of living of the poor. The economy *has* taken off and India stands on the brink of great possibilities. Yet, there is no denying that there are deep faultlines beneath the surface. With a literacy rate of below 70 per cent, we trail behind not just industrialized nations but many much poorer countries, like some sub-Saharan African nations. Even though poverty has probably declined a bit over the last seven or eight years, having close to 300 million abysmally poor people is a blot on a country that is otherwise doing well. (And, I am here not going beyond economics to matters like the massacre in Gujarat and the shame of the Modi government's inaction.)

India needs to invest more in interventions to combat illiteracy, morbidity, and poverty. It should also provide a social welfare system for workers who are unable to work, or who are out of work. While a law guaranteeing full employment is not a good idea (it will either clutter the courts or join the ranks of India's many unused laws), a system of social security is possible and desirable. If this is combined with the revoking of some of our archaic labour laws and customs, there can be gains all round.

Spending on education, health, and social security will cost money. But if we add up the huge subsidies that are given indirectly to the rich and the powerful (just consider how well maintained are the urban areas where these people live), we will find little excuse to skimp on the poor. Moreover, the total revenue (from taxes and other sources) collected by the Indian government is 13 per cent of the national income. The figure for most Scandinavian nations is around 40 per cent, for Singapore 25 per cent, and the US 21 per cent. If we work on correcting this, even as we raise spending on the poor we can keep budgetary pressures under control.

14

Has Poverty Declined in India?*

There is an old story of Stalin visiting a school in Moscow and asking the clever kid, Boris: 'Who killed Julius Caesar?' Boris burst out crying, 'Not me sir.' A furious Stalin met the teacher and asked him to explain. The teacher, trembling, said, 'Sir, I have looked into the matter and can confirm that, incredible though it may seem, Boris did not kill Julius Caesar.' An exasperated Stalin called on the headmaster. But the headmaster's response was the same. Boris had not done it. And this continued—the same question being asked of different authorities, and the same answer. Finally, Stalin sent for the KGB chief and asked him to look into the matter. The following day, the chief returned to say, 'Sir, the KGB has solved the problem. The boy has confessed.'

Has India's poverty, as measured by the percentage of people living below the poverty line, gone down during the 1990s? The same answer, no, for many years and then a sudden dramatic change, caused by a different method of calculation by India's National Sample Survey (NSS), seemed to have a strange parallel with the Stalin story.

Few economic debates have been as charged and murky as the one that tries to answer the question concerning India's poverty. For a lot of people (foolishly, in my opinion) the answer to this question is tantamount to an evaluation of the success or failure of the economic reforms that were started in 1991.

Because of the change in the method of data collection, one needs considerable ingenuity to be able to distil a clear answer from NSS

*First published in *Business Standard*, 2 April 2002.

statistics. Fortunately, a number of skilled econometricians have been researching these poverty trends. And, for the first time, I believe, there is a satisfactory answer: India's poverty rate was virtually unchanged during the first five or six years after the reforms. But during the last two years of the 1990s it declined. In fact, the drop is so sharp that not only has the *percentage* of people below the poverty line fallen, there has been a drop in the *absolute* number of people who live below the poverty line.

Here I discuss not the cause of this recent decline in India's poverty but the fascinating story of how this 'fact' was deduced from the NSS data.

The Indian NSS, started in 1950 through the initiative of Nehru and Mahalanobis, is one of the world's most celebrated organizations for tracking the performance of an economy by collecting data from a random sample of the population. The NSS collects data from a large sample approximately every five years, and does a 'thin' sample survey virtually every year in between the large surveys. The poverty controversy began with the 50th Round Survey, which was one of the large surveys, conducted in 1993-4. Being the first large NSS survey after the reforms began, there was a lot of expectation in the Indian government that poverty would have declined sharply. But the 1993-4 poverty rate turned out to be 37.3 per cent for rural India and 32.4 per cent for urban India, which were virtually the same as the poverty rates in the 1980s. Then came the thin rounds and the same question was asked again and again, and the answer was the same—the changes in poverty were negligible.

Anticipation built up for the next big round, the 55th Round, held in 1999-2000. As the results started pouring in, the NSS declared that poverty had fallen sharply. Rural poverty was down to 27.1 per cent and urban poverty to 23.6 per cent. But foul, cried critics, arguing that the NSS had changed its method of collecting data in this 55th Round.

The whistle-blowing was not without reason. In India, consumption data used to be collected by asking people how much they had consumed over the previous thirty days. This practice, which is at variance with that in most other parts of the world—where people are asked about their consumption over the previous seven days—had been under fire for some time. As the late Pravin Visaria and others had pointed out, small studies in the 1990s showed that people have a notoriously poor memory. People's daily consumption computed from the thirty-day question turns out to be close to 20 per cent less than that computed from the seven-day question.

Pressure started building up on the NSS to switch to a seven-day questionnaire. But a sudden switch would make it impossible to compare earlier rounds of statistics with the new ones. So the NSS decided that in the 55th Round people would be asked about their consumption in the previous thirty days *and* in the previous seven days. The answers were duly recorded in two adjacent columns in the survey questionnaire. The NSS used the thirty-day answers to estimate poverty in 1999–2000, and the celebratory announcements by the Indian government concerning the decline in poverty were based on this.

This was, however, problematic, for an unexpected reason. If you use the 1999–2000 survey and check how much less the daily consumption of various goods turns out to be by the thirty-day method as compared to the seven-day method, the answer turns out to be a mere 2 or 3 per cent—nowhere near the 20 per cent we know from previous studies. And it is clear what happened. When you ask people how much they consumed in the last seven days and then follow up this question with what they consumed in the last thirty days, it is natural for people to do mental checks to make sure that the two answers are roughly consistent. In other words, the answers to the thirty-day and seven-day questions had been contaminated by each other, and the trouble is we do not know the extent of the contamination.

What do you do lumped with these seemingly incomparable data sets? Angus Deaton, economist at Princeton, came up with a neat idea. For some goods, which people buy in a lumpy manner and only occasionally—such as fuel and light and some other goods—all rounds of the NSS ask only a thirty-day question. It turns out that these goods form a fairly substantial part, approximately 20 per cent, of a typical person's total consumption. Now, by using data from uncontaminated samples, we can estimate how the proportion of income that an average person spends on these select items varies as his income changes. Once you have estimated this relation, you can use it in reverse to make a guess about a person's income from data on the amount a person spends on these select items.

So, what one can do now is use the consumption data from the 55th Round on these select items to estimate incomes, and, from that, to estimate the number of people with income below the poverty line. Deaton's method yields the following findings: rural and urban poverty in 1999–2000 are 30.2 per cent and 24.7 per cent. In brief, the decline in poverty is not as sharp as the Indian government claimed, but it is pretty sharp nevertheless.

Whatever the cause, it is satisfying to know that India's stubborn poverty statistic has been dented a little at last.

Postscript

More recent research by Abhijit Sen and Himanshu, as available in December 2004, suggests that the proportion of money spent by consumers on the 'thirty-day' goods may have risen. If this is verified then the decline in poverty would be less sharp than suggested here.

15

Infant Mortality
and the Anti-Female Bias*

Much has been written about the bias against the girl child in India. A cursory glance at the data can be telling. In 1998, of every 1000 girls born in India, 77.2 would die between the ages of one month and five years; whereas for boys the figure was 59.9. This ratio of 1.3 to 1 seems large; but in itself a ratio means very little.

It is too large or too small only when compared against some standard. On 14 May 2002, in Philadelphia, President George Bush is supposed to have remarked (according to a list of 'Bushisms' published in Slate.com): 'For every fatal shooting, there were roughly three non-fatal shootings. And, folks, this is unacceptable in America.'

One reason why this observation is ambiguous is that it is not clear whether the speaker wishes to emphasize the poor marksmanship of those doing the shooting or the high rate of fatality.

Is India's relatively high girl child mortality rate the symptom of a malaise? By all accounts, it is. Detailed studies, done under controlled circumstances and in developed countries, suggest that if there is no difference in the treatment between girls and boys, a girl is more likely to survive than a boy during the first month of her life. Then, from the age of one month to five years, girls and boys have equal survival chances. So, India's ratio of infant mortality between the age of a month and five years, based on gender, does seem to suggest some form of bias

*First published in *Business Standard*, 17 April 2004.

against the girl child. Exactly what form this bias takes is an interesting question and I shall come back to that later. Let us first take a look at some of the facts.

Thanks to the availability of data from Demographic and Health Surveys (DHS) and other related surveys we now have comparable statistics on births and child mortality from a variety of countries. The DHS itself has been conducted in more than seventy countries, of which around sixty are developing nations. If we compare against the standard mentioned above, we find that there is excess female child mortality in only six countries or regions: Bangladesh, Egypt, Nepal, Pakistan, and parts of India and China.

While Africa has much higher mortality in general one finds no systematic bias against females. On the other hand, in the age group one month to five years, girls are more likely to die than boys by 9 per cent in Nepal and Pakistan, 14 per cent in Bangladesh, and a shocking 20 per cent in Egypt and India. Within India there are large regional differences, with particularly adverse ratios in Haryana, Punjab, Uttar Pradesh and in fact much of northern India; and with much smaller ratios in the south and the east.

All this, it must be noted, takes no account of gender-specific foeticide, which has been on the rise in large parts of India and China over the last few years, encouraged no doubt by the easy availability of amniocentesis.

What is the cause of the poor life chances of girls in India? Researchers have hazarded guesses ranging from the outright murder of little girls to the denial of adequate food and medical attention to the girl child. However, while all these things have happened in some measure, the evidence of such gender discrimination does not seem large enough to explain the big mortality differences. Some carefully done empirical studies suggest that, when it comes to food, parents do not in fact significantly discriminate against the girl child.

How then does one reconcile the two 'facts' about India, namely (1) the well-documented phenomenon of girls doing worse than boys at the macro level, as evident from their sharply higher mortality; and

(2) the less-well-documented but plausible feature of there being not enough direct discrimination against girls within the household to match the larger dismal picture.

While (2) will need to be investigated much more thoroughly in the future, a young economist at Harvard, Richard Jensen, has produced a clever theory for reconciling (1) and (2). To understand this we need to distinguish between 'discrimination against girls' and 'son preference'. 'Son preference' refers to the strong preference for having boys rather than girls. If a couple decides that they must have at least two boys and, if necessary, will produce up to ten kids to achieve this target, or that they will keep having children till they get at least one boy, they are expressing a son preference.

This is, however, totally different from discriminating in favour of boys, which involves giving boys better and more food or taking them to the hospital when they are ill more readily than girls. A family can thus express son preference but be resolved not to discriminate against girls once the children have been born.

Note, now, that in a society characterized by son preference, girls will in general belong to larger households. This is caused by the pursuit of producing children till the target number of boys has been achieved. The easiest example is to take the case where couples want to have one boy and are willing to have up to two children to reach this target. In other words, if the first child is a boy they stop; otherwise they have another. In such a society, all girls will have one sibling, whereas, on average, two-thirds of the boys will have no sibling. Next, note that a family that has a large number of children will, other things remaining the same, have less income per person.

In a poor country, this can make a substantial difference to the quality of life and care. Now, if a society has son preference but does not discriminate against girls, by the above argument girls will nevertheless be worse off, since girls will, on average, be born in larger families. Clearly we have reconciled (1) and (2).

Now, with this theory in the background, if we look at some of the facts, they are quite revealing. If we look at the ratio of the number of siblings that girls have to the number that boys have, this is virtually one in the Americas and even in Africa. However, in India this is significantly greater than one. On average, in India girls have 0.22 more siblings than boys have—and the gaps are particularly high for Himachal Pradesh, Haryana, Punjab, and Rajasthan. The only regions where one does not observe this kind of son preference are Kerala and the far eastern states, such as Assam, Meghalaya, and Manipur.

So, clearly Jensen's hypothesis has plausibility. There will still have to be a lot of empirical research before it can be confirmed. What is likely to be found is that there is some discrimination against the girl child, but this combines with a strong son preference. This will then explain why the indicators of disadvantage to girls are bigger at the level of macro data and mortality statistics than at the micro level of treatment in the household.

16

Labour Laws and the Role
of Contracts*

The months of July and August in 2004 saw announcements from India's BJP-led government preparing citizens for major changes in the country's labour laws. This is an important undone task from the reforms initiatives of the early 1990s. I have, over the years, written about the need to revise our labour market policies, and welcomed these announcements. At the same time, the statements from the government were so conflicting that I could not help feeling apprehensive that the effort would be botched once again.

A proper reform of labour laws requires intimacy with the field of law and economics, and a modicum of understanding of the role of incentives in markets. But there is no sign of the Indian government wanting to marshal the kind of research and knowledge needed for this purpose.

Judging by past laws and policy debates, the Indian policy-maker's understanding of the role of labour legislation is deeply fallacious. The first fallacy is to view the marketplace as a zero-sum 'game', where, as I said earlier, one person's gain is invariably another person's loss. This has led to the oft-repeated observation that for India to progress, organized labour must be prepared to make sacrifices. So the reform

*Based on 'Reforming India's Labour Laws', *Business Standard*, 14 August 2002 (Section I); 'Contracts versus Contacts', *India Today*, 6 March 2000 (Section II); 'Words Don't Feed the Poor', *India Today*, 8 September 1997 (Section III); and 'Trust and Economic Progress', *Business Standard*, 12 June 2002 (Section IV).

is presented as something that will hurt organized labour but is justified in the interest of the nation's overall growth. In fact, a properly revised labour policy can help us achieve faster economic growth and at the same time benefit all workers, including organized workers.

The second misunderstanding concerns the hiring and firing of labour. There has been much debate on whether employers should have the right to fire workers. Currently, the Industrial Disputes Act, of 1947, requires that any firm employing more than 100 workers must obtain prior permission from the government before laying them off. There is talk of raising this limit to firms employing 300 workers or even 1000 workers. This obsession with a cut-off misses the point: what we really need is to move towards a system where workers and firms have greater flexibility of contract at the time of employment. This simple fact has proved extremely difficult to explain to the common politician and to the trade-union leader. But before explaining the role of flexible contracts in market economies, let me briefly review how India's labour market has performed.

Between 1977 and 1999 the aggregate Indian labour force grew from 277 million to 387 million. Given that population growth during this period was a little higher than the labour force growth, the section of population dependent on the working population has grown. Unemployment is very difficult to measure in a developing country such as ours, but based on National Sample Survey data one finds, somewhat surprisingly, unemployment falling slightly over this period, with a marked upward spike in 1987-8, which was a year of severe drought.

Finally, here is the indicator of the poor performance of our labour markets: Real wages (that is, wages after weeding out the effects of inflation) of Indian workers have close to doubled during these twenty-two years. Just in case you wonder why I am calling this a 'poor' performance, recall that during the same period the wages of workers in several Asian countries increased sevenfold, which of course means a total transformation of the lifestyle of workers.

There are, no doubt, many reasons for this. But the most important contributory factor behind this dismal performance is the utter short-sightedness of our policy-makers—and I am defining this broadly enough to include scribes and economists. In a modern growing economy, especially in this age of globalization, one has to contend with the fact that the forces of demand and supply will swell and ebb in various sectors. A particular segment of the computer industry may see its demand rise sharply and then suddenly collapse as a technological breakthrough renders that segment obsolete. If the various sectors are prevented from growing and shrinking in tandem with these forces, firms in the volatile sectors will have to decide whether they can make profits enough in the good periods to be able to survive through the bad periods—when they need to downsize but cannot because the law does not permit them to. It is entirely possible that many firms will close down altogether in such circumstances. Moreover, there may be firms that never come into existence because of this anticipation. The latter fact is particularly worrying because people will not realize the cost of these bad laws—because there is no visible consequence. And my contention is that this is exactly what has happened in India, leaving Indian workers vastly poorer than other Asian workers.

One simple piece of statistic shows how the Industrial Disputes Act may have influenced labour markets. It was in 1982 that the Act was amended, making it mandatory for firms employing more than 100 workers to seek prior permission before retrenching workers, as mentioned above. In 1982 there were 898,000 workers employed in firms that employed 100 or more workers. By 1990 the number had fallen dramatically to 569,000 workers. So the amended Industrial Disputes Act, far from shoring up jobs, had the opposite effect. The reason is not difficult to see. New firms coming into existence after 1982 tried to make sure that they did not cross the 100-workers mark so as to not come under the ambit of the new law. They managed this by hiring contract workers or simply by moving to more capital-intensive technologies. Old firms refused to expand their workforce as labourers left through natural attrition. And overall, employment in firms with more than 100 workers fell.

What we strictly need to do is not to make hiring and firing easier or harder, but make room for flexible contracts between workers and firms. That is, they should be given the right to negotiate the terms of the contract and then have the government enforce whatever it is that they have agreed upon. The National Labour Commission has recently suggested raising the severance package to sixty days' salary for every year in the job. What is not being understood here is that different firms and different workers have varying needs, and for efficiency we cannot have terms like these exogenously fixed by the politician or the bureaucrat. These need to be left to workers and their employers. We will find some sectors paying high wages but retaining the right of quick dismissal of workers with little severance benefits, while other sectors will guarantee employment or huge severance but offer lower wages.

It is true that people can at times get exploited by failing to recognize complex clauses in a contract. To prevent this, the government can specify the limits within which contracts must occur. Thus, it may say that severance must be between thirty and eighty days' salary for every year on the job, and leave it to employers and firms to choose specific contracts within these limits; and then the role of the law will be to enforce these contracts.

This will have the additional value of teaching people about contracts and the need to adhere to contracts. The effect of the law is not just through its literal meaning. What the law 'expresses' influences behaviour even when there is no formal enforcement—the so-called expressionist function of law that has been written about in recent times by Cass Sunstein and others. In India much of labour market behaviour lies, strictly speaking, beyond the arm of the law. This is the reason why we need to be aware that the reach of the law frequently goes beyond its literal application.

II

Today, as the Indian economy undertakes reform and makes greater room for enterprise and initiative, it is not surprising that we are suddenly seeing a flowering of talent and success stories, such as in the software sector with the remarkable success of Infosys, Wipro, and Tata.

I have written in the past about specific reforms. In this essay I want to discuss a single underlying principle—the 'principle of free contract'—which, properly understood, can help craft many separate reforms (Section I, above, discussed this in the context of labour regulation). This 'principle of free contract' asserts the need to give people room to sign contracts as they wish—as long as these have no negative fallout on uninvolved third parties—and for government to provide a credible machinery to enforce these contracts.

Unfortunately, India's existing legal system does very poorly on this front. Our rental laws specify the 'standard rent' and the conditions under which a tenant can be evicted, instead of leaving it to individual landlords and tenants to decide on their own conditions, based on their special needs; our labour laws specify the terms and conditions for retrenching or laying off workers. Such pre-specified terms as we saw above, can dampen a lot of business and industry. In the fashion products industry, for example, the demand is by definition volatile. So potential workers should have the freedom to receive a high wage as well as be laid off at short notice. If a nation's law or, for that matter, custom, makes this impossible, entrepreneurs will never go into business in this industry in the first place. And, to reiterate: industries that never started do not appear in our records, which means the cost of violating the principle of free contract is hidden, or easy to overlook, and vastly underestimated.

In the US, many who do not have ready money for higher education nevertheless manage to get an education because they can get loans against their future income, which they can pay back over many years. These loans are not given by government but by ordinary, profit-making firms who know that the nation's laws can be reasonably relied upon to ensure that the loans are repaid. If the law or the courts exempted the poor from having to repay loans, it would look benevolent on paper, but it would in fact be a very harsh law because it would ensure that the poor never got loans.

If you express these concerns to a hardened bureaucrat, the response is that our laws have enough flexibility. This response is founded on a total misunderstanding of the extent and range of flexibility that modern businesses require in a globalizing world, where they have to forge alliances with other companies, including foreign ones. The complexities are impossible to anticipate till the occasion arises.

I should emphasize that I do not advocate this principle just for efficiency and growth, but also for equity. The Indian economy is characterized not just by widespread poverty but also by exclusion. There are millions—the market outcastes—whose lives have remained virtually untouched by the progress of India's market economy. There is no doubt that we need direct government interventions on behalf of these disadvantaged people, but there is also much that can be achieved by strengthening the principle of free contract.

In India, since we cannot rely on the state to enforce contracts, what we have come to rely on, disproportionately, is contacts. A landlord looking for a tenant tries to find one through friends and relatives. A businessman seeking collaboration tries to find a partner within his community or sub-caste or golf partners. Hence, for a newcomer it is very difficult to break in, and it is not surprising that many who are dismissed in India as lacking in 'business talent' have gone on to prosper in industrialized nations. This is because 'business talent' in India is a euphemism for the ability to nurture contacts, to wheel and deal through our labyrinthine bureaucracy.

An efficient system of contracts may *look* harsh, but by providing a more anonymous environment for commerce it enables newcomers to break into the system and encourages many such to invest in the first place. So, as the process of globalization opens up new opportunities, we need to re-examine our legal environment to make it easier for more people to enter our marketplace.

There is no denying that the principle of free contract has important exceptions, involving reasoning too intricate to go into here. But the bottom line is that, in drafting legislation and economic policy, it is better to start by adhering to this principle and then working in the exceptions, instead of starting with the presumption of its denial.

III

Among the major political parties in India, the Marxists (i.e. the CPM) are arguably the least corrupt and most well meaning. Despite their long hold on power there, West Bengal's economy has, overall, performed poorly, not only in terms of income but in removing poverty and illiteracy. This is because of the CPM's failure to understand that economic policy has to be guided by research, hard-headed reasoning, and statistical analysis. Economic policy should be for the people but not by the people. Just as it would be foolish to design a dam by majority opinion, it is folly to design economic policy by a show of hands, as our politicians effectively do. Pro-market or anti-market can be a straw man, an empty slogan, because 'market forces' in economics refers to a set of laws of aggregate behaviour. No matter what one's ideology, these laws cannot be ignored.

The CPM was right in making poverty removal and empowerment of the poor its primary objectives but wrong in thinking that the state could ignore individual incentives and suppress the laws of the market. What it ended up doing was to drive capital out of West Bengal. With this, the demand for labour fell and the ultimate loser was the working class. Seeing China's pragmatism, which has resulted in sharp increases in real wages, the CPM leadership is now trying to reverse its economic policy; but it has lost precious time.

Thorstein Veblen, who studied the rich with the zeal which anthropologists reserve for tribals, reached the conclusion that the rich are mean, vulgar, and ostentatious. There are exceptions, but as a ball-park description this is quite accurate. Time and again, I have seen evidence of this and especially remember one occasion when, after giving a lecture to a certain chamber of commerce, I had to spend the evening socializing with the chamber's president. I regretted not having Bertrand Russell's foresight or courage. When he was asked to write for an American newspaper, Russell agreed on condition that he would not have to hobnob with the newspaper's millionaire owner, William Randolph Hearst.

Especially in a nation as poor as ours, the consumerism and profligacy of the wealthy are jarring. But we must realize that in trying to curtail a rich person's wealth we may hurt the conditions of the poor. When we stop the production of a luxury item, it *may* hurt the rich but it *certainly* hurts the poor worker who produces it. To divert money from the rich to the poor, it is not enough to be well meaning. It is not surprising that, despite so much progressive rhetoric, the poor remain so deprived in India.

One class of well-meaning people who could do with a lesson or two in economics are our judges. Given the widespread corruption and criminalization in Indian politics, the increasing activism of our judiciary is welcome. I consider the judiciary, along with the press, among the most valued institutions of modern India and therefore worthy of special responsibility. But an important principle of economics, which the judiciary has repeatedly ignored—and journalists frequently misunderstood—is the sanctity of the contract. To get the most out of the market, we need institutions which enforce voluntary contracts between individuals.

There are exceptions to this principle. We must make sure that the contract does not adversely affect uninvolved outsiders. Civil society also places limits on the range of allowable contracts. It will not, for example, tolerate giving away Draupadi as part of a contract. But subject to such limits, the feasibility of credible contracts is the backbone of a modern economy and a modern economy cannot exist without a credible judiciary.

One reason why the Indian worker is so much poorer than his East Asian counterpart is that our law and the judiciary make it so difficult for workers and employers to sign credible contracts which have a severance clause. Both parties know that when the time comes to enforce such a contract, there are a variety of ways to renege. This inability to sign contracts has kept the demand for labour, and therefore wages, low in India.

True, statute laws cannot be changed in a hurry. However, to the extent that a lot of law in India is jurisprudential or judge-made, our activist judges can help not only with the maintenance of law and order but also with the progress of the Indian economy.

IV

Visiting the city of Bergen in May 2002, accompanied by a Norwegian economist and friend, Magnus Hatlebakk, I went to a jazz concert.* Before entering the auditorium one comes upon a cavernous hall with rows of hooks, each labelled with a number that corresponds to a seat in the auditorium. My friend hung up his jacket and bag on his designated hook, and, realizing that the same was expected of me, I, trying not to betray signs of hesitation, did the same. For anyone brought up in India on a staple of lost footwear during temple visits, my state of mind would be easy to understand. As I entered the auditorium I gave my leather sling bag a last lingering look, fearing that was the last I was seeing of it. Surely, in such a large audience there would be some individuals rational in the sense in which economics textbooks tell us all people are.

But my expectations turned out to be wrong. After two hours of exhilarating jazz by the Norwegian composer and saxophonist Jan Garbarek (Garbarek was deeply influenced by Ravi Shankar and blends jazz with oriental strains), I found my bag and jacket exactly where they had been left. As we walked out into a magnificent Bergen evening, with the fjords on one side providing contrast to the mountains on the other, and the beautiful central plaza, Torgalmenningen, with its street musicians, dancers on stilts, and tourists, I wondered about the Norwegian economy. Norway is today among the richest and most equitable countries in the world. In terms of per capita GNP data, it

*Bergen is in fact best known to lovers of Western classical music as the home of Edvard Grieg (1843–1907), Norway's greatest composer.

stands ahead of the United States and behind only two or three other nations.

But it was not always like that. Norway was in fact poorer than most other countries. Its history effectively began when the Vikings went sailing and plundering faraway nations, including—now it is almost certain—the United States 500 years before Columbus. Development started in a small way in the thirteenth century, when Bergen became a major trading port for the Hanseatic League of traders from Germany. Even today, one can see rows of coloured houses of the Hanseatic traders, with narrow façades and stacked-stone foundations in the Bryggen waterfront area. And some Bergeners are known to affect a certain Germanic style to signal their bourgeois German ancestry.

More recently, in the 1960s, there was the discovery of North Sea oil and this now comprises more than a quarter of Norway's national output. All this must have contributed to Norway's economic success. But what economists tend to forget is that economic success often has social and political roots. The hunch that I had as I left the concert hall in Bergen was that a society's ability to trust people must be an asset on which economic growth can be founded.

Indeed, recent research shows that trust is a major ingredient of growth. Consider the question: 'Do you agree that most people can be trusted?' A rough and ready method of measuring the level of trust in a society is to compute the percentage of people who answer yes and treat that as an index. This is roughly what is done by the World Values Survey. What the survey finds is that trust is highest in Norway, which has an index of 65 per cent, and lowest in Peru (5 per cent). The US scores a moderate 36 per cent and the UK 44 per cent. Hovering very close to Norway are all the Scandinavian countries and Singapore. This index of trust is admittedly crude, but other statistics, such as the number of times a person's lost wallet is returned with the contents intact, have been found to correlate well with this index. Hence, economists have been using this index to study the causes and consequences of trust. Research by Paul Zak and Stephen Knack shows that trust is indeed a major ingredient of superior economic performance.

This stands to reason. The basis of a nation's economic activity and success is the ability to sign contracts and honour agreements. 'I will deliver raw material to you now and you will pay me a certain promised amount thereafter.' 'You give me money to buy a house, and I shall pay that back to you over the next twenty years.' 'I will give you a high-paid job now but you must agree to quit at short notice if my business slumps.' Agreements of this kind provide the foundation of modern market economies.

If there is trust, you save a huge amount not having to have these contracts enforced by courts, judges, and policemen. However, the biggest cost of the lack of trust is not these visible monitoring costs but the much larger and more invisible cost of trade not performed, houses not bought, goods not produced, and firms not started—all because people anticipate in advance that they cannot rely on contracts. In societies where these trusts are high, such as in the Nordic countries, Singapore, and Japan, economic growth has been high. Conversely in other societies, such as India.

India, and some transition economies such as Russia, have an additional problem. Even if a society does not have a high amount of trust, one way of compensating for this is to have a system of law and courts that enforce contracts between consenting adults which have no negative fallout on others. But the role of contract enforcement by the state is totally underestimated by policy-makers in developing countries and transition economies. The laws wantonly overrule contracts with exogenously stated principles and we use a variety of criteria to not enforce a contract when one party reneges (the anticipation of which, in turn, encourages the reneging). But the damage done by this, via the thousands of contracts that are therefore not made, is poorly understood. It is not as if all contracts should be allowed and enforced, but my belief is that many of these nations have erred grossly on the side of disrespecting too many contracts and poor economic performance is partly the result.

Indeed it is arguable that if courts respect and enforce contracts efficiently and without nepotism, people will also learn the value of fairness and the importance of being able to rely on one another. This can create a society of trust which will, in turn, obviate the need for continuous monitoring and bureaucratic enforcement at every stage.

Postscript

Since I began on the subject of theft in public places and rationality, let me end with a scheme that I have invented for the prevention of loss of footwear when visiting Indian temples. It relies crucially on the rationality of thieves. My friends and relatives assure me that my method has worked well. No longer do they have to leave their shoes in the car and walk barefoot on dirty streets to get to the temple or risk losing them by leaving them at the temple entrance. So, here is the time-tested prescription: most Indian temples have several entrances. Choose one, and leave one shoe in the heap of footwear inevitably found in front of these temple entrances. Then, hobble a few steps along to another entrance, and deposit your other shoe in the pile of shoes there. Walk in and let providence have your undivided attention: your footwear will be safe.

17

The Reform of Small Things*

When, on 28 January 1986, 73 seconds into the flight, the US space shuttle Challenger exploded, killing all astronauts aboard, the first thought in everybody's mind was that something major had gone wrong. But investigations revealed that the entire tragedy occurred because of the malfunctioning of some tiny 'o-rings', which are, literally, little rings used to seal joints.

Amidst our larger concerns for the Indian economy—the fiscal deficit, inflation, exchange rate—it is easy to forget that an economy's success depends also on the o-rings, the small things. In India there is immense frustration among people about the bureaucracy, the police, and governance in general. As the Draft Approach Paper to the Tenth Five Year Plan notes: 'People perceive bureaucracy as wooden, disinterested in public welfare and corrupt. The issue of reform in governance has acquired critical dimensions.'

To break out of this bureaucratic gridlock, it is important to turn our attention to the o-rings of our economy, which get ignored because they are not part of any of the larger schemes of economic policy.

In most Indian universities, after a student submits his PhD thesis, it takes between a year and two years for the final examination, the viva, to be held. Most students and professors have come to accept this as natural. But if one thinks of it objectively, the delay is unpardonable. Most European universities conduct the viva within three months of submission, and American universities do so literally within weeks.

*Based on 'Reform of Small Things', *India Today*, 21 July 2001 (Section I); and 'India's Economy: Oil the Nuts and Bolts', *BBC News Online*, 29 June 2004 (Section II).

Hardly any resource is needed to change this. It simply requires the university's top boss, the VC, to *want* to change this. It will require the university to send the thesis by courier to the examiner, a few phone calls to hurry him or her. It may require changes like dropping the rule that the thesis be sent to at least one examiner abroad. This is quite an absurd rule anyway, which is frequently fulfilled by sending the thesis to some sub-par professor whose only qualification is that his address is Not-India.

Even if this change means that one or two unworthy theses slip through, the countervailing benefit of thousands of students saving one or two years each would more than make up for it.

The Indian software industry was raring to go from the early 1980s. What held it back was nothing major, such as a shortage of skilled personnel or other resources, but our arcane import restrictions. To import a computer, a company had to designate officers to run to Delhi, persuade customs personnel why it could not manage without a computer, plead with the commerce ministry; this process could take up to two years. Changing this bottleneck needed no resources, just some thought and wanting. The change happened in 1991. Infosys Technologies grew five times from 1881 to 1991 and five hundred times from 1991 to 2001.

For the last several years I have been travelling regularly to Stockholm for work. On arrival at Arlanda airport I would, like most locals, take the airport bus to the city centre and wait there for 5 to 10 minutes for a taxi. A few years ago I was surprised to find the airport bus driver ask me if I needed a taxi on reaching the city centre. Having gathered this information from all the passengers, he relayed it to the information desk at the city centre by phone. Upon arrival there we had our taxis waiting. This has been the system ever since. This change of system needed no parliamentary debate, no money, just a clever and considerate bureaucrat to think it up. Ten minutes for each person is nothing, but when you add it up for the thousands travelling through Arlanda, it amounts to a considerable saving of resource.

Can these o-rings never be fixed in India? Recently, in Bangalore I visited the corporate headquarters of Infosys on Hosur Road. The experience was beyond my expectations. The sprawling campus with thousands of young employees, tonnes of computer facilities, cafes, coffee stalls, and state-of-the-art gym resembled an American Ivy League university. As India's leading software company it had, naturally, the best computers, excellent boardroom, and wired-up lecture theatres. But the secret of Infosys's success was not just these big things. It was, as Forbes magazine noted, its 'fanatic attention to detail'. This has enabled it to become the company of choice at all levels. Last year it received 183,000 applications for 3000 jobs. This is not a surprise given that Infosys has created close to 2000 rupee-millionaires in its short history. Even for the women who do the sweeping and cleaning, it has been worked out that they can come in very early in the morning so that they have the option of going back home to attend to their children setting out for school. There should be organized tours of the Infosys campus for ordinary Indian citizens to see what is possible in India.

Popular writers often naïvely equate economic liberalization with the withdrawal of government. But government regulation is an essential prerequisite for the functioning of markets. From street vendors to the functioning of the foreign exchange market, there is need for regulation. By all accounts the American economy is highly regulated. Its success lies in having cleaned the regulatory system up relentlessly, plugging holes and punishing the corrupt.

There is no reason why it should be so hard to pay one's income tax, lodge a complaint about one's electricity bill, and get a new passport— as happens in India. The market in itself cannot solve these problems. For these to change we have no option but to work through the nuts and bolts of our system of governance.

II

In Singapore, if you wish to set up a new business, clearances take 8 days, in Hong Kong 11 days, in India 88 days. Purely in terms of time, let alone the costs of getting the legalities sorted out and bureaucratic hurdles cleared and the inching up of the diastolic count, it is not easy starting a private business in India.

If you do get started and your firm runs into a dispute over contract violation, contract enforcement in India takes a year. In Hong Kong it would have taken 180 days, in Singapore less than 60 days.

The real catch in India is neither starting nor running a business but getting out of it. If a firm becomes insolvent, in Hong Kong it takes a year to clear formalities and close the firm; in Singapore less than 7 months; in India a little over 11 years. Even if you had managed to keep the systolic count in check, by now it will have blown its lid.

Little wonder that Singapore and Hong Kong have new businesses springing up all the time and economies that have been surging ahead. In India, politicians and their economic advisers spend a lot of time holding forth on the grander issues of the economy, like privatization and monetary policy, but each of the three matters and the accompanying numbers that I mentioned above relate not to these *grand* policy issues, they pertain to the nuts and bolts of the economy. How long it takes to start a business has virtually no connection with a nation's privatization or fiscal policies. The cost of resolving a contractual dispute is a matter that lies beyond the ambit of a country's budgetary policy.

Of course, the grand policy matters are important. But what is often overlooked in India is that the success of a nation depends also, and critically, on what happens to its nuts and bolts. The Indian economy currently has an unparalleled professional team heading it, starting with the Prime Minister, Manmohan Singh. If government can seize this opportunity and fix these little things on which an economy runs, it will have a lasting effect on the well being of the common person. If people can find reward for their enterprise, rely on contracts and promises, and pay their bills and taxes without having to battle a labyrinthine bureaucracy, government would not have to shoulder the burden of driving the economy. Ordinary and honest people would be able to go into business, which they typically cannot in contemporary India, and the economy would run on its own steam.

My recommendation to the Indian government would be for it to concentrate on a few things and do these well. First, make a fetish of efficiency. Study the legal structure that causes such long delays in starting a new business and restructure it to achieve the efficiency of Singapore or Hong Kong. Find out how many days it takes for various embassies to issue a new passport or to give out a visa and instruct the relevant administrator to do whatever is needed to streamline the procedure and cut down the time to a quarter of what it takes now.

Second, go on an all-out drive to control corruption. This will need a lot of intelligence and professional skill. In the past, India has been so single-minded in trying to control corruption that it has ended up bringing certain industries to a virtual halt by creating endless regulations (and often having no perceptible effect on the corruption it set out to control). The design of corruption control has to be crafted very carefully but if top functionaries of government are determined to control it, corruption in India *can* be brought down substantially.

Tightening the nuts and bolts can push up the country's annual growth rate to 8 per cent or 9 per cent for a few years. But to *sustain* such growth it is essential to boost the investment rate from the current level of just over 20 per cent to over 30 per cent. Through good fiscal planning this can be achieved in five years' time. And this should be the third policy target.

There has been much debate in academic journals about what caused India's growth rate to rise to the current average annual rate of over 6 per cent. Ideologues give easy answers. In fact, this was caused by a complex of many factors, but the precondition without which this would not have been feasible was the rise in India's investment rate from 12 or 13 per cent in the late 1960s to 22 or 23 per cent ten years later. What India desperately needs now is one more boost to this to take it to the levels found in East Asian economies.

Finally, it must be remembered that the ultimate reason for growing faster must be to help the poor. And so the fourth target has to be to craft policies to help and support the economically disadvantaged.

To see what a poor country can achieve, one does not have to look far. What many people do not know is that Bangladesh, despite being much poorer than India, is catching up on some basic standard-of-living indicators, and, in some dimensions, it *has* already overtaken India. In 1990, the percentage of primary school children who were actually enrolled in a school was below 65 per cent for Bangladesh and Pakistan, and around 80 per cent for India. Ten years later, Pakistan reached 67 per cent, India 83 per cent, while Bangladesh reached 87 per cent.

Being poor is, of course, a disadvantage, but Bangladesh's experience with education shows that to say 'nothing can be done about basic needs till one has overcome poverty' is an alibi.

18

Is India's e-Economy for Real?*

The numbers are quite stunning. In 1998-9 the volume of India's software exports was $2.7 billion, in 1999-2000 it was over $4 billion and in 2000–1, from the estimates coming in, it is expected that the exports will be $6.2 billion. This trend has been there for the last eight years—an annual growth rate of approximately 40 per cent. This, given the compounding involved, means that every two years India's exports get virtually doubled. A study by NASSCOM and McKinsey in 1999 predicted that India's exports will reach $50 billion by the year 2008. Since India's total current exports are around $35 billion, and nothing like this has happened in any other sector in India in living memory, these estimates and predictions are giving rise to much scepticism.

Are the numbers a result of jugglery? I myself was initially sceptical, but having checked and compared various sources I am convinced that, give or take a margin of 5 per cent, the figures of the volume of exports are right—the performance in this sector has been spectacular over the last eight or ten years.

What about the forecast? This has met with harsh criticism. One argument has to do with pure deduction. If we assume that India's current export growth rate will persist, it is easy to check that in about sixteen years our exports will exceed our national income (assuming

*First published in *Mantram*, June 2001.

that income also grows at the current rate). But a part cannot exceed the whole, so goes the argument, and hence this is impossible; and so we cannot extrapolate from current trends. This reasoning is based on a false step. There is no reason why exports cannot exceed national income. Not only can this happen, it has happened. Singapore's exports are about 25 per cent larger than its national income.

But even though the forecasts are not technically impossible, is it not foolish to predict by extrapolating from past data? There is the old British joke about the Tory psephologist who came out of a counting centre, all excited, and spoke into the television cameras: 'The first vote has just been counted; it has gone to the Conservatives. If this trend continues, the Conservatives will have a landslide victory.' Yes, forecasting by pure extrapolation, based on very short evidence, is foolish. But in this case the evidence pertains to eight years and, moreover, the forecast is not based on mere extrapolation but on a study of the global and Indian situation and trends.

The most serious criticism is based on the observation that the global situation has changed since 1999 in ways that beckon us to revise the forecast downwards. First, there is the downturn in the US stock market, especially in the IT sector. This is indeed a matter of some concern, since 66 per cent of India's exports end up in North America. However, what must be realized is that the stock market need not be correlated with the size of the industry, and exports depend mainly on the latter. One reason why the technology stocks are doing badly is precisely because the IT sector in the US is such an attractive industry and growing so rapidly. As the number of firms increase, profits go down; and so the stock market does poorly—especially since market players did not understand this and overinvested in technology stocks. So this in itself should have very little effect on India's exports. If, however, the US economy goes into a slump and US growth stops or becomes negative, then the projections can go wrong. Fortunately, though some slowing down of the US economy is expected, no proper study predicts a major depression. But this is something that we need to be cautious about.

The second worry pertains to the supply side in India. With the large flight of computer professionals out of India, there is going to be a supply bottleneck forming in India's software production. This problem is likely to be exacerbated with increases in the US quota of H1B visas. For the next three years the US is going to let in 200,000 professionals under the H1B category each year. Moreover, there is no reason to believe the number will decrease after three years. Typically, about 45 per cent of these visas go to Indians (the second largest category being the Chinese—9 per cent) and 53 per cent of the ones who get H1B visas are computer professionals. This means that roughly 50,000 computer professionals will leave India for the US each year. When one adds to this the (admittedly smaller) flows to Germany, Sweden, and even Japan, it is evident that the next years will test the limits of how many computer professionals India can produce.

While this is reason for some concern, it must be recognized that IT is the one sector in which India has actually benefited from the brain drain. This is what has enabled establishing links between Bangalore and Silicon Valley. In fact, NASSCOM predicts that the larger the outflow of personnel from India, the greater will be the demand for software exports from India. So, this increased demand for Indian computer personnel should be treated as a blessing and government should simply work hard to educate larger numbers of Indians appropriately.

This brings me to the question of policy. The software export market is highly competitive and bungled policy can easily erode India's initial competitive advantage. The right policy environment is no easy matter and in this area many a received wisdom gets turned on its head. Many economists, and this includes me, argue for greater openness for India. Yet there can be no denial that it was an act of closing the economy that spurred our domestic IT sector. In 1977 the Janata government asked IBM to leave India and, as Infosys's Narayana Murthy has written, 'this was in some sense a blessing in disguise', encouraging the production 'of smaller, state-of-the-art but cheaper minicomputers and microcomputers'. But after that, the boost to this sector came from the opening up of the economy in the 1990s and the need now is to move more strongly in that direction, allowing Indian companies to go for larger acquisitions abroad.

Whatever the details, what is paramount is an active and intelligent involvement by government in promoting this sector, which may just turn out to be the philosopher's stone that at last pulls all of India out of poverty.

19

India's Trade Policy and the WTO*

On 31 March 2001 India will witness a dramatic change in its foreign trade regime, when quantity restrictions on the import of virtually all goods are removed. The only permitted exceptions will be a few special goods on grounds of security and religion.

Broadly speaking, there are two methods of curbing imports—the first is to charge a tariff on the commodity being imported, and the second is to rule that the commodity is not allowed to be imported. The latter is described as a 'quantity restriction'; and it is just as well it has a popular acronym, QR, since it has been used so widely in India. A whole range of agricultural, consumer, and some capital goods—a total of over 700 goods—are prevented from entering the country under this criterion.

Once QRs are removed on all these 700 items, a host of new goods will flow into India. Unsurprisingly, a lot of Indian businessmen are exercised over this imminent policy shift.

It is true that, left to ourselves, we would have phased out QRs more slowly. But we had no choice. Ever since the conclusion of the Uruguay Round of GATT in 1993 there has been pressure on India to open its borders. In 1997 India proposed a nine-year phase-out plan to the WTO, arguing that it should be given temporary shelter under Article XVIII B of GATT which allows developing countries to use QRs to

*First published in *India Today*, 19 March 2001.

counter balance-of-payments problems. But the industrialized nations contested this, referring the matter to a WTO dispute settlement panel, which ruled against India, giving us up to 31 March 2001 to end all QRs.

In assessing the imminent regime change, it is worth noting that it will not be as momentous as some fear. From July 1991 India has been steadily dismantling its trade barriers. This has already put India on the road to integration with the global economy. India's total foreign trade (export plus import) as a percentage of national income has risen from less than 16 per cent in 1990 to 21 per cent in 1999. When these QRs are removed, we will still have the right to slap a tariff, subject to some upper limits, to protect the indigenous industry. And government should provide a reasonably high tariff cover for the new product lines being opened up for imports, along with a commitment to lower these over the next few years as our domestic industry adjusts to the new open regime.

The benefits of this opening up can be numerous and, in my opinion, outweigh the costs. First, there is the standard benefit of trade, which allows for specialization and thus greater production. This also helps improve the quality of domestic production, which in the long run should enable us to increase our exports. Second, the use of a tariff instead of a QR has the advantage of generating revenues to the government through customs collections.

But apart from all this, there is another benefit of openness which is often overlooked. Openness draws our attention to the failings of our government and domestic policies. When products from other nations come in at a lower cost, we are forced to examine our comparative failures. Our indigenous producers become conscious of the fact that they may not have access to as much credit as the Chinese producers do, or that we face more obstructive bureaucracy than the Korean firms. We realize that subjecting our indigenous producers to the restrictions of small-scale industry (SSI) and expecting them to compete against large-scale Chinese manufacturers is like asking someone to fight with his hands tied behind his back. As these pressures build up, the opportunity arises for government to clean up its act—by curtailing bureaucracy and corruption, relaxing SSI regulations, and so on—so that our producers are not handicapped when competing against foreign entrants.

Nimbleness and efficiency on the part of government are important to this new regime. It is naïve to think that openness has no negative consequences. With openness we will encounter a variety of damaging business strategies that companies and governments use when breaking into new markets. Much ink has been spilled on the problem of dumping. Dumping pertains to the act of unfairly lowering prices to win over customers. Now, if a country *consistently* keeps the price low (perhaps because its government subsidizes its exports), this should be no problem. We should simply make room for such foreign producers and allow them to subsidize our consumers. The problem arises when prices are lowered temporarily to out-compete indigenous producers, who may not have deep enough pockets to take the losses, with the idea of putting prices back up after these indigenous producers are driven out of the market. Government will have to be vigilant, countering such practices with tariffs, and, if need be, taking such dumpers to the WTO.

Apprehension is often expressed in India that the WTO is a rich country's handmaiden. There is some truth to this. WTO procedures are so expensive and so knowledge intensive that rich countries are better able to exploit them. But despite this it is important for us to take part in the global system rather than withdraw into a shell, crying foul, as we tended to do in the past. First, our indigenous businessmen are no fonts of virtue. Second, even if the global system is unfair, it is better to engage and try to change it than to withdraw and thereby more or less ensure it is never changed.

20

The Coming Textile Turmoil*

The end of country quotas on textile exports marks one of the most major events of the world economy—one that can cause tectonic shifts in the global economic landscape.

The Multi-Fibre Agreement (MFA), under which these quotas were organized, was put in place in 1974 to protect the textile industries in the US and in Europe. The MFA expired in 1994, but the quotas were continued and managed by the WTO, with the understanding that these would be terminated at the start of 2005.

That has happened now and the winds of change are palpable. The US is expected to lose a large number of jobs in this sector, which has anyway dwindled over the last decades. In 1974 there were 2.4 million workers in the textile sector in the US. By 2000, 40 per cent of these jobs were gone.

What is more worrying is that there are many poor countries that could lose out. Anticipating the end of quotas, exports from El Salvador collapsed by 30 per cent last November. It is expected that the apparel sector of the Dominican Republic will lose up to 40 per cent jobs.

Currently, global textile and apparel exports are just short of $500 billion per annum. To put this in perspective, India's national income is just over $500 billion; Bangladesh's and China's close to $50 billion and $1300 billion. With the quotas gone, total global exports are expected to cross $1200 billion by 2010. Shifts in shares of this huge industry can lift entire nations out of poverty and, equally, plunge whole regions into joblessness.

*First published in *BBC News Online*, 2 March 2005.

While the gains for China are certain and enormous, India is also expected to reap substantial benefits. In the first six weeks of the quota-less world, India has made big gains. Sears and Marks and Spencer are setting up operations in India and Gap Inc. is expected to expand its sourcing from India. It seems likely that in the first quarter of this year garment exports will get a spurt of 50 per cent.

What happens over the next few years will depend critically on government policy. Currently, India exports $14 billion worth of textile products. Even without doing much it should reach an export of $40 billion by 2010. But with a proper blend of policies, it is possible to reach the figure of $80 billion. This, apart from the benefit of bringing in foreign exchange and boosting growth, can make a visible dent on unemployment.

For Bangladesh and Pakistan, which rely on textiles for about 70 per cent of their export earnings, it will be a harder struggle but they—especially Bangladesh—could also benefit from a quota-less world. All these countries have cheap labour; the additional advantages that India has are those of size and large foreign-exchange reserves that can (and, I believe, should) be used to boost infrastructure.

Last month I met Sudhir Dhingra, Chairman of Orient Craft, one of the largest Indian exporters, and toured one of his factories in Gurgaon, outside Delhi. The unit had 3800 workers, sitting in modern, assembly-line arrangements in a clean, well-lit factory. They were producing little dresses and skirts that would be sold by Orient Craft at $4 a piece and would be retailed in the US for $45. With margins like this it is not surprising that the global garment manufacture is expected to move entirely to developing countries over the next few years. Orient Craft had a turnover of $118 million last year and this year is expected to cross $160 million.

While the Gurgaon factory that I visited is one of India's largest, to take full advantage of scale factories need to be several times its size. To achieve this government has to play an important coordinating role. It has to remove its small-scale industry size restrictions, modernize its ports, and allow more flexible labour markets.

For a product to travel from a factory in India to a retail outlet in New York takes around thirty days. Most East Asian countries take half that time: this is where the ports come in. Indian ports are small and riddled with bureaucratic delays. Large liners do not dock in them. Most exports have to go out on feeder vessels and are transferred to a mother vessel in some other port. Moreover, goods are required to be delivered at the port seven days prior to shipment. In most East Asian ports this cut-off is one day.

The modernization of ports and transport infrastructure will need money. One possibility is to use a small fraction of India's foreign exchange reserves, say $10 billion, for this and other infrastructural investment. This would help not just the textile sector but all traded goods; and the initial investment could be recovered in a few years in terms of not just money but jobs; and it could also help the global trade of other South Asian countries.

PART III

Social Norms
and Political Economy

21

Social Norms, Law, and Economics*

Social Norms and the Law

After one eats in a restaurant, that one has to leave a tip is a social norm, and that one has to pay for the food is law. As is evident from this, both norms and the law influence our behaviour. What we say, for instance, can be curtailed by having laws that restrict freedom of speech. But not having such a restrictive law, or having a law or a constitutional requirement—such as the First Amendment in the US—which gives individuals the right to say what they wish or believe in, does not automatically guarantee freedom of speech. *Social* restrictions can also curtail our freedom. If there is a social norm against a certain opinion or viewpoint or against the explicit mention of certain facts of life, then through the threat of ostracism and other 'social' punishments the individual freedom to express a viewpoint or fact can be limited.

The goods that we buy, the food that we consume, the services that we render are all influenced both by the law and the norms of society. But in traditional economics there was little recognition of this fact, especially the influence of norms. In recent years this has been changing and there have been several initiatives to integrate the analysis of norms and institutions with markets and the provision of public goods (see, for instance, Ullmann-Margalit 1977; Elster 1989). Indeed some

*First published in *New Palgrave Dictionary of Economics and the Law*, edited by Peter Newman (London: Macmillan, 1999).

of the clues to important economic phenomena—for instance, why one nation has rapid growth and another stagnates—may lie in these extra-economic factors.

This essay begins by discussing what social norms are and how they influence economic functioning. It comments on the relation between norms and evolutionary processes and the interconnections between social norms, the law, and the state, and in particular the much-discussed question: to what extent can social norms or voluntary community-based effort be a substitute for law?

Social Norms

Like cows, social norms are easier to recognize than to define. Most existing definitions are suggestive rather than exact. Consider Axelrod's definition (1986: 1097): 'A *norm* exists in a given setting to the extent that individuals usually act in a certain way and are often punished when seen not to be acting in this way.' This is a useful working definition but clearly it is understandable only by those who already know what a norm is. Likewise, Elster (1989: 99-100) defines 'social norms by the feature that they are *not outcome-oriented*'; and he adds that for 'norms to be *social*, they must be shared by other people and partly sustained by their approval and disapproval'. He then goes on to distinguish these from 'legal norms', which are 'enforced by specialists who do so out of self-interest: they lose their job if they don't. By contrast, social norms are enforced by members of the general community.' It is worth adding that at times social norms can get internalized to the extent that they do not need social enforcement and are adhered to by individuals of their own accord. With these suggestive ideas in the background, it is convenient to study norms by distinguishing between three kinds of social norms: rationality-limiting norms, preference-changing norms, and equilibrium-selection norms.

A '*rationality-limiting norm*' means a norm which stops us from doing certain things or choosing certain options, irrespective of how much utility that thing or option gives us. Thus most individuals would not consider picking another person's wallet in a crowded bus.

This they would do not by speculating about the amount the wallet is likely to contain, the chances of getting caught, the severity of the law and so on, but because they consider stealing wallets as something that is *simply not done*.

In traditional economics the 'feasible set' of alternatives facing an individual (from which the person makes his or her choice) is defined in terms of technological or budgetary feasibility. Thus a consumer's feasible set is the collection of all the combinations of goods and services that the consumer can purchase given his or her income. From the above discussion it should be evident that a rationality-limiting norm further limits the feasible set, because now certain alternatives may be infeasible to an individual not just because they are technologically infeasible (like walking on water) or budgetarily infeasible (like buying a Jaguar) but because they are ruled out by the person's norms. Indeed a person endowed with norms may forego options which could have enhanced his utility and thus such a person would be considered irrational in terms of mainstream economics. Basically, such norms limit the domain over which the rationality calculus is applied.

Some may argue that instead of thinking that such norms limit individual rationality, we can simply redefine our utility function so that what I described as infeasible gives a very low utility, perhaps negative infinity. But doing this *invariably* runs the risk of reducing utility theory to a tautology. Moreover, in reality there are certain things we would love to do but our norms get in the way. Nevertheless, this does not mean that norms never change our preferences or utility functions. Certain norms do get internalized. There are many individuals whose religion requires them to be vegetarian and they tell you that they find non-vegetarian food revolting anyway. More often than not this is no coincidence; a religious norm adhered to over a stretch of time often gets internalized so that one begins actually to prefer what the norm requires. This can explain why one finds systematic variations in taste across regions and nations. What starts out as a norm or a custom can over time become part of one's preference. Such a norm may be referred to as a '*preference-changing norm*'. The only reason for being aware of this kind of a norm is that it can give us an understanding of how some of our preferences are formed. This can enormously enrich the traditional model of economics, which treats preferences as primitives.

Finally, consider the norm, in many countries, of driving on the right. It is true that this norm is additionally fortified by the law; but it is arguable that even if this were just a norm or a convention and not the law, people would still drive on the right. This explains why the police have to be vigilant in enforcing the stop-sign rule or the speeding rule but not the drive-on-the-right rule. The first two are laws which are not in people's self-interest (they may of course be in their *group* interest). But the third is a norm which, once it is in place, happens to be entirely compatible with self-interested behaviour. In the absence of such a norm, there are at least two possible equilibria— everyone drives on the left and everyone drives on the right. The norm is very different from the two discussed above because it simply helps people *select* an equilibrium. It is for this reason that I call such a norm an '*equilibrium-selection norm*'. This is the norm the study of which is currently in vogue in economics and has generated a lot of literature, to the extent that economists tend to forget about the other kinds of norms—conveniently so, since the equilibrium-selection norm is the one which is most compatible with conventional economics.

According to this terminology, Akerlof's (1976) conception of caste is that of an equilibrium-selection norm. More recently, Cooter (1997), in discussing the connection between norms and law, identifies norms entirely with equilibrium-selection norms. He describes a 'social norm' as an 'effective consensus obligation' and goes on to identify a consensus obligation with an equilibrium of a game. All these are special cases of the general idea of a social institution as in equilibrium of a game (Schotter 1981; Calvert 1995).

Some writers have distinguished between 'conventions' and (equilibrium-selection) norms, by treating the latter as special conventions, the adherence to which is additionally fortified by the human desire for peer approval (Sugden 1989; see also Warneryd 1990). Thus Sugden (1989) has described the norm which used to exist in a fishing village in Yorkshire, whereby the first person arriving on the shore after a high tide had the right to collect the driftwood. Moreover, if she placed two stones on top of the pile, she could leave the pile and take it away at leisure. Sugden explains how such a rule can emerge initially as a convention which is an equilibrium, in the sense that, once it is there, it is in no one's interest to deviate from it unilaterally. Then, over time, as people get used to it, they develop a sense of rights associated with this convention; so that anybody violating it meets with social disapproval. That is how the convention becomes a social norm. While recognizing the scope for this kind of categorization, I shall nevertheless proceed by using the terms 'convention', 'custom', and 'norm' interchangeably.

The simplest example of such an equilibrium-selection norm may be illustrated with the prisoner's dilemma. If the game is played once, no rational player will cooperate, as is well known. But suppose the game is being played by two players repeatedly and without end. Then it is possible for the two players to adopt strategies such as the tit-for-tat strategy or the trigger strategy, which result in cooperation and which are in each player's self-interest. A trigger strategy is one where the player begins by co-operating and then co-operates if and only if no one has defected in the past. Evidently, if each of the two players play trigger strategies they will end up co-operating throughout. If one of them deviates in one period by playing non-cooperatively, then (given that they are playing trigger strategies) from then on they will both play the non-cooperative strategy. Hence, unless the discount rates of the players are so high that the future losses forever do not offset the one-time gain from sudden defection, no player will deviate. Hence, the trigger strategy can be thought of as a social norm which, once in place, survives because of self-interest (given that the time discount rate is below some critical level). So, far from being contrary to one's self-interest, these kinds of norms are parasitical on self-interest. Hence, they sit rather comfortably with conventional economics and its *homo oeconomicus*.

The distinctions discussed above may not always be self-evident.

Consider the norm of reciprocity, whereby human beings exchange favours over time. For instance, a person in need can expect help from other members of the tribe or the village, the implicit understanding being that the help will be reciprocated at other times when their fortunes are reversed. This norm can be thought of as a rationality-limiting norm since the person who helps out the destitute seems to do so against his *self*-interest. But we can also take a long-run perspective on this and argue that if an individual refuses to help when it is his turn, the whole system can collapse. So, in a manner akin to the case of cooperation in the repeated prisoner's dilemma, the norm of reciprocity may be an equilibrium-selection norm. In other words, it is foolish not to recognize that there may be compacting explanations for the same norm.

Norms, the Law, and the State

At one level there is a lot in common between social norms and the law. Both place restrictions on individual behaviour. Both tend to work through sanctions. It is not surprising that there has been a large literature that compares and contrasts these two related forms of control over the individual (Hart 1961; Raz 1980).

To understand the role of law in economics it is helpful to think of an economy as a large 'game'. That is, every citizen in the economy can be thought of as a 'player' who has available to him or her a set of actions (also called strategies). The final outcome that occurs in the economy depends on the choice of strategy by each player, and each player's 'payoff' or utility depends on everybody's choice of strategy. It is the latter, which allows one person's strategy to affect another person's utility, that gives the game-theoretic approach its distinctness. It recognizes that externalities may be ubiquitous rather than the exception. An economy described as above may be called an 'economy game'.

What role does law play in such a game? The traditional view is that the law either limits an individual's set of available strategies or changes the payoff function. Consider two laws: (a) one that bans cigarette smoking and (b) one that declares that anybody driving at a speed above 100 km per hour has to pay a fine of 200 francs. Now, (a) can be thought of as a law that limits the set of strategies or actions open to an individual and (b) can be thought of as a law that changes the payoff function of individuals. Earlier, the payoff from driving at 140 km per hour would be the sum of the joy of arriving early at the destination and the thrill of speed. But now (that is, once law [b] is in place), we have to subtract from that the expected cost of the fine (that is, 200 francs multiplied by the probability of getting caught) to compute the payoff of driving at 140 kmph. So, it does seem that the law can affect the feasible set and the payoff function.

Note however that it is also possible to think of the ban on smoking not as a restriction on the set of what a person can do but as a change in the payoff function, because we can say that even after the smoking ban a person *can* smoke, but has to pay a huge penalty if he is caught. Baird, Gertner and Picker (1994) take exactly this view. They think of laws as invariably affecting only the payoff functions of players. This is a plausible alternative characterization.

More controversially, it is possible to go a step further and argue that strictly a law cannot affect either the strategy sets or the payoff functions. We have the impression that the law changes the payoff function because, unwittingly, we treat the enforcers of the law as agents exogenous to the economy game. We assume that they mechanically enforce what the law lays down. Once the state is endogenized, however, and the enforcers of the law are also treated as players with their own motivations, it becomes evident that the law cannot change the payoff functions or the strategy sets. This is because all players taken together are free to ignore the law and do exactly what they were doing in the absence of the law, and in so doing get the same payoff as before. So, according to this argument, the law cannot change the game. It can only influence the *outcome* of the economy game and it does so by influencing the beliefs of players concerning how other players will behave, and by creating new focal points (Basu 1997).

Much of the above description of the role of law in economics can be translated to social norms as well. The way in which norms differ from the law is in terms of their origins and enforcement. According to one classic view, usually associated with Austin (1861), a law is a command from the sovereign to his subjects. In Austin's model the sovereign is 'illimitable'—he can legislate any law into existence and in the exercise of his legal powers he is not himself limited by the law. While Austin derived many of his views from Bentham, Bentham did not consider the sovereign to be illimitable.

This view of the law as something that can only come from the state or the sovereign and is enforced by the agents of the state can, however, be taken too far, as when some commentators do not regard 'primitive law' as law at all. On the other hand, anthropologists and historians have contested such an interpretation. Gluckman's (1995) classic work outlines the legal system of the Lozi people of Barotseland and though it is not formally the law of the state it is very much a legal system. Similarly ancient laws, such as the Code of Hammurabi in Mesopotamia which dates back to more than two thousand years BC or the laws outlined by Kautilya for the Maurya Dynasty in India in the book *Arthashastra*, written some time between the fourth century BC and AD 150, are by any standard legal systems. They are codified, have procedures for implementation and are enforced by well-defined agents.

It is true that some norms shade into laws and the boundary between the two is not always sharp. A good example is caste or race discrimination. Are these matters of law or norms? In contemporary India, for instance, caste is clearly a matter of norms, since the law does not recognize caste differences (excepting for some kinds of affirmative action to reverse historical disadvantages). But if one goes back in time a thousand or two thousand years, the status of caste becomes ambiguous. If we recognize Kautilya's *Arthashastra* as specifying the laws of that society, then caste, we have to admit, was a matter of law. As Kautilya states in no uncertain terms (1992: 484): 'A *Svapaka* (a dog-breeder and an outcaste) man having sexual relations with an *Arya* woman shall be condemned to death. A *Svapaka* woman having relations with an *Arya* male shall be mutilated by having her ears and nose cut off.' (I leave it to the reader to decide which of these was considered the bigger crime.) But if one goes even further back in time the caste system is simply an informal social system or norm, not enforced by the 'state' as law. Leaving such troublesome cases aside, we can, in general, assert that norms are either enforced by the community or society at large or by the individual's own sense of shame and embarrassment, whereas the law is enforced by the state or some organization resembling the state.

Second, the *origins* of norms and laws are usually different. Laws typically *can* be enacted; and so dates *can* be associated with particular laws. There are no doubt laws which do not take the form of legislative statutes. This is true, for instance, of English common law, and of the US practice of relying on interpretive principles and judicial rulings. As Ferejohn notes (1995: 193), 'Many nonstatutory legal materials [. . .] bear a formulaic resemblance to statutory commands, while having a different pedigree.' Nevertheless, laws *can* be adopted through acts of parliament, even if (at times) only to codify what is already accepted by custom. Social norms, on the other hand, almost always emerge gradually. Repeated patterns of behaviour gradually ossify into custom and then into a social norm, the violation of which causes eyebrows to be raised and is seen as an aberration. The origins of many norms, such as caste norms, disappear into the mists of distant history.

As with all distinctions, this is not one without its problems. Legal theorists talk of 'natural laws' and 'positive laws' (for discussion, see Goldsmith 1996). The former consist of that which stems from our natural sense of morals and justice, whereas the latter refer to codified laws of the state or some comparable organization. First of all, to the *extent* that 'natural laws' are also laws, their roots may be as difficult to locate as the roots of norms. Moreover, even for many positive laws, the origins often lie in the gradually hardening norms of society. Thus the law can at times be simply a codification of norms. Not surprisingly, legal scholars and philosophers have differed on whether laws, especially natural laws, are invented or discovered (Olafson 1961).

This conflict recently arose in the case of Miriam Wilngal, an eighteen-year-old woman in Papua New Guinea, whose clan agreed to give her away to another clan as part of a traditional tribal contract. The trouble arose because Miriam refused to go, taking the case to court and citing the 'written law' of the state. The court ruled in her favour.

But the clan that has failed to secure Miriam has threatened to press counter-charges for the violation of contract and the denial of traditional tribal rights. As the *New York Times* (6 May 1997) noted: 'In effect, they are threatening to use the modern legal system to demand their traditional tribal rights.'

The origins of many norms are more difficult to understand than their persistence (Basu, Jones and Schlicht 1987). As Akerlof (1976) has argued, a norm persists if it is no one's individual interest to violate it. Hence, as in the prisoner's dilemma game, norms can survive as long as they are individually rational, even though they may harm the group as a whole. On other occasions some norms may be in the interest of one group and hurt another. These, at first sight, seem to amount to a rejection of 'functionalism', which claims that institutions exist to fulfil useful social functions. However, one can bring back a minimal functionalism by recognizing that norms must have some properties of evolutionary stability.

Evolution and Norms

Where these norms come from is difficult to explain but we can, at least partially, understand why some norms exist and why some do not, in terms of *evolutionary* stability. Indeed evolution and norms are topics that have for long been discussed as closely related to each other (Hayek 1960; Axelrod 1986; Boyd and Richerson 1994). According to this argument, we do not see any society with the norm that one must not eat proteins simply because such a society would perish along with its norm. Similarly we do not find any society where stealing anything from anyone is considered legitimate because such a society would soon be in complete chaos, become impoverished, and wither away.

On Forest Home Drive in the city of Ithaca, New York, there is a bridge on which two cars cannot cross at the same time. When we were children we were told how in the Andes there are pathways along steep mountains, which are so narrow that two persons cannot pass; and so when two persons found themselves face to face on one of these paths, the one with the quicker draw survived by shooting the other person. In Ithaca a different norm is used. Cars pass in little convoys, three or four at a time, and the convoys from the two directions alternate. That is, after the third or the fourth car goes, one just stops and waits for an oncoming convoy and then starts once again. This is against one's self-interest; so it is indeed a rationality-limiting norm. However, the reason why we find some norm of this kind and not the Andean custom of a shoot-out is that it is evolutionarily more stable. This is also the reason why the 'Andes custom' probably exists nowhere outside children's tales. A society practising this norm would not survive and neither would the norm. In brief, the evolutionary argument explains why certain norms cannot exist by demonstrating why societies which carry such norms cannot survive.

There are different ways of formalizing this institution. Let me here follow the route of evolutionary game theory *a la* Maynard Smith and Price (1973). In their model agents play a certain game pairwise, but unlike in the economist's game in their 'game' (a) each agent plays a fixed strategy, and (b) the payoffs do not really indicate utility but are fitness indices, whereby a higher payoff implies a faster reproduction of the agent playing that strategy. Assumption (a) is justified by the fact that in these 'games' the players are typically animals or phenotypes who cannot choose rationally but are programmed to behave in certain ways. A hawk always plays the aggressive strategy; a dove the accommo-dating one. Now think of a society in which all players are identical, that is, they play the same strategy. Into this society occasionally other strategies (that is, players using other kinds of strategies) enter as mutants. If the mutants earn a greater payoff when they play the incumbents they kill off the original population. Otherwise, the mutants get killed off and we say that the existing population is 'im-mune' against the particular mutant in question. If a particular strategy is immune against all possible mutants we say that strategy is 'evolu-tionarily stable'. That is, agents programmed to play that strategy will survive the process of natural selection. From this to explain the evolu-tionary survival of norms is a small step.

Consider what has been described above as a rationality-limiting norm. Hence a social norm is a restriction on what people choose. This is the view that Boyd and Richerson (1994: 72) take in their anthropological study of norms: 'A culture's norms determine which behaviours are permissible and which are not.' Hence, if we start with a game in which each person has a feasible set of strategies, then a 'norm' is a subset of that set. For instance, *i*'s norm may allow *i* to choose anything from that set, except the strategies of picking pockets in buses and jumping queues. Hence, a person with a norm is between the textbook *homo economicus* who is free to choose any strategy and Maynard Smith and Price's player who has to choose one specific strategy. Now instead of looking for *strategies* which are evolutionarily stable we can look for *norms* which are evolutionarily stable (Basu 1996). Such an approach can yield interesting insights. It can explain certain kinds of cooperative behaviour and altruism. Stable norms can earn payoffs greater than in a Nash equilibrium.

A related question that in recent times has exercised the minds of many researchers working in the area of law and social norms is this: can social order be achieved through social norms and community efforts, *without* the intervention of the state and its laws, and without bringing in the effects of natural selection and evolution?

Law and Order

'Legal centralism' is a phrase that has been used by Williamson (1983) to express the belief that all law and its enforcement come from the government. From such a belief it is easy to jump to the belief that the order that we see in the world—to the extent that we do—emanates from the law and its enforcement. This belief has in turn given rise to a large literature, both theoretical and empirical, which challenges this assumption (Taylor 1976; Sugden 1989; Ellickson 1991). With the rise of game theory the theoretical ideas are now easy to grasp. First, we can often shape the behaviour of another person by using the threat of 'exit' from a relationship. Secondly, many games or strategic environments in which some suboptimal outcome seems inevitable turn out differently when repeated interactions are considered. As already noted, if the prisoner's dilemma is played repeatedly the players may be able to cooperate without the need for third party intervention. The threat of future retaliation keeps the players in line. Unfortunately, and this is important to keep in mind, this method cannot explain cooperation in the prisoner's dilemma but only a variant of it, namely, when it is played an infinite number of times.

Whether for these reasons or not, there are many examples of societies or groups ushering in order without recourse to the law. Bernstein (1992) has described in detail how the diamond industry organizes its own system of punishment and monitoring without seeking legal help. Ellickson (1991) documents how the ranchers of Shasta County, California, have evolved their own rules and sanctions to bring order in their lives and professional pursuits. Interesting though these facts are, one has to be careful in posing these examples and arguments as part of the debate on state intervention and non-intervention. There is no reason why we must think of the state as a force opposing private efforts. After all, the state itself emerged gradually, from the atomistic actions of individuals. So in some ways the state is itself like a norm. Hence, the state may be viewed as one of the many different instruments through which individuals create order among themselves. Instead of thinking of the law and social norms as alternative systems, or worse, as adversaries, it is possible to treat the legal system as part of the general theory of norms.

Bibliography

Akerlof, G.A. 1976. 'The Economics of Caste and of the Rat Race and Other Woeful Tales, *Quarterly Journal of Economics* 90: 599-617.

Austin, J. 1861. *Lectures on Jurisprudence*. London, John Murray (1911 edition).

Axelrod, R. 1986. 'An Evolutionary Approach to Norms'. *American Political Science Review* 80: 1095-1111.

Baird, D.G., R.H. Gertner, and R.C. Picker, 1994. *Game Theory and the Law*. Cambridge, MA: Harvard University Press.

Basu, K. 1996. 'Notes on Evolution, Rationality and Norms'. *Journal of Institutional and Theoretical Economics* 152: 739-50.

————. 1997. 'Prelude to Political Economy: The Role of Norms and Law in Economics'. Paper presented at the Conference on 'Social Science and Social Change' at the Institute for Advanced Study, Princeton, 9-11 May 1997.

————. E.L. Jones, and E. Schlicht. 1987. 'The Growth and Decay of Custom: The Role of the New Institutional Economics in Economic History. *Explorations in Economic History* 24: 1-21.

Bernstein, L. 1992. 'Opting out of the Legal System: Extralegal Contractual Relations in the Diamond Industry'. *Journal of Legal Studies* 21: 115-57.

Boyd, R. and P.J. Richerson, 1994. 'The Evolution of Norms: An Anthropological View'. *Journal of Institutional and Theoretical Economics* 150: 72-87.

Calvert, R.L. 1995. 'The Rational Choice Theory of Social Institutions'. In *Modern Political Economy*, ed. J.S. Banks and E.A. Hanushek, Cambridge: Cambridge University Press.

Cooter, R.D. 1997. 'Law from Order'. Mimeo: University of California, Berkeley.

Ellickson, R.C. 1991. *Order without Law: How Neighbours Settle Disputes*. Cambridge, MA: Harvard University Press.

Elster, J. 1989. 'Social Norms and Economic Theory.' *Journal of Economic Perspectives* 3: 99–117.

Ferejohn, J. 1995. 'Law, Legislation, and Positive Political Theory.' In *Modern Political Economy*, ed. J.S. Banks and E.A. Hanushek, Cambridge: Cambridge University Press.

Gluckman, M. 1955. *The Judicial Process among the Barotse of Northern Rhodesia*. Manchester: Manchester University Press.

Goldsmith, M.M. 1996. 'Hobbes on Law'. In *The Cambridge Companion to Hobbes*, ed. T. Sorell, Cambridge: Cambridge University Press.

Hart, H.L.A. 1961. *The Concept of Law*. Oxford: Clarendon Press.

Hayek, F. 1960. *The Constitution of Liberty*. London: Routledge & Kegan Paul.

Kautilya. 1992. *The Arthashastra*. Edited by L.N. Rangarajan, New Delhi: Penguin Books.

Maynard Smith, J. and Price, G.R. 1973. 'The Logic of Animal Conflict.' *Nature* 246: 15–18.

Olafson, F.A. 1961. 'Natural Law and Natural Rights.' In *Society, Law and Morality*, ed. F.A. Olafson, Englewood Cliffs, NJ: Prentice Hall.

Raz, J. 1980. *The Concept of a Legal System: An Introduction to the Theory of a Legal System*. 2nd edn, Oxford: Clarendon Press.

Schotter, A. 1981. *The Economic Theory of Social Institutions*. Cambridge: Cambridge University Press.

Sugden, R. 1989. 'Spontaneous Order.' *Journal of Economic Perspectives* 3: 85–97.

Taylor, M. 1976. *Anarchy and Cooperation.* London: Wiley.

Ullmann-Margalit, E. 1977. *The Emergence of Norms.* Oxford: Clarendon Press.

Wärneyd, K. 1990. 'Economic Conventions: Essays in Institutional Economics.' PhD dissertation. Stockholm School of Economics.

Willamson, O.E. 1983. 'Credible Commitments: Using Hostages to Support Exchange'. *American Economic Review* 73: 519–20.

22

Methodological Individualism in the Social Sciences*

A social science which explains social regularities and phenomena, such as reciprocity and inflation, wholly from the decisions and behaviour of *individual* human beings is described as adhering to methodological individualism (henceforth, MI). Whether this is the right methodology for social science or not was once a matter of considerable dispute, which engaged the minds of leading economists and sociologists. Gradually, interest in the subject died down, individuals continued to do social science research without, mercifully, trying to explicitly articulate the method that they were in fact using. But with this developed the feeling, especially among economists, that the problem of MI was either trivial or resolved in its favour. There is, however, a revival of interest in the rights and wrongs of MI as evidence from the works of Bhargava (1993) and Arrow (1994). The aim of this essay is to evaluate this resurgence of interest, by critically examining some of Bhargava's ideas, and to present the reader with an open-ended and somewhat paradoxical problem concerning methodological individualism and normative judgements.

Rajeev Bhargava's book is meant to be a challenge to orthodoxy. In this book, which is a revised version of his PhD thesis submitted to Oxford University, Bhargava argues that MI is not trivial, there are

*First published in *Economic and Political Weekly*, vol. 31, 3 February 1996. I have benefited greatly from some comments I received from Kenneth Arrow in response to an early version of my argument.

versions of it which are intellectually sophisticated and deserve our attention; however, MI can be challenged and he goes on to construct non-individualist methodologies which according to him are at least as satisfactory as MI. In brief, the aim of this book is not to hammer in the last nail but to resurrect the old debate. And this he does with remarkable command over the discipline—its history, its philosophical roots, and its moorings in economics and sociology. Bhargava is one of the most graceful *writers* of social science and the philosophy of social science. There are criticisms, important ones, to be made and I do so, below; but that does not change the fact that this book belongs to the highest genre of books written on the philosophy of social science. There are many places where one is left feeling that his arguments are not precise enough, that deductive reasoning is used well but without that final finesse which clinches a theorem or destroys some conventional wisdom. At the same time what is remarkable and so rare in contemporary writing is Bhargava's flair for expressing the philosopher's anguish and elation. A variety of philosophers and scientists have suffered the anxiety of self-doubt, of not knowing whether what they are grappling with or have actually established is something profound or trivial. One has no difficulty in seeing that Bhargava means every word when he writes (p. 5): 'On reading the literature one is swung between exuberance and despair, from feeling that all problems have been resolved to one that none has . . . Gradually an intense frustration overwhelms the reader: perhaps there was nothing worth discussing in the first place. What on earth was all the fuss about?'

Rajeev Bhargava's agenda is a very clear one. He first surveys the myriad schools of methodological individualism, isolates what he considers its strongest version and then attempts to construct a non-individualist methodology which challenges it. His sympathies are clearly anti-MI, even more between the lines than in them. He nevertheless does a very good job of presenting the various historical arguments *for* MI. In fact, the only criticism one can make of this initial part of the book is its taxonomic indulgence. Thus, one soon encounters ontological individualism, semantic individualism, and explanatory individualism. The latter is, in turn, split between its 'nomological and non-nomological' (I must confess to an occasional feeling that 'she sells sea shells' is easier) variants. And there are more subdivisions and categories.

What Bhargava settles for as the best face of MI is what in this book is christened 'intentionalism'. The intentional man is somewhere between the well known but 'yeti'-like *homo economicus* and equally rare *homo sociologicus*. He can choose and decide individually but he is not a relentless, maximizing agent. He has psychology and a sense of social norms, which distinguishes him from the computer-like *homo economicus*. I do not know about sociology, but his view of economic man does oversimplify the characterization of human beings that occurs in the modern economics literature. I shall return to this later.

Then, after going through some discussions of the limitations of MI, the author develops the idea of 'contextualism' as a challenge to MI, including intentionalism. The challenge consists of arguing that a variety of beliefs and practices in everyday life make sense only in the *context* of the society where they occur. Hence, in describing society or an economy we are compelled to use concepts which are *irreducibly social*.

The problem with this thesis is not that it is unacceptable but that it is *too* acceptable, and it is not clear that the critique of social science on which it is based is a fair critique. To be on safer ground while making this argument, I shall confine my attention mostly to economics. Indeed Rajeev Bhargava pegs a lot of his analysis on the writings of economists like Hayek and Schumpeter. Joseph Schumpeter is the person who coined the term 'methodological individualism' and is at times treated (not by Bhargava) as the original defender of this method. This is wrong because there were others using the method and espousing its cause even before the term had been coined. The Austrian economist Carl Menger, for instance, published a book in 1883 where he makes a vigorous case for this method. This in itself is enough to deprive Schumpeter (despite his famous precocity) of any claims to paternity for this idea, 1883 being the year of Schumpeter's birth.

As an aside, Hayek's position is not very representative of modern economic thinking since he seems to have concluded, in violation of a well-known dictum of David Hume, that the normative case for individualism and non-intervention can be based on methodological individualism.

The reason why Bhargava's case that certain beliefs and concepts are inextricably social is unlikely to stir a hornet's nest is that though many economists claim to be rigid adherents of MI, they do use and have always used social concepts and categories. This has been very convincingly argued recently by Kenneth Arrow in his Ely lecture (Arrow, 1994). Arrow points out how a variable such as price in a competitive model is an irreducibly social concept. Each individual takes price to be given but the price that comes to prevail is an outcome of the choices of the *collectivity*. So economists constructing equilibrium models, who claim to be hardened methodological individualists, are actually not so. They unwittingly follow a method which uses social categories and, therefore, is not too far away from what Bhargava is recommending, thereby making the recommendation partly futile. Hence, despite the excellence of his style and plenty of thought-provoking passages and sections, his ultimate position reinforces some of his early fears—it is not clear that it actually makes a difference for the practitioner.

To me it seems that the more contentious and substantial methodological debate concerns the permissibility of a certain class of propositions in social science. Bhargava discusses this in the context of the works of Elster and Roemer but does not give centrality to it. Consider the following proposition:

'The landlord will undertake action A, *because* it is in the landlord's class interest to do so.' (Action A could, for instance, be: 'refuse to hire a servant who has fled another landlord's employment and offers to work for this landlord for a very low wage'.)

I shall call this proposition P. There are many social scientists who believe that P is not permissible. I have sympathy with this. People do occasionally behave in certain ways simply because those are in their group or class interest. But as an axiom to be generally applied, I find P unacceptable. If I am to use an axiom like proposition P, I would usually want to first satisfy myself as to why it may be in the landlord's *self*-interest to behave in a way which is in his *class* interest. Or, at the very least, I would go along with P only insofar as there is no direct evidence or reason to believe that in this case the landlord's class interest does actually conflict with his self-interest. Hence, in explaining behaviour, I consider the reduction to individual interest to be of some importance. However, this does not negate the use of beliefs, concepts and variables which are irreducibly social. It is not clear that a researcher who does both (that is, resists explaining individual behaviour solely in terms of its ability to serve group or class interests but uses concepts and beliefs which are inherently social) is an MI person or an anti-MI person and neither is this a very important question. The important and contestable question seems to me to be whether assumptions like proposition P should not be used. And, as I just explained, I would prefer to avoid such assumptions as far as possible.

In closing, I want to discuss one more contentious matter. This concerns how even in our normative statements we make use of elements of non-individualism, unwittingly. To those who insist on MI, and perhaps even to others, the problem that is outlined below constitutes almost a paradox and certainly a challenge. I present it here without offering any 'solution', as an open-ended problem for the reader.

It seems arguable that we often pass moral judgements on groups of people which cannot be reduced to the individuals in the group. Observations of the following kind are clearly not uncommon.

1. 'It is a shame that no one in JNU does research on poverty', or
2. 'It speaks very poorly of the economics profession that so few economists in the nineteen thirties were writing on the unemployment problem despite that being one of the most important problems of that time.'

I should clarify that I did not choose 1 and 2 for their empirical validity—I would not dare—but purely for illustrating certain kinds of normative judgments, though 2, I know, is true.

Let us here concentrate on 1. If a person making this observation were asked: 'Do you therefore feel that it is wrong that Professor X in

JNU does not do research on poverty?', the answer would typically be: 'Of course not. I am not blaming any *individual* for not working on poverty'. So presumably when we make an observation such as 1, we are not casting moral aspersion on any individual in JNU, though we are clearly casting aspersion on JNU as a whole. Hence, by analysing our 'language of morals' we find that we do use non-individualistic judgements, since we do often make observations like 1.

There is one possible chink in the above argument. Some may want to say that 1 does amount to a *small* moral criticism of each person in JNU. I shall, however, argue that this is not a valid line. Assume it is valid. Now, if a few persons in JNU began working on poverty, then clearly criticism 1 would cease to be true. Hence, the *others* in JNU would be exonerated of the small moral criticism without having changed their behaviour at all. This does not seem an acceptable method of moral evaluation. Hence the claim that everybody in JNU is morally guilty is wrong. Therefore we may conclude that 1, which belongs to a common class of moral judgements, shows that moral judgments are not always reducible to individualism. My own inclination is not to pass moral judgements on groups unless we can reduce it to all its members or, at the very least, to some of them.

A similar dilemma but with a possible solution has been suggested by Dworkin. He argues that in situations of shared or group responsibility it may be reasonable to personify the group or the community. Thus, when a corporation produces a dangerously defective good but it is not possible to pin down the responsibility on any particular individual in the corporation, we may need to treat the corporation as a moral agent and apply 'facsimiles of or principles about individual fault and responsibility to it' (Dworkin 1986, p. 170). And *then*, by virtue of the *corporation's* responsibility, we may proceed to hold the *agents* and *members* of the corporation responsible. This is methodologically interesting. Individuals are still essential units in his analysis but, unlike in standard MI, judgement on the group *precedes* the individual.

He demonstrates with a very elegant example how we, unwittingly, do often use this method. This happens, for instance, when we talk of the state's or the community's responsibility for certain kinds of individual rights. Thus we talk of the state's obligation to ensure that no one is assaulted by others. Moreover, we do this even before agreeing on how this responsibility is to be apportioned across various units of the state, for instance, the police, the bureaucracy and the military. Dworkin (p. 171) points out how we discuss the community's responsibility and 'leave for *separate* consideration on the different issues of which arrangement of official duties would best acquit the communal responsibility' (my italics).

I find this bifurcation of discourse troublesome. To talk of a group's responsibility without knowing how it is to be apportioned out to the individuals in the group seems to me to be useful only to the extent that such an apportionment is eventually possible. If it were not possible, then we should turn back and question whether it was reasonable, in the first place, to think of the group as having that responsibility. In other words, the bifurcation of discourse is merely a matter of convenience and there may well be situations where the outcome in the second part requires us to revaluate our conclusions of the first part. This, in turn, means that the personification of the corporation or the community can only be an interim construct, which may need to be dismantled if we are eventually unable to spread the responsibility in some reasonable way across the members of the corporation or the community.

Returning to my example, this means that we cannot first decide that the personification of JNU is responsible for a certain neglect and then, by virtue of that, hold every JNU professor culpable. So the dilemma mentioned above continues to persist: We have to either admit that methodological individualism does not extend to normative judgements (which in Dworkin's example would mean that we may personify the group but have to stop there and not carry the judgement over to the individuals) or take the position that, though we do in practice pass judgements on groups, these are, in fact, meaningless and best resisted.

References

Arrow, Kenneth (1994). 'Methodological Individualism and Social Knowledge', *American Economic Review*, vol. 84, May.

Bhargava, Rajeev (1993). *Individualism in Social Science: Forms and Limits of a Methodology*. Delhi and Oxford: Oxford University Press.

Dworkin, Ronald (1986). *Law's Empire*. Cambridge, Massachusetts: Harvard University Press.

23

Left Politics
and Modern Economics*

When Manmohan Singh was Finance Minister of India, his critics pointed out that (a) his early writings had given the impression of his being a left-oriented economist who would wield his pen in favour of the underdog in any context, be it international politics or domestic policy debate; whereas, (b) once he became Finance Minister, he tried to liberalize the economy, encourage free trade, and make more room for market-based policies. To many, especially to the Indian Left, these facts seemed contradictory. They criticized Singh for not living up to his writings.

This was a mis-assessment. There is no real contradiction between (a) and (b). In fact, I supported Singh's reforms precisely because he combined both (a) and (b). Economic liberalization without concern for the disadvantaged gives rise to right-wing policies of the kind seen in Ronald Reagan's America and Margaret Thatcher's Britain—and to a certain extent even in India in the 1980s. I have no sympathy for it.

On the other hand, compassion without the ability to conduct clear-headed analysis can prove to be very costly. The world economy today is extremely complex; but there is also a large amount of analysis and statistical information available on this intricate organism. To ignore this information and to live by slogans and rhetoric is to court disaster. By failing to distinguish between Singh's reforms and right-wing economics, which ought to be abhorred, the Left has done us a great disservice.

*First published in *India Today*, 19 January 1998.

In these days of alignment and realignment, there is time to make amends. While I appreciate the ultimate objectives of the Left, I cannot but feel disappointed by the actual policies that the Left establishment has espoused in India. Ideology seems to have dulled its common sense and robbed it of pragmatism.

There are exceptions, especially among some of the CPM's politicians. When I was at the London School of Economics (LSE) in late 1993, I attended an informal meeting between some LSE social scientists and Jyoti Basu, then visiting London. The discussion ranged from taxation policy in West Bengal to Singh's reforms. My impression was that Basu, personally, understood and supported the reforms; even though—and this is unfortunate—he would not take such a public stand because that would be unpopular among his party cadres. Basu's other handicap was that for drafting economic policy he had around him more ideologues than professional advisers.

Let me give an example of how compassion without reason can be harmful. Calcutta's Salt Lake urban development was a noble enough idea. In response to housing needs, large tracts of salt marshes to the east of the city were land-filled and developed. To ensure the land did not end up with the rich, it was sold in small plots at heavily subsidized prices to individuals whose antecedents were allegedly checked to confirm that they were deserving.

This was, I believe, a good idea. Then, to make sure that these relatively worse-off individuals did not lose their land to the rich who would be able to offer them high prices, a well-meaning government legislated to make it virtually impossible for people to sell their property in Salt Lake.

This kind of legislation is not special to Salt Lake, Calcutta. It exists all over India. Land and apartments are sold by the government at subsidized rates and then the law is used to prevent the property from being resold.

This is such an ill-conceived policy that it surprises me how so many people can be brainwashed into believing it is fine. A commonly heard remark among Salt Lake residents is, 'So and so has sold his house.' What is unusual is that this is uttered *sotto voce*, as if one is reporting some crime. What our legislators have failed to realize is that making people keep their property by outlawing its sale does not help anybody, except perhaps some meddlesome bureaucrats who can exercise power and collect bribes.

If a prospective buyer offers the owner of a property a price at which the owner prefers to sell it, she can only be better off by having the option of selling it. In other words, if the government does sell land at subsidized rates to people it considers disadvantaged, there is no reason not to allow them to resell the land and make more gains when the need arises.

It is no surprise that the Salt Lake housing market is a cesspool of corruption. The rich have anyway muscled their way in and bought a lot of the houses. In addition, there is chaos, bribery, and the trading of favours.

This is an instance where (after the initial allotment of land and flats) allowing the free market to function without bureaucratic fetters would have been a policy that helped people whom the government had set out to help in the first place. In many other areas, too, there is no reason for the bureaucracy to stand between market demand and market supply. Yet, the term 'the market' is often such an anathema in India that large sections of our population have been made to believe that supporting market-based policy is tantamount to selling out to big business.

What India needs is a Left that does not pretend it can transcend the laws of the market but uses and directs the market for the ends it believes in.

24

Hung Parliament: A Voting Scheme for Preventing It*

A major concern for all Indians today is the repeat appearance of hung parliaments. If after an election no party manages to establish a majority in parliament, the standard recourse has been to call another election. However, with around 600 million voters, elections are expensive, and there is no guarantee that the new parliament will yield a majority. So I suggest a new voting system which, without sacrificing the basic principles of democracy, will almost always guarantee that one party will come out with a majority.

In suggesting this scheme a few criteria are worth bearing in mind. First, the new system must be simple, so that even the illiterate voter can understand it. Second, it must not be so different from the present system that it gets rejected out of hand as too alien to Indian democracy. Indeed, I believe India would be better served by a presidential system, and we could then use the system of run-offs that many countries use to ensure that the elected president has majority support. But this would involve too major a change for it to be immediately implementable. Finally, it must not be too expensive.

What I am about to suggest meets all these criteria and can be adopted in the very next election, which, given the current prognosis, may not be too far away.

On every ballot paper voters will be asked to mark their most-preferred candidate and, if they wish, their second-most-preferred

*First published in *India Today*, 9 March 1998.

candidate. To start with, only the information concerning the first-preference votes will be used to find out which party has got how many seats in parliament. If a party gets a majority of the seats, that party will form the government, and there will be no difference with the existing system.

The difference will occur if, on the basis of the first-preference count, no party emerges with a majority. Then the following procedure will have to be followed: check which party has the fewest seats—let us call this the Marginal Party. In all constituencies from where a member of the Marginal Party was elected, reopen the ballot papers, and wherever it is found that the first-preference vote was given to the Marginal Party, ignore that and treat the second-preference vote of the voter (wherever a second-preference is expressed) as the voter's choice. With this correction, find out the winner from each such constituency.

While I say 'reopen the ballot papers', that is simply a manner of speaking, since all the information (that is, concerning first- and second-preference votes) in the ballot papers should have been collected during the initial count. Hence, this second count will involve no extra effort. Indeed the information from the ballots from all over India can be entered into a computer and a program can be written so that, should we need to recount votes from some constituencies because the first-preference votes gave us a hung parliament, the procedure outlined above can yield a result in minutes.

If, with this recount a majority party emerges in parliament, the party forms the government and that is the end of the matter. If not, we look at the party which *now* has the fewest seats in parliament and repeat the process described above.

Barring some very special events, this system of voting will invariably result in a government which commands a majority in parliament. It does not involve repeat elections, it will be marginally more expensive than our current elections (voters will have to exercise their forearms twice and the vote-counting will have to take account of second preferences), and it will give us the political stability that we all seek.

My expectation is that, once a system like this is instituted, the very fact of it being there will make it much more likely that the first count will yield a majority. The reason is that, under this system, it will be in the interest of small parties to enter into formal alliances with other parties before the parliamentary elections because they will know that if they get too few seats on the first count, they may end up with no seats in the final count. With the rise of regional parties, it is likely that over the next decades India will see a diverse set of parties in power in the states. What the new voting system will ensure is that these parties will, at the time of parliamentary elections, seek out like-minded parties to form large formal coalitions.

What I have just sketched is an outline. Lots of details will have to be worked out before this can be put into effect, and we may also want to debate some variants of the above system before settling on one. Moreover, there is no reason why India should not revisit larger debates, such as switching to a presidential system of government. For this we will not have to work from scratch because there is today a large literature on voting theory.

In the nineteenth century Lewis Carroll—he was a mathematician by training—investigated the properties of alternative voting systems. Before him the French philosopher and mathematician Condorcet had uncovered a paradox of the majority voting system. The big breakthrough occurred in the 1950s when the economist Kenneth Arrow proved one of the most dramatic theorems in the social sciences, popularly called the 'Arrow impossibility theorem'. This showed that all voting systems must suffer from fairly major defects, so the choice of a voting system is basically a trade-off in defects. Arrow's theorem assures us that the new system cannot be a panacea for all evils, but with some thought and debate we should be able to do better than we have thus far.

A major culmination of this line of work occurred in the books and papers of Amartya Sen in the late 1960s and 1970s and, thanks to his influence, in the research of a subsequent cohort of Indian economists such as Prasanta Pattanaik, Bhaskar Dutta, and Rajat Deb. It is testimony to our innate conservatism that we do so much research on voting and social choice but refuse to seriously re-evaluate our voting systems.

25

Money, Music, and Harmony*

Traditional economics downplayed the role of culture and social norms in the progress of nations, and was dismissive of anybody who evinced an interest in these topics. A joke that did the rounds among mainstream economists was the one about an expert on culture and economics who said, 'There are three kinds of economists, those who can do mathematics and those who cannot.'

The same is true in other disciplines. The anthropologist Clifford Geertz observed that 'The term "culture" has by now acquired a certain aura of ill-repute in social anthropological circles.'

Fortunately, this is changing. A whole lot of serious economists and anthropologists are now interested in the role of culture in economic and social life. This is partly because of the rise in the study of evolutionary game theory, which has given us a handle for modelling and understanding culture; and partly for the practical reason that with globalization, different cultures—once far apart—are today rubbing shoulders. At times this gives rise to new bursts of creativity, at times to friction and occasionally to amusement.

Travelling by train and bus in the West and in India can give one fascinating glimpses of cultural differences. In the West, it is impolite to ask the stranger who happens to be sitting next to you personal questions. So you make inane conversation about the weather. In India it is in fact impolite not to ask personal questions: it shows you're being standoffish.

*First published in *India Today*, 20 April 1998.

In the days when I used to travel regularly between Delhi and Calcutta by train, I was often impressed by the rapidity with which my co-
passenger managed to extricate information on my marital status,
whether I owned my apartment or was a tenant, my salary, and whether
I had any other sources of income—that final question prompted no
doubt by dismay at learning my salary.

Sanjay Subrahmanyam, well-known economic historian and one-
time student of mine, once made the shrewd observation to me that,
in Delhi buses, when one person tells another, '*Main aapse* request *kar
raha hoon*' (I am requesting you), it is usually the last attempt at verbal
resolution of a conflict between you and him, and is uttered moments
before the speaker takes recourse to violence. Thus, a newcomer to
Delhi or an Indian travelling by train abroad can get into misunder-
standings for no reason except failure to appreciate another culture.
The important thing to understand—and what at the high point of
Western colonialism was utterly misunderstood—is that cultures are
seldom superior or inferior to one another. They are simply different.

The increasing tendency in India to resist globalization by impeding
foreign investment and putting up barriers to imports is sought to be
justified in the name of protecting our cultural heritage. It is eminently
understandable for people to be proud of their culture. So, using culture as an alibi to practice protectionism invariably finds support. In
Denmark, Pia Kjaersgaard, the right-wing politician, tried this ploy in
the recent elections. She and a band of 'pianists'—as her followers are
called—preached that immigrants were diluting Danish culture and
whipped up considerable support. Similar movements have been witnessed in Germany, France, and other nations.

In India, there is today a risk that we will reverse some of the gains
of economic liberalization in the name of saving our culture. This is
unfortunate. Anybody who tries to protect his culture by closing its
doors to outsiders, far from being proud of his culture, betrays a lack
of confidence in it. Indian culture is far too robust for us to fear that
it will perish if our people have access to other cultures.

Actually, the real danger to a culture comes from economic decline.

Talented people often live in poverty. We know of eminent artists and scholars who have flourished in the midst of penury; yet, if a whole society or nation suffers acute poverty for a long period of time, its music, arts, and philosophy also begin to flounder. So, if we want Indian culture to prosper, we cannot neglect our economy. The main reason why American culture is spreading is not the strength of its culture but its economy.

True, in a globalizing world some parts of one's culture will be lost. As the world links up technologically more and more, an early casualty may be language. It is very likely the world will ultimately have only one active language. This is unfortunate because so many languages have so much to offer. But it would be a greater pity if we close our nation's doors and run down the economy, to try and resist the inevitable.

On the other hand, the increasing globalization of the world can nourish and strengthen much of our own culture, generating new ideas in science, music, and dance. Globalization also brings with it immense opportunities for the Indian economy. We must seize them.

What Swami Vivekananda wrote on 10 July 1893, in a letter to some friends in India, while travelling abroad, has not lost its relevance: 'Come, see these people and then go and hide your faces in shame. . . . Sitting down these hundreds of years with an ever-increasing load of crystallized superstition on your head . . . Come out of your narrow holes and have a look abroad. See how nations are on the march!'

26

Rules of Engagement*

The Kargil War marks the start of a new era for India's international relations. Never before has a third world government been quoted so widely by the world press on the facts and figures of a war in which the government itself was involved. This is partly a consequence of India's democracy, which makes it easy for independent observers to verify the government's pronouncements, thereby making it costly for the government to deviate too much from the truth. But it is also in part a reflection of improving Indo–US relations.

During John F. Kennedy's tenure the US had moved to make India its ally in the region. The compulsions of world politics and a succession of hawkish regimes in the US prevented this from happpening. Now, with the Cold War over, the US concern shifting from war to terrorism, and increasing reports of terrorist groups operating out of Pakistan, America's new India tilt is not surprising. This presents an opportunity for India not just in regional politics, but in shaping a more dynamic economy.

Kargil also shows us that conventional wars between India and Pakistan will never be the same again. The knowledge that both countries possess the nuclear bomb has changed the rules of the game. One reason why India could not retaliate with more air power across the Line of Control (which would mean smaller casualties) was the fear that Pakistan would respond with a nuclear attack. This would be irrational on the part of Pakistan because India would retaliate immediately,

*First published in *India Today*, 23 March 1999.

resulting in a mutually destructive nuclear war. But we could, in any case, not rule out such a reaction from Pakistan.

Did the 1998 nuclear tests make a difference to this war? At one level, not very much, since both countries already knew the other had the bomb. What the tests did was to take this mutual knowledge to higher orders. Not only does India now know that Pakistan has the bomb but Pakistan knows that India knows that Pakistan has the bomb.

Game theorists and scientists working on artificial intelligence have analysed the role of higher-ordered knowledge and shown how these can have huge effects on behaviour. In this case Pakistan could provoke India, knowing that India's reaction would be measured, because it knew that India knew that it had the bomb. These intricate considerations are no longer an academic matter between India and Pakistan but may have life-and-death implications.

It is believed Bill Clinton brought pressure on Nawaz Sharif only after US intelligence analysts and strategic experts, studying elaborate simulations of the Kargil conflict, reached the conclusion that if left unchecked the conflict would go nuclear, with Pakistan as the initial transgressor.

We now know a lot about war games between nuclear nations because of the release of the Kennedy tapes—the secret recording of discussion among experts in the Oval Office during the Cuban missile crisis of 1962 (*The Kennedy Tapes*, edited by E. May and P. Zelikow, Harvard University Press). An important principle learnt during the Cuban crisis was that of 'second strike'—the ability to launch a counterattack after the enemy's initial nuclear attack. This second-strike capability is important not because it will have to be used, but precisely because having it may mean that it will never have to be used. It is the fear of this capability that deters a rational enemy from launching the initial attack.

It is for this reason that US planes have standing instructions to take to the air, loaded with nuclear weapons, when a major enemy attack is expected. This is by way of precaution against a massive initial attack destroying America's counterattack capacity on the ground. It is believed that during the most critical moments of the Cuban crisis US planes were in the air, ready to go. And this must have figured in Russia's calculations.

While on the one hand India must strive for total nuclear disarmament, till that happens it has to develop and maintain second-strike capability. Unfortunately, India has an additional problem, which the US and the USSR did not have, at least not in any significant measure. It is known in game theory that it is often more difficult to play against an irrational agent than a rational agent, because the former is less predictable. This theoretical argument has suddenly jumped out of textbooks and stares India in the face, since Pakistan has the advantage of irrationality. Because its governance is in a shambles and its command and control structure so chaotic, its behaviour is unpredictable. It may use the bomb in contexts that no rational power would. India, therefore, has to use extra caution and Pakistan, knowing this, will take advantage of it.

From now on Pakistan will probably provoke India in small ways more frequently than it did before 1998. The only way to contain this is to use our new credibility to bring international pressure on Pakistan. In designing our policy and setting targets, our ultimate aim must not be to win a war but to prevent it from happening. As we have seen in the case of Kargil, now that we are back to square one, the loss of human lives, both Indian and Pakistani, is a meaningless tragedy. No matter who wins, the fact of having had a war is a form of defeat for all involved. In the end the costs of war must be counted not in terms of Indian lives lost, but lives lost.

27

The Enigma of Advertising*

To most lay persons, few economic phenomena are as puzzling as advertising. It seems impossible to believe that anyone with an iota of sense would be induced to purchase products by the tall claims made about them in glossy magazine and television ads. But when profit-seeking firms and multinational corporations spend millions advertising, we can be sure that they have done their calculations right. In 1995 the top 100 firms in the US spent 50 billion dollars on advertising. Each year, during the SuperBowl, the final match of American football, a 30-second TV commercial costs more than a million dollars.

Over the next few weeks we will, in India, witness one of the largest advertisement campaigns that occur anywhere in the third world—the advertising of politicians and their parties. The BJP alone is believed to be ready with Rs 10 crore in its coffer. It is a sad fact of our political life that the marketing is as important as the content—often more.

So, though we may dismiss the ads we see on television and on hoardings, and believe that we are immune to them, the fact is that a vast majority of us is not. In 1994, soon after we arrived in the US, my family would watch on TV the commercial for a cumbersome fitness machine and laugh at gullible Americans. A few months later I was outvoted and the machine arrived. Another few weeks and everybody stopped using it. I must admit, however, that it has not been all loss, because the fitness machine with its multiple handlebars has turned out to be exceptionally handy for drying clothes.

*First published in *India Today*, 13 September 1999.

Industry is forever discovering new ways to advertise goods. The rich and the famous are often plied with free clothes and footwear by various brand-name companies because of the realization that the loss of a few items is more than made up by the masses who will try to buy the product seeing the famous in them. The famous of course include the infamous: companies apparently vied with one another to make Monica Lewinsky wear their product when she went public to confess her misdemeanours.

A lot of advertising is simply wasteful. In 1994 cigarette manufacturers in the US spent 5 million dollars advertising their products. Then in 1997 the US government, in an effort to contain health hazards, prohibited cigarette companies from advertising. The companies were angry and had their lawyers challenge the order. But they soon discovered that the prohibition on advertisements caused no drop in their profits. What much of the advertisements had been doing was cancelling one another out. It is a bit like the custom of saying 'thank you' at every turn. In a society which has this custom, these phrases come to mean nothing. But people still say thank you, even when they do not mean it (which is usually the case), because not to say thank you amounts to being offensive. When all tobacco companies were stopped from advertising, no single company faced a special disadvantage, and of course they saved the massive amount they were earlier competitively wasting on commercials.

Another new twist in advertising that we see today is among groups of firms, who were traditionally rivals, colluding in their advertising effort. The milk producers of the US have got together not to advertise any specific brand of milk but milk, itself as a drink worth consuming. It is believed that single-malt whisky producers stole the limelight from popular blended whiskies by sinking their differences and marketing single malt as the best kind of whisky.

There is a lesson in this for India as a whole. In the export market, buyers look for brand names all right but they also look at the label saying where the product is made. And, just as the brand name shapes our opinion in advance, the 'Made in . . .' label also influences our view of the product. If it is made in France, it must be fashionable; if it is made in Japan, it must be durable. These opinions can help and hurt individual producers. Indian products are generally believed to be shoddy, and this belief handicaps Indian producers. They find it very difficult to sell their product, no matter how good it is, because buyers pre-judge its quality. Individual Indian producers are helpless against this negative belief: advertising their product is competing against settled prejudice. This being so, many exporters do not even try to supply the best. One way out of this belief-trap is for the Indian government to advertise and market not this or that product but, more generally, products from India. In other words, India needs to act like the milk cartel. A small part of our foreign exchange reserves can be profitably used for this purpose.

This can have a beneficial fallout. It is known that it is not typically worthwhile for a company to advertise substandard products, because advertisement can draw people to a product but not keep them with it unless the product is above a certain cut-off quality. Hence, given how expensive advertising is today, it is not worthwhile marketing a product unless you know that once a buyer tries it out, he will stay with it for a long time. This means that for the advertising of India to be profitable we must first ensure a certain minimum quality. These efforts, sustained over some time, can become self-sustaining; and so, once this initial effort is made, India may actually be able to sell more and better stuff.

28

The Truth About Lying*

On being asked by Bertrand Russell if he ever told lies, the famous Cambridge philosopher G.E. Moore answered, 'Yes.' Russell believed this was the only time Moore had lied. It is possible to argue that Russell's deduction was, for once, wrong, and that Moore had got the better of him. If Moore had told lies before giving that answer to Russell, then clearly his answer was not a lie. Now suppose that he had never told a lie before, then in answering yes he ensured that his answer was right.

Lying and honesty are intriguing subjects that have engaged philosophers for centuries. Social scientists took very little interest in them. This has suddenly begun to change. It is a much more mundane concern with lying and honesty that has been engaging economists and political scientists in recent times, but it's a concern of some pervasive importance.

Social analysts, notably Francis Fukuyama and Robert Putnam, have argued that societies with a high level of trust—i.e. where people tend to be honest, adhere to promises, and respect contracts—tend to prosper. So, faster growth is not just a consequence of appropriate economic policy, savings rate, human capital, and fiscal deficits, but, somewhat surprisingly, the level of honesty in the citizenry.

This is one area in which the Indian citizenry can do with a little bit of brushing up. The damage usually gets done early, when children are taught that 'honesty is the best policy'. As they grow up, they realize

*First published in *India Today*, 10 July 2000.

whoever taught them that lesson was not quite honest. There are many situations in life where a quick lie, a broken promise, or a reneged contract can bring gains.

Many people may try to cash in on these gains too often, not realizing that each time one does it, one tends to damage one's reputation a little. If a person breaks too many promises, people will be wary of getting into agreements with him. In other words, excessive dishonesty and corruption, as in our society, is a sign of several things, but, importantly, of myopia. To a person interested in nothing but his own welfare, the Machiavellian lesson would be simple: try not to tell lies so that you can get away with the rare one when you have to. So, even if people were entirely selfish, if they calculated their own interest rationally (that is, without being myopic), they would be more honest than they typically are.

Collectively, people may have an interest in being even more honest and trustworthy than selfish rationality calculus requires. This is not always easy to understand. Let us begin by noting that people use group characteristics to judge individuals. Thus people hold views on how trustworthy Indians are and how punctual Latinos are; on the ethics of Protestants and the materialism of Calvinists; on how dependable the Japanese are as business partners and how untrustworthy such and such people are (let me leave the identity of this last group to the reader's imagination); on how good South Indians are as tenants and how bad . . . once again, let me leave this to you.

These are, essentially, opinions about the average traits of different groups. But they have important implications for the individual. They can mean that people will hesitate to get into a business deal with you if you belong to a group considered untrustworthy; or you may be more likely to get hired because people believe that your community is hard working. So you could gain or lose through no fault of yours.

This also means that your actions can influence the prospects and well being of others in your group. If you cheat, you bring down the average evaluation of your community. Economists have a name for this: it is called an 'externality'. If an action by one person brings down the welfare of others, it is called a negative externality; if it raises welfare it is a positive externality. Free markets malfunction when there are excessive externalities, positive or negative, bringing down everybody's welfare.

Something similar happens in the domain of corruption and dishonesty. Each such act hurts the nation or the community that one belongs to, but since that hurt does not enter the individual's calculations (especially so when the individual is selfish), people tend to overindulge in corrupt and untrustworthy activities. Hence, nations where people are habitually (that is, not prompted by rational optimization) more honest will tend to get more investment, trade, and business.

Most economists direct their advice at the government—to politicians to act in certain ways, or to bureaucrats to carry out certain responsibilities. This new research in economics on the role of trust is a reminder that some of the responsibility lies with ordinary citizens.

29

Rationality: New Research in Psychology and Economics*

A 'rational' person, so went the assumption in economics, could have any aim in life, but, *given that aim*, he or she invariably chose the option that best furthered that aim. Over the years this assumption became part and parcel of mainstream economics. Predictions concerning economic life were deduced from this assumption and policy design was based on it. Every now and then some critic would remind us that the assumption was not robust. The reminders would be absent-mindedly acknowledged and promptly forgotten.

The last few years have, however, witnessed a dramatic change in this regard. It began with a set of trespassers into economics. Psychologists Daniel Kahneman, Amos Tversky, and others, through a series of laboratory experiments, showed that not only are human beings often irrational (as most of us already knew), but that they are systematically so. This has given rise to one of the most exciting areas of modern economic research, called 'behavioural economics'. It is widely expected that this area of inquiry will, within the next few years, be recognized with an economics Nobel Prize being awarded to the pioneers of this field.[1]

Suppose you have a ticket for a cricket match and someone comes up to you and asks the minimum price for which you will be willing

*First published in *Business Standard*, 20 March 2002.
[1] Daniel Kahneman did go on to win the Nobel Prize, along with Vernon Smith, later in the same year, 2002.

to give up the ticket. Next, suppose you do not have a ticket for the match and someone comes to you with a ticket and asks for the maximum you will be willing to pay for it. If you were perfectly rational, your answer to both questions would be approximately the same. If you considered the pleasure of watching a match to be equal, for instance, to Rs 200, your answer to the first question would be something like Rs 201, and to the second, something like Rs 199. However, laboratory experiments have now revealed that the answers to such questions differ by a very wide margin—usually a factor of two. In other words, it is not uncommon to find people asking for Rs 300 to part with the ticket and offering Rs 150 to acquire the ticket.

Another commonly observed behaviour is the following. Suppose you have bought a ticket worth Rs 250 for a concert and, just before setting out for the concert, discover that you have lost the ticket. It is found that most people, under the circumstance, would forego the concert rather than buy a ticket again. Now consider an alternative scenario in which you were planning to buy the concert ticket but, just before you did so, you discovered that Rs 250 had been stolen from your wallet. Experiments show that most people would still go for the concert.

Another kind of irrationality that has received a lot of attention, with contributions from George Akerlof, Matt Rabin, Robert Pollak, and others, is as follows. Suppose, some time in April, you are asked to choose between having a necessary surgery on 1 August and having it on 2 August. The surgery, you are told, is going to be painful, and, moreover, for every day that the surgery is delayed there will be a slight increase in the level of pain you will have to suffer. Very few people, in this situation, will opt for 2 August. Since one will have to suffer pain, why postpone it and suffer more, even a tiny amount? That is how most people will reason. Now assume that the same choice is given to you by the doctor on the morning of 1 August. It is found that many more will now opt for having the surgery on 2 August. This reversal of preference, or 'dynamic inconsistency' as this phenomenon has come to be called—resulting from our preference for postponing pain (when the decision is about an imminent matter) even when the postponement is expected to compound the pain—has found powerful confirmation from laboratory experiments. In fact, elaborately crafted experiments by the well-known psychologists G. Ainslee and R.J. Herrnstein revealed that even pigeons have this tendency to postpone pain or, equivalently, to seek immediate gratification even when a delay would increase the level of pleasure. This suggests that dynamic inconsistency may be hardwired into our brains and not just a matter of *human* frailty. These findings have helped economists explain a variety of phenomena, ranging from stock market crashes to drug addiction.

I believe that this new research in economics is just beginning to scratch the surface of an important area and a lot more will come. And this is likely to have important consequences for the way economic policy is crafted.

In a modern economy no one is supposed to have to pay a price for being physically weak. If a strong person comes and snatches food from a weak person, this is not considered tolerable behaviour. And, indeed, the physically weak do not feel particularly insecure in today's world. But what about a person who is irrational or miscalculates the benefits and losses of actions? Modern society provides little protection to such a person. Mainstream economics is partly responsible for this. Its assumption that human beings are always rational became so ubiquitous that it was forgotten that people could be irrational. Hence, very few provisions exist to protect the irrational.

However, there is reason to believe that people get systematically 'cheated'. People in rural India take loans, which entail interest rates as high as 200 per cent per annum. Is this just a reflection of their preference, or miscalculation? Standard economics treated this as a matter of preference, but I think there is reason to believe that this is a reflection of dynamic inconsistency. Jean Dreze, an economist with extensive experience of rural India, tells me how people in a village in Uttar Pradesh take one-evening loans with an interest rate of 10 per cent, to participate in gambling sessions. Now, 10 per cent for one evening means an annual interest rate so high that it is difficult to comprehend. A similar phenomenon has been observed in New York, where unscrupulous 'financiers' encourage old widows living in nice houses to take large home-improvement loans, knowing that there is a good chance that they will not be able to repay, and the lender will be able to foreclose on the property.

Once we view such behaviour on the part of the borrower as irrationality rather than preference, it urges us to think of new policy instruments to protect people from their own follies. Of course, the policies have to be carefully designed and prevented from becoming alibis for mindless government intervention in market transactions, of which India has seen so much.

To recognize human irrationality is to pave the way to protect the irrational from the rational. This may seem a strange idea today, but I believe and hope that in the future this will look no more strange than the belief that the physically strong must not be allowed to snatch away the belongings of the weak.

30

Higher and Lower Education*

I

One of the domains in which India belongs conspicuously with the developed world is higher education and research. Go to an international conference on physics, statistics, economics, and, increasingly, even English literature; or open a journal in any of these disciplines and you will find an Indian presence in a way that no other Third World country matches, and just a handful of developed countries do. Nevertheless, it is time to rethink our education policy. This advantage in higher education, especially in the sciences, is beginning to get eroded. The deterioration of the libraries and laboratories and the students' lack of access to computers are now causing a competitive disadvantage. Second, India's remarkable achievement in higher education is matched only by its notable failure in primary education.

Suppose you construct a house in which the ground floor has as many square feet as the number of persons who have primary education in the country, the first floor as many square feet as the number who have secondary education, and continue the same way constructing a floor each for high-schoolers, undergraduates, and postgraduates. For most countries, the house will look like a pyramid, tapering off rapidly as one goes higher. In the case of India, the building is relatively like a tower.

*Based on 'Paying for Education', *India Today*, 17 November 1997 (Section I); and 'Combating India's Truant Teachers', *BBC News Online*, 29 November 2004 (Section II).

In 1995, only 52 per cent of Indian adults were literate.[1] This is in sharp contrast to, say, China's 81 per cent. We cannot blame it all on poverty. There are a number of countries much poorer than India that have markedly higher literacy rates: Vietnam (94 per cent), Kenya (78 per cent), and Rwanda (60 per cent).

The erosion in higher education and the lack of scope for erosion in primary education are both matters in which we need the government to act. India has 197 universities, 34 deemed universities, 2.87 lakh teachers (some of them presumably only deemed teachers), and around 50 lakh students. Even governments in rich countries would throw up their hands in despair if faced with the prospect of financing such a large system. The university has become infrastructurally one of the most expensive institutions in the world. Running a library, a computer system, and labs is capital intensive.

One thing that has remained constant in India is the tuition fee charged to students: officially, less than Rs 25 per annum. In a good American university, the annual tuition fee is $21,000, over 28,000 times India's. Given that nearly half of all Indians do not get primary education and are poor, it is clear that those who go to college are by and large better off. Moreover, after getting this education most of them get decent jobs and so can afford to borrow against their future and pay more for their education. In a country where the vast majority of the rural poor gets no education for want of money, it is a shame that the state should subsidize so liberally the education of those who have the money.

Our failure with primary education is not all a question of money. What many urban people do not know is that, in terms of teacher truancy, India is one of the worst performers. Some years ago a study revealed that a school built by 'Food for Work' labourers in rural Bihar had such small doors to classrooms that adults could not pass through them. Was this a case of architectural lapse or were the labourers simply better informed than us?

[1] The figure, as of now, December 2004, is above 65 per cent, the last decade being the one of fastest growth in literacy that India has seen.

Truancy must be corrected quickly through monitoring. It is true that monitoring costs money, but that brings me to my second point. India spends far too little on primary education. All the Asian economies that are performing well devote about twice as large a fraction of their governments' expenditure on education as we do. The Finance Minister should massively step up spending on primary education. This is a must if we are to sustain a 7 per cent to 8 per cent annual growth rate.

For higher education, we need the opposite. The government should withdraw much of the massive subsidy. The state-run university system should be shrunk while private universities and colleges should be allowed to come up. These private universities should be left free to fix student fees and teacher salaries. My expectation is they will charge very high fees and also pay very high salaries to teachers. But this should not be worrying if we still have a state-run higher-education sector where one can get a decent education for a low fee.

The current policy of discouraging private colleges and striking down the charging of capitation fees is wrong and causes market pathologies all too glaring. Many small universities, mainly from Britain, are setting up branch campuses in India. They charge students up to Rs 3 lakh per year. The legality of these ventures has come up in the Madras High Court because only institutions recognized by the University Grants Commission are allowed to give degrees. The foreign universities are arguing that they are not giving degrees 'in India'.

Whichever way this is settled, the very existence of these universities shows there is scope for expansion in quality higher education at no cost to government. There is no reason for government to stand between this market demand and supply.

II

For a country in which higher education is so valued, India's record in primary education is dismal. With a literacy rate (percentage of adults who can read and write) of 65 per cent, India compares poorly even with much poorer economies: Vietnam, Zambia (80 per cent), Tanzania (77 per cent), and Cambodia (70 per cent).

If India's growing prosperity is to spread beyond the urban elites, battling illiteracy has to be treated as top priority by government. A critical step in getting children to school is to get teachers to school.

The so-called PROBE Report, led by the economist-activist Jean Dreze, has drawn attention to the fact that the majority of parents who kept their children away from school did so only because there were no schools of minimal quality in their vicinity. The study of 188 government-run primary schools in central and northern India revealed that 59 per cent of the schools had no drinking water facility and 89 per cent no toilets; and, most alarmingly, a large number of teachers were found to be absent at the time of the survey.

The latter problem has now received detailed scientific scrutiny from a team of economists (Michael Kremer, Kartik Muralidharan, Nazmul Chaudhury, Jeffrey Hammer, and Halsey Rogers) from Harvard and the World Bank. On the basis of three surprise visits made to 3700 randomly selected schools in twenty Indian states, they concluded that teacher absenteeism in India is 25 per cent. That is, at any random time, 25 per cent of the teachers are absent from school. Comparable studies, done in other countries, show India as one of the worst cases. Bangladesh, for instance, has a teacher absenteeism or truancy rate of 16 per cent, Zambia 17 per cent, Papua New Guinea 15 per cent. Among the known studies, only Uganda does worse than India, with 27 per cent.

The study reveals other facts of interest. 'Head teachers'—true to their designation—are in the lead. They are, on average, truant 5 per cent more often than ordinary teachers. Salaries do not make any significant difference to truancy. Better infrastructure improves teacher attendance a little.

The big differences are regional. Maharashtra has the best record with a truancy rate of 14.6 per cent, followed by Gujarat (17 per cent) and Madhya Pradesh (17.6 per cent). The worst offender is Jharkhand (41.9 per cent), followed by Bihar (37.8 per cent) and Punjab (34.4 per cent).

What is the cause of these dispiriting statistics? Lack of accountability and proper economic incentives are no doubt factors. But I believe it is not entirely a matter of economics. If that were so, then, given that salaries and the formal rules of the game are so similar all over India, we would be hard pressed to explain the regional differences.

It is important to recognize the role of factors like norms, work culture, and stigma. Sociologists, from Erving Goffman to Mark Granovetter, have long stressed the importance of these variables in determining human behaviour. Fortunately, a few modern economists have also begun making room for these in their work. Stigma, for instance, can explain many of the things that human beings do, such as wear brandname jeans (in American high schools), give dowry (in parts of India), wear trousers when they go out (in the British Isles) and not wear trousers when they go out (in parts of the Trobriand Islands). Further, once we recognize that the extent of stigma for some behaviour depends on how many other people indulge in this behaviour, sociology begins to interact with economics in interesting ways. A teacher contemplating missing school will no doubt have to incur some stigma cost. But if lots of teachers miss school, then the stigma cost is less for each individual, since he will no longer be singled out as especially antisocial.

In this set-up, if very few teachers miss school, the stigma cost of missing school will be high and so it will not be in the self-interest of teachers to miss school, unless there is a compelling reason. As a consequence, only a few teachers will miss school, corroborating the initial assumption. Likewise, if lots of teachers miss school, the stigma cost of missing school will be small and that in turn will ensure that lots of teachers will play truant.

Hence, the same society, facing the same economic and legal environment, can be caught in two very different equilibrium situations. This can explain why Maharashtra and Jharkhand exhibit such different behaviour.

The Indian government needs to urgently consider policies to cure this problem of our times. Once we bring sociological dimensions into the picture, the range of policies that opens up is much larger, and implementing some of these policies may not involve a big fiscal burden either.

PART IV

Persons

31

Amartya Sen*

Lamont and Harvard

Some years ago, when Amartya Sen, then Lamont University Professor at Harvard University, was on a lecture tour abroad, a journalistic write-up listing his many achievements noted that he taught at two famous American universities, Lamont and Harvard. It must have seemed a shocking mistake to all those who knew Amartya Sen or Harvard University (I cannot tell what it seemed to those who knew Lamont University). But over the last few months, ever since won the Nobel Prize in economics, reading the popular press prodigiously interpreting Sen's work and why he won the Nobel Prize makes one realize that errors of this kind, while disturbing, are the least of it. The more significant mistakes are the ones made in interpreting his work.

One source of many such mistakes is Sen himself. He has comfortably straddled two worlds, that of academic, technical economics; and that of policy and pamphleteering. Since the laity and ordinary journalist have some familiarity with the latter, it has been easy for them to jump to the conclusion that it is for the latter that Sen won the Nobel Prize. A mistake of this kind could not have occurred, for instance, with Gerard Debreu, also a Nobel laureate, because journalists would not understand *any* of his papers.

One of the most common assertions has been that Sen was given the prize for showing how famines can occur during times of plenty, or how famines are unlikely in a democracy, or for his work in development

*First published in *Challenge*, 1999.

economics. The exception is the official Nobel citation released by the Royal Swedish Academy of Sciences, which states that Sen has been given the prize 'for his contributions to welfare economics'. The accompanying write-up mentions a whole range of his work, but it gives primacy of place to Sen's work on social choice theory, axiomatic welfare economics, and individual decision-making. This is the work he had done from the mid-1960s to the late 1970s, mostly in Delhi and London. A part of this work is reported in his classic book, *Collective Choice and Social Welfare (CCSW)*. This is, in my judgement, his most important book; it is a work of immense elegance. It combines formal logic, welfare economics, and moral philosophy. The book had many new theorems (or at least reported on new theorems which Sen had first published in journals), but, more importantly it influenced the *way* many economists thought about welfare economics and collective decision-making.

Welfare and Social Choice

Amartya Sen did not start out with welfare economics. As an undergraduate student at Trinity College, Cambridge (where he later returned as Master), Sen wrote a dissertation on choice of technology. The dissertation, with small modifications, won him a PhD and in 1960 was published as a book *Choice of Techniques* that became a celebrated book which students of development, planning and growth read, researched on, and modified. This work had many spin-offs for Sen himself. He contributed to growth theory, cost-benefit analysis, and development; he became a full professor at the Delhi School of Economics in 1963, at the age of 30, and a little thereafter he became Fellow of the Econometric Society.

During this time his interests were, however, beginning to shift as he became intrigued by the problems of welfare and the conundrums of voting and social choice. There was a small literature on the latter at that time. It had all begun in the early 1950s with the publication of Kenneth Arrow's path-breaking 'impossibility theorem', which showed that all systems of voting, existing or conceivable (for example, the majority-decision rule or the two-thirds-majority-or-status-quo rule), will violate some elementary and desirable norms of democracy. I consider this one of the most profound breakthroughs in economics. It required no hard mathematics, as so much modern economics does, and that is precisely what made it such a challenge. There were no standard results to fall back on; the theorem had to be proved through plain reasoning, of which, in principle, everybody is capable. Yet the reasoning had to be sustained relentlessly over such a long stretch that few could, in practice, have done it.

When Arrow began working on voting theory, the subject had a negligible history. This is not to deny that it had attracted some colourful personalities. Almost 200 years before Arrow, the Marquis de Condorcet and Jean Charles de Borda had been intrigued by a strange feature of the majority-decision rule, which allows it to generate cycles, so that, for *every* candidate, we can find another candidate whom the majority prefers. The problem, which had later attracted the eccentric genius of Lewis Caroll (who did mathematics using his real name, C.L. Dodgson), is easy enough to illustrate.

Suppose three persons, 1, 2, and 3, have to choose between three presidential candidates, Adlai (A), Bush (B), and Clinton (C). Suppose 1 prefers A to B to C, 2 prefers B to C to A, and 3 prefers C to A to B. If they agree to use the majority-decision rule, it is easy to see that between A and B, A will win the election (because voters 1 and 3 would vote for A); between B and C, B will win; and between C and A, C will win, thereby yielding no clear verdict on who the winner is. Note that, for each of the three candidates, we can find someone else whom the majority would prefer.

Arrow's shatteringly important theorem and the problem with the majority rule set the agenda on which Sen's work on social choice was based. One set of papers that he wrote, alone and with Prasanta Pattanaik of the University of California at Riverside, specified the conditions under which the majority rule 'works', that is, does not yield to the above problem of indecision. An important direction that he explored was to place restrictions on voters' preference. It is arguable that in most societies preferences are not quite as varied across voters as in the above, imaginary example. Sen showed that, given some natural restrictions on the variation in human preference, the paradox of majority decision-making illustrated above may be averted. Given the widespread use of the majority rule and its obvious practical importance, these papers attracted a lot of attention.

Another direction that he pursued was to introduce a new axiom into this framework, that of individual liberty, capturing the notion, which goes back to John Stuart Mill, that every individual should have some 'protected sphere' over which he or she has the *right* to decide, without being constrained by what others feel. For example, whether or not person i reads *The Satanic Verses* could be said to belong to i's personal sphere. This work turned out to be extremely influential, drawing the subject of rights and liberty into the domain of social choice.

Sen's book, *CCSW*, played a very significant role in the coming together of welfare economics and moral philosophy. Like liberty, other concepts and ideas from philosophy, such as fairness and justice, came to be analysed using the tools of social choice theory. Arrow had written about an alleged inscription on a grave in England:

Here lies Martin Engelbrodde.
Ha'e mercy on my soul, Lord God,
As I would do were I Lord God
And thou wert Martin Engelbrodde.

This is an illustration of putting oneself in another's shoes; it is the basis of a new approach to comparing the well-being of different individuals. Economists had, for long, acknowledged the deep difficulty of making interpersonal comparisons. How can we ever know what goes on in a person's head? Can we really say that a poor boy in the street is unhappier than the wealthy tycoon in his mansion? The new method of interpersonal comparison relied on making the mental experiment of putting oneself in the shoes of each of the characters involved. Would you rather be a rich tycoon than a poor boy in the street? If you can answer this, then, even though you are still in the dark about what goes on in the heads of the boy and the tycoon, this gives you *some* insight into the well being of the two individuals. This method of making interpersonal comparisons was formalized into a new approach—that of 'extended sympathy'—and, through the efforts of Sen and other economists and philosophers, has helped us better understand the foundations of utilitarianism and John Rawls' moral philosophy.

With such a diverse set of ideas crowding the pages of *CCSW*, the book became a classic. It drew the attention of not just economists, but professional philosophers, and it is just right that it is the spreading influence of this book which was ultimately honoured by the Nobel Prize.

Delhi and London

Much of this work was done at the Delhi School of Economics, where Amartya worked from 1963 to 1971. This was a remarkable time for the Delhi School. Jagdish Bhagwati was there teaching and researching trade theory and development, Sukhamoy Chakravarty had returned from MIT to be professor, and the eminent econometrician A.L. Nagar provided leadership to the quantitative economics group.[2] The Delhi School was conceived of as a multi-disciplinary institute. This is all the more impressive when one realizes it was run on a shoestring budget. Its economics community was matched by an outstanding collection of sociologists.

I got to know Amartya Sen as a student at the London School of Economics, where Sen had moved in 1971. He was already quite well known and his lectures drew full houses, with students squatting on the floor and perching on windowsills. Those were heady days, days of unbridled idealism, and his blend of economics and philosophy appealed to students. One of the greatest lectures I have heard in economics was Sen's inaugural lecture at the LSE, which was later published as 'Behaviour and the Concept of Preference' in *Economica* in 1973. (It helped shape my own PhD research agenda, a PhD which I would later do with Sen as principal adviser.) In this paper Sen puzzled about the meaning of individual rationality. Was rationality simply a matter of consistency—as many economists had come to believe following Samuelson's famous work on revealed preference (in which a person's preference was taken to be simply that which was revealed by her choice)—or was it something else? Also, what was the relation between the various kinds of consistency axioms that were floating around at that time? The lecture raised more questions than it answered but it led to a series of formal papers on rational choice theory and consistency.

Philosophy

Throughout the time that Sen was working on the choice of technology and social choice theory, one of his enduring passions was philosophy. The roots of this passion are not difficult to fathom. His mother's father, K.M. Sen, was a philosopher of distinction who wrote on religion and Hinduism and lectured at Viswa Bharati University (founded by the literature Nobel laureate, Rabindranath Tagore) in Shantiniketan, a small town outside Calcutta, where Amartya was born and grew up. K.M. Sen belonged to a generation which upheld the oral tradition and his grandson must have learnt philosophy talking and listening to him.

The first evidence of Sen's interest in philosophy was a paper he wrote in 1959 in *Enquiry*. This is a little-known paper; for a long time I had the smug satisfaction of not knowing anyone apart from myself who had read it. The paper consisted of a compelling statement on determinism and free will. Sen may have moved away from the position taken in the paper, but it is a paper I would recommend to the reader, if for nothing else but its lucidity.

Sen's philosophical interest continued to grow in Oxford, where he interacted with philosophers. In addition to the journals mentioned earlier, his papers appeared in *Philosophical Quarterly, Philosophy and Public Affairs, Theory and Decision,* and *Journal of Philosophy.* He also lectured to philosophy students at Oxford and later at Harvard, where he offered a course jointly with Robert Nozick.

Poverty and Campaign

During his stay at the LSE, Sen's interest moved to an area which had always, though somewhat subliminally, existed within him—poverty and inequality. Towards the end of his seven years at the LSE, and after he moved to Oxford as professor in 1977, Sen worked on these subjects. One branch of this interest was concerned with the technical problem of how best to measure poverty. The standard method in those days was to consider an income level—the poverty line—below which a person could be called poor, and then to find the percentage of a nation's population that lived below the poverty line. This was the so-called 'headcount measure'. Sen noted that this had an obvious restriction. If you take away ten dollars from a person way below the poverty line and give it to someone *just* below the poverty line, the head-count measure of poverty will fall, since the recipient will cease to be below the poverty line. But surely, in an important sense, such a transfer (from someone poor to someone better-off) cannot be thought of as a poverty-*reducing* act. Hence, governments that were using the headcount measure to design policy risked crafting faulty policy.

Sen drew on his expertise in choice theory and constructed a new measure of poverty, approaching the problem by setting down a set of axioms of poverty that a good poverty measure should satisfy, and then deducing the measure. Sen's measure was sensitive not only to the number of people below the poverty line, but to how far below the line they were, as well as to the distribution of poverty. The paper that resulted was published in *Econometrica* in 1976 and it immediately caused a groundswell of interest in the subject.

The other branch of Sen's work on poverty was related to more practical concerns: what causes famines, and how best should famines be controlled or avoided. This resulted in the book *Poverty and Famines*, which is arguably his most widely read work. This is an extremely important book, beautifully written, and full of practical policy implications and insights (some of which he pursued further in his subsequent work with Jean Dreze). Its significance is, however, different from that of his earlier work. My guess is that the same book written by a less famous person would not have caused as much of a stir as it did. This was an area where Sen was using his already established renown to campaign for causes that he believed in, to urge for state action to eradicate poverty and to leaven the burden of the weaker sections of society. And of course he was bringing an enormous amount of scholarship to bear on the subject, so that this book on famines has today come to be regarded as an important work in economic history.

Working on poverty and basic needs, Sen gradually came to challenge the pervasive use of income to measure and compare human welfare. Thus, the most popular way of ranking the economic performance of countries is in terms of per capita income. Sen argues repeatedly for the need to bring in other indicators of the standard of living in order to evaluate the overall well being of societies. This work has had enormous practical implications ever since the UNDP, openly acknowledging Sen's influence, began computing the Human Development Index (HDI) to evaluate societies. The HDI is constructed by taking account of three aspects of each nation or society: the life expectancy of its people, the average level of literacy and education, *and* the per capita income. But would it not be the case that a nation with a higher income will also have better health facilities, and therefore higher life expectancy, and better educational facilities, and therefore higher literacy? The answer must be no, because moving away from using solely the per capita to using the HDI makes enormous differences to the ranking of nations. Canada, for instance, which has a lower per capita income than the US, Switzerland, Kuwait, Norway, Singapore, Denmark, and Japan, turns out to have the highest HDI in the world. At the poorer end, Sri Lanka and Vietnam, for instance, move up considerably when they are assessed in terms of their HDI, instead of their per capita income alone. The shifting of attention away from only income has led to policies being evaluated in terms of their impact on education and health as well. The *Human Development Report*, which reported the HDIs of various nations, began as a sort of alternative publication to the World Bank's immensely influential *World Development Report*. A sign of the spread of this larger concept of well being is how close the two reports have moved to each other in recent times, with the World Bank laying increasing stress on the importance of *human* development.

In certain newspaper articles, Sen's normative work has come under attack. A mindlessly virulent one was by Robert L. Pollock in the *Wall Street Journal* of 15 October. Fortunately, Pollock's partisanship comes into display early in the article when he says that, to him, 'seemingly every winner' of the Nobel Prize for literature is a Marxist. Clearly he himself must be positioned somewhere very outlandish for the world to appear all on one side! Another mistake that he makes others have made too. From the fact that Sen has written repeatedly about the need for public action to help the disadvantaged, some have jumped to the conclusion that Sen does not appreciate the role of the market and of incentives. But that is like concluding that since Mr E wrote only about relativity, he does not believe in government intervention; or, alternatively, that he does believe in government intervention.

A careful reading of Sen's *oeuvre* shows that the body of policy that he believes in is not very different from that which would be prescribed by a large number of eminent economists, such as Kenneth Arrow, Paul Samuelson, and Joseph Stiglitz, though each of them may have concentrated on some specific policy—the one closest to his expertise.

It has been said that Sen's recent work is repetitive and populist; and there is, I believe, some truth to that charge. But it has to be kept in mind that a large part of the recent work is that of a person with a cause, and Sen II must be evaluated differently from Sen I. While the former may not have added to the *scientific* worth of Sen I, it does not detract from it either. In addition, while it is true that the Nobel citation emphasizes Sen's early work, the prize may well have eluded him were it not for the build-up of popular acclaim—a lot of which was a consequence of his later work.

32

John Nash: Paranoid, Schizophrenic, Nobel Laureate*

John Nash was, arguably, a genius. He certainly believed he was one. Most of his papers in game theory—the work for which he won the Nobel Prize in economics—were written by the time he was 25 years old. Subsequently, he wrote some fundamental papers in mathematics and theoretical physics. But it all ended by the time he was in his late twenties. Nash began suffering from delusions. At the age of 30 he had to be confined to a mental asylum and, for the next thirty years, he was in and out of mental homes, unable to work, incapable of relating to people, a hostage to the demons in his head, paralysed by fear and paranoia.

Unlike other Nobel laureates in economics, John Nash was not prodigious. Depending on how one counts, he wrote a total of three or four papers in economics and game theory. But these papers grew to be classics. 'Nash' became an adjective. When a group of self-seeking individuals interact—for instance, several producers of a commodity, deciding how to set prices and what marketing strategy to follow— what outcome can we expect? Nash described a general method for locating the outcome, which came to be known as the 'Nash equilibrium'. This and the 'Nash bargaining solution' became standard tools of modern economic analysis. In classrooms and seminars people talked about the properties of the Nash equilibrium and used his ideas, but very few knew anything about the reclusive man behind this work.

*First published in *India Today*, 3 August 1998.

Then by the late 1980s, his mental illness seemed to be in partial remission, as often happens with schizophrenia. He could be seen pacing the yards of Princeton University or sitting in the 'dinky' train, travelling back and forth between Princeton and Princeton Junction, absorbed in his own thoughts. I was a Visiting Professor at Princeton in 1989 and, while the regular faculty there were quite used to him and so had ceased to notice him, another Visiting Professor, Jorgen Weibull, and I found it unbearable that the man behind the Nash equilibrium that we talked about so much in class was the solitary figure out there. So, through the perseverance of Jorgen, a luncheon appointment with Nash was set up.

It was an unremarkable afternoon. We were, of course, tense, given his genius. But he was also visibly tense, probably because of his shyness. He seldom made eye contact with us. There was no sign of his early arrogance. He spoke softly and seemed sad and vulnerable. One wanted to reach out to him. That was the last time I saw Nash,[1] but Jorgen Weibull kept in touch with him.

By the early 1990s the Nobel committee began deliberating over whether it could give Nash the Nobel Prize. Was he well enough to be able to receive and appreciate the honour? Some argued that he was essentially a mathematician and so should not get the prize for economics. Others argued that even though his own passion was for mathematics, his contributions had turned out to be too important for economic theory for him to be denied the award. In 1994 the announcement came: John Nash, along with two other game theorists, John Harsanyi and Reinhart Selten, had been conferred the Economics Nobel Prize.

Once that happened, the glare of publicity was impossible to avoid. And last month, with the publication of his biography, *A Beautiful Mind*, by *New York Times* journalist Sylvia Nasar, the life of John Nash is now available to all. It is a book that weighs down on one: it describes

---

[1] This needs revision. Since I wrote this essay, I met Nash and his wife once more in Mumbai, at a conference on game theory in January 2003. It was in fact a great honour for me to see him in the audience when I presented my paper, and I did not mind at all the fact that he had to be woken up at the end of it.

a community of mathematicians at Princeton and MIT, brilliant and obsessed but troubled by neurosis and insanity. There was Norbert Weiner, the father of cybernetics and an avuncular presence in Nash's life, who fluctuated between manic excitability and depression, and frequently contemplated suicide. There was also the brilliant Norman Levinson, who provided Nash with some of the kindness he craved but was too awkward to ask for. Levinson himself suffered from hypochondria and acute depression and also the pain of watching his daughter slide into mental illness, a suffering made worse by the fact that he was a Communist sympathizer and so had to bear some of the brunt of McCarthy's witch-hunt.

The book records well the life of John Nash, his insensitivity to other human beings, his obsession with intellectual excellence to the exclusion of everything else, and the tragedy of his long confinements in mental homes. But the people who emerge as true heroes in this biography are the women: Virginia, Nash's mother; Eleanor, his brief lover who bore him a son; and above all Alicia, his wife and the mother of his other child.

Alicia was from El Salvador and, as a student at MIT, she was known for her beauty and intelligence. She fell in love with Nash and married him. But within years, as his insanity and rudeness to everybody, including Alicia, became unmanageable, she had no option but to divorce him. She divorced him but could not abandon him. She took him back in her house as a live-in guest.

That is where Nash continues to live now. It is clear from Sylvia Nasar's account that Alicia's immense strength and compassion have played a role in Nash's survival. And, in the end, when we encounter John Nash at an informal lecture, joking that he was pleased about the Nobel Prize because that would improve his credit rating and enable him to get the credit card he never had, it becomes clear that this book, which is dedicated to Alicia, is also, in a way, a tribute to her.

33

Nobel for Market Failures:
Akerlof, Spence, and Stiglitz*

As soon as the Nobel Prize in Economics of 2001 for George Akerlof (Berkeley), Michael Spence (Stanford), and Joseph Stiglitz (Columbia) was announced, I got a flurry of emails from students and friends. The reason they were congratulating *me* is that these were among the five or six names I had for the last several years been predicting and hoping would get the prize. And I must admit feeling mighty chuffed by the announcement. The work of Akerlof, Spence, and Stiglitz is among the most creative research that my profession has seen. Their papers involve a blend of logic and social observation which is very rare and hard.

The paper that gets the first mention in the Nobel citation is, rightly, George Akerlof's classic, 'The Market for Lemons: Quality Uncertainty and the Market Mechanism'. Much of this paper was written during the year 1967–8 that Akerlof spent at the Indian Statistical Institute in New Delhi; and it suffered the fate common to a lot of truly original research—it was initially rejected by leading journals as being sub-par. It was eventually published in the *Quarterly Journal of Economics* in 1970.

The 'lemons' in the title refer to second-hand cars or duds that used-car sellers often try to pass off as if they were of superior quality. This paper, written mainly in the form of examples, illustrates a point of

*First published in *India Today*, November 2001.

immense importance. Much conventional economics used to be done under the assumption that buyers and sellers are fully informed and rational. Of course, sensible economists always knew that these were merely convenient assumptions, seldom true in fact. But even then the final results and theorems that emanated from these assumptions were believed to be valid. What Akerlof showed was that, if these assumptions were invalid *in a particular way*, namely, if, among the buyers and the sellers, *one* side happened to be worse informed than the other (a phenomenon now referred to as 'asymmetric information'), a lot of conventional economics gets turned on its head. In particular, the belief that the 'invisible hand' of the free market always leads to the efficient outcome turns out to be false.

Once one looks around, it becomes evident that asymmetric information is a very common characteristic of markets. In the used-car market, clearly the seller knows more about the vehicle than the buyer; in the labour market the worker knows better about her skills than does the potential employer. Hence, all these markets, left to themselves, are likely to exhibit inefficiencies.

In the presence of this phenomenon in the labour market, what would workers do? The more skilled among them would somehow try to 'signal' their higher skill. Hence, even if education did not increase human productivity, if higher education were achievable only to those who happened to be *innately* high skilled, it would be worthwhile for them to get such degrees in order to signal their higher skill to potential employers. It was this insight that Michael Spence got as a PhD student at Harvard and wrote up in a classic paper in 1973 and then, more elaborately, in a book in 1974. This gave rise to the huge literature on 'signalling', which gave us deep insights into a variety of phenomena, including why there can be sustained discrimination against some groups (like a caste category, gender, or race) even when these groups may be as skilled, or even more skilled, than others. This was contrary to the 'Chicago School' view that free-market competition eventually wipes out unfair discrimination.

Akerlof has worked on an array of original topics—procrastination, cognitive dissonance, and social identity—and reached some stunning insights into a variety of important phenomena, such as why people get addicted to certain habits, why India's caste system has such staying power, and why youngsters join gangs.

Spence is an unusual economist who, after producing a relatively small body of research, surprised the profession by abandoning full-time academics for administration. In 1984, at the age of 41, he became Dean at Harvard, and later Dean at the Stanford Business School.

Of the three laureates, Stiglitz's work is the hardest to describe because his productivity is legendary and intuitive creativity immense. He has contributed papers to virtually every field of economics. I worked closely with him during the year 1998–9 when I went to the World Bank at his invitation. He was then Senior Vice President of the Bank. He would eventually be eased out of the Bank for being too critical of the 'Washington Consensus' and the IMF. I saw during that year his frenetic level of activity. But he managed it with a sense of humour and warmth which is rare in high office.

Those days, because of his heavy bureaucratic responsibility, he had a team of research assistants who dotted the i's and compiled the bibliographies of his papers. (Unlike many other intellectuals known for their fastidiousness, Joe Stiglitz was unfussy about these finishing touches.) One of his assistants would drop by my office asking, one day, for 'two non-Stiglitz references on share tenancy', another day for 'one non-Stiglitz reference on peer monitoring', and so on. Eventually, curiosity caught up with me and I asked him what was behind these unusual queries. He said Stiglitz had told him that no paper of his should have more than 50 per cent of the references to his own work. But then, every time Joe Stiglitz revised a paper, he remembered works he had done many years ago and inserted the references. That brought his assistant scurrying to me to keep the balance right.

34

Nietzsche Century*

25 August 2000 passed uneventfully. There were notices here and there, in a British newspaper, in a German magazine. Yet a century ago, on this very day, one of the greatest philosophers of the last millennium died. For a few years prior to his death he had become a celebrity. His books were selling in their tens of thousands. His writings were being analysed, worshipped, and vilified. The only person who did not know of his fame was Friedrich Nietzsche himself, because for the last eleven years of his life he had been bedridden, stricken with insanity and paralysis.

Since his death, the Nietzsche legend has continued to grow, and though his thought may not be the stuff of popular media, there has been an unbelievably large amount of writing on him—on his work and on his influence in the world of politics. The last is ironic, because he detested politicians, political parties, and ideology. Nevertheless, a variety of politicians, many of them with completely contrary views, have claimed allegiance to his philosophy.

It is not difficult to fathom why this is so. Nietzsche did not write with the precision of an analytic philosopher. He had instead a rabble-rousing style, full of lyricism, delightful in ambiguity.

What made Nietzsche so attractive as a philosopher was his passion. Plagued by migraine, poor health, and spurts of insanity, living like a nomad in cheap apartments in European cities, he poured out his thoughts in books, pamphlets, and letters. He wrote prodigiously,

*First published in *India Today*, 25 September 2000.

fearlessly trampling on conventional thought, almost as if he knew the end was near and so must put out in a hurry whatever he had to tell the world.

Nietzsche had many passions that failed him. He loved the music of Wagner and admired him but eventually fell out with him. He was deeply attached to his sister from childhood but later grew distant because he had no sympathy for her and her husband's anti-semitism. He was very critical of the German treatment of Jews; it is therefore ironic that the Nazis later claimed to draw inspiration from Nietzsche's philosophy. He was brought up in a religious family but came to denounce Christianity. Yet he admired Jesus. 'In truth', he once wrote, 'there was only one Christian and he died on the cross.'

Through all these ups and downs, the enduring influence on Nietzsche's thinking was Vedanta philosophy and the Upanishads. He had read these early in his life and his interest was reinforced through his admiration for Schopenhauer. Though he later outgrew this infatuation, he remained close to his schoolmate, Paul Deussen, one of the best-known interpreters of Indian thought at that time. In many of Nietzsche's passages there are allusions to 'maya'. Thus he wrote about the world being 'transitory, seductive, illusory'.

Despite the power of his intellect and the insightful aphorisms that litter his work in his famous books—notably *Beyond Good and Evil* and *Thus Spake Zarathustra*—it is undeniable that his tragic life fuelled interest in Nietzsche.

He was born on 15 October 1844. Four years later his father became mentally ill and, a year later, died. The son was brought up in a house consisting of a doting mother, a grandmother, two maiden aunts, and the boy's sister. In school and later in college in Bonn he was recognized for his prodigious mental capacity. At the precocious age of 24 he was appointed professor of philology in Basel and three years latter he published his first book.

Everything seemed glorious and green. But all the while into his 'green valley' was drifting 'the apalling snow'. He lived throughout in the fear that his father's mental illness would also afflict him. His father's ailment was perhaps not hereditary. Nietzsche's own mental illness was possibly due to syphilis, picked up during one of his two encounters with prostitutes. This was the greater pity because he had lived a near-celibate life. When he did fall in love with Wagner's wife Cosima—she was doubly famous because her father was the incredible pianist and famous composer Franz Liszt—he could not get himself to admit this to her and almost not to himself. There is pathos in Nietzsche's entry in the asylum book, written in a state of delirium, that he was brought there by his 'wife, Cosima Wagner'.

Nietzsche became convinced that he would die in 1880, at the age of 36, just like his father. He retired from his work in 1879, citing poor health. When 1880 passed without event, he got a new lease of life and his classic, *Zarathustra*, was written in a last flash of enthusiasm.

The irreversible mental breakdown occurred on a cold January morning in 1889, when he collapsed on a street in Turin, clutching desperately to the neck of a mare. Within days he lost his sanity completely and for eleven long years was looked after by his mother and, after her death, by his sister, as he slid 'gentle into the good night'.

PART V

On the Road,
Around the World

35

Notarizing in Delhi*

Last week I went to a notary public in Ithaca to have my signature on a document attested. I had phoned in advance and when I stepped into her office, she guessed: 'Professor Basu?' In about ten minutes I was out of there, job done. As I drove back to Cornell I could not help feeling impressed by the efficiency. But I must admit, there was also a feeling of nostalgia for India.

Last August my wife and I had to get a document notarized in Delhi. Dodging a procession of banner-waiving protesters of some sort, near the crossing of Sansad Marg and Ashoka Road, we entered an open arena resembling what I imagine the bazaars of ancient Babylon must have looked like during the decline of the Mesopotamian civilization, where notaries public (I just checked—that *is* the right way to write the plural) keep their offices. 'Offices' here means a cluster of ramshackle desks and chairs beneath makeshift sheds and tarpaulin to keep the sun out. Right in front of this arena is a garbage dump, with additions to it appearing like missiles every now and then from a window in an adjacent building. Chai-wallahs and peons weave their way through rows of desks where an assortment of men in black coats sit, some working, some staring vacantly, some dozing.

We were in a hurry and so we thrust the document into the hands of the first notary we came across, a man who was somewhere between staring vacantly and dozing. He was annoyed by the haste. 'Not like

*First published in *India Today*, 4 December 2000.

this. Everything has to be done in proper order.' Those words brought into existence an assistant with a Dev Anand hairdo, who took the paper from our hands and gave it to 'Mr Sharma'. During the course of that afternoon we discovered that that was the only job of Dev Anand, and every notary public seemed to have one such person. Someone with a sheer genius for job creation must have thought of this arrangement.

We were told to return after an hour.

'One hour, to type so little?' I asked.

The notary's gaze, now directed at me, was like that of the fabled basilisk. 'Sir, notary work is no *faaltu* work. It has to be done properly.'

When we returned after a little over an hour, during which we lunched in Connaught Place, the document was lying exactly where we had left it. I could not help being angry, but Mr Sharma was unruffled, 'Kindly understand. Only we are not taking lunch. Typist is also eating.' To contest that would sound too mean, so my wife and I sat on the two chairs that Dev Anand had produced, before vanishing with the document 'to get it typed'.

We would be there for the next two hours, watching the ebb and flow of this Kafkaesque theatre. The monotonous clatter of old-fashioned typewriters would fade into the background every time some customer lost his patience and shouted for his document to be produced forthwith. The humid heat of August added fuel to frayed nerves. 'You keep mum', shouted one notary to another, the latter responding with Wodehousean civility: 'Rather, you keep mum.'

After an hour a lady in *salwar kameez* and white sports keds came to Mr Sharma to have a signature verified. Dev Anand intercepted and gave the papers to Mr Sharma. Her husband had lost his B.A. degree and the Delhi University office had instructed her to bring a letter from him saying that he had lost it, with a notary public's attestation.

But where was the husband who would have to sign it? She explained that they were NRIs and her husband could not come to India; but she could do his signature exactly. As I warmed to the thought of witnessing a forgery being notarized, I realized that corruption was not among Mr Sharma's failings. He insisted that her husband would have to come to his office and he would be happy to wait till 'tomorrow'. 'But he is in Vancouver', she pleaded. This went on for a while, till I, to break the stalemate, suggested that she could type out a letter in her own words saying that her husband had lost his BA degree and so she would like to collect a duplicate on his behalf.

After a short silence—or perhaps a nap—Mr Sharma said, 'The suggestion is not without merit.' And soon Dev Anand had vanished again in the mélée of typists to have another letter typed. I later felt quite guilty for I just could not see the hardened bureaucracy of Delhi University issuing a duplicate degree to some lady who came in with a letter saying she was the wife of someone who had lost his degree.

Anyway, she was quite cheerful. She berated Mr Sharma for the garbage dump in front of his desk, which, she assured him, could never exist in Vancouver.

'What you are saying? Everywhere there is garbage', countered Mr Sharma. 'Even in Kashmir.' It was not clear why he thought garbage particularly unexpected in Kashmir.

'Have you been to Kashmir?' I queried.

'Otherwise how I am saying there is garbage there? I will not speak about any place unless I have been there and seen with my own eyes.'

A little later the Vancouver lady mused that there was too much corruption in Delhi. 'Why only Delhi?' countered Mr Sharma with his unerring Delhi-loyalty. 'There is corruption even in Russia.'

'Have you been to Russia?' she asked. 'No never', he replied, slightly annoyed, 'How can you go to every country?'

36

Traveller's Bihar*

An Afghan commoner of uncommon wisdom, Sher Shah Suri, built it around 1540 during his brief tenure as Emperor of India. The British rulers coated it with asphalt and used it to haul their colonial pickings across the subcontinent. The Grand Trunk Road of India has seen it all. But between the towns of Dhanbad and Bagodar in Bihar what you will not see is the Grand Trunk Road. The tar has vanished, the edges have merged into the open fields, and with its potholes and boulders the road resembles images of moonscape that one sees in science magazines. For three hours, our Ambassador snorts and grunts along the 'highway', past lyrical little towns like Isri and Dumri, with the magnificent Parashnath mountain and its pinnacled Jain temple as backdrop.

We would have forgotten that this was mafia country had it not been for rows of glistening swords and *trishuls* being sold openly on the roadside. This went on for more than a mile—a series of horizontal bars with swords hanging from them.

I ask my driver why these are being sold in such large numbers. 'Naturally, for self-defence', he replies, making me feel silly for my ignorance. I wonder where one goes if one wants to buy a sword for offence but keep the query to myself.

Our driver, who had picked us up at Dhanbad station and would be our companion for the next three days, was in his early twenties, a dignified person with a touch of pathos. It was only on the third day

*First published in *India Today*, 9 February 1998. Since this piece was written, the state of Bihar was partitioned into Jharkhand and Bihar, and several places mentioned in this essay straddle both states.

that he told us that he was a student when his father died, less than two months earlier. His mother and sister were devastated and, given that the father had been the sole breadwinner in the family, he had no option but to start working and the only job he could get was that of a driver.

At Bagodar we turn north, off the Grand Trunk Road. The 35 km from here to Hazaribagh Road is a pretty route with hillocks and forests on both sides, interrupted occasionally by villages. I have been on this road many times—first as a child with my father, who loved this part of Bihar and would drive up once a year from Calcutta, and, later, with friends and students to do fieldwork in the village of Nawadih. Hazaribagh Road is the name of an overgrown village—a small cluster of houses that mushroomed around a railway station on the Grand Chord—where people had to get off to go to Hazaribagh Town, about 48 km south of there.

Somewhat tired after the dusty ride, we have an early dinner in the dim glow of hurricane lanterns and go off to sleep. There is a string of visitors next morning. This includes someone from the village of Nawadih who had met me during one of my field trips and an old man who knew my father. For most of them, it is not clear why they want to see me, but seeing people for specific reasons is probably an urban custom. Many of them say a few things and then just sit quietly. That may seem odd to us, but from their perspective, what is odd is our modern urban norm whereby we feel embarrassed by silence.

One of my visitors that morning is Mr Haldar, a Bengali gentleman who lives in Hazaribagh. He begins by saying that he has come to ask me for a favour and then stays on for two hours, talking about Laloo Yadav, sharing with me his thesis on the decline of England *and* assuring me that to travel in Bihar nowadays one needed protection, adding promptly that if, however, 'someone targets you, then even with protection you don't stand a chance.' This last, I realize, is something he feels strongly about for he continues to elaborate on how protection is fine only as long as no one is 'targeting you'. After several minutes, as my mind drifts, I hear him say how he 'can give it in writing' that a targeted person is as good as dead. He never asks for the favour.

In sophisticated urban society, people say they have come for a chat and ask for a favour. But, evidently, here saying that you have come to request a favour is the alibi, when the real intention is to chat.

Bihar is a land of breathtaking contrasts. It was once the seat of one of the great civilizations, with its grand capital in Patna, formerly Pataliputra. The region has made important contributions to art and literature. As individuals, the people here are gentle, and it is impossible not to notice that the women are of exceptional beauty. On the other hand, barring a few pockets of excellence, such as the Steel City of Bokaro, there is hardly any infrastructure and the towns are in disarray. In many areas, gangs and private armies rule the streets. This other Bihar depicts Hobbesian anarchy and chaos. It is a grim reminder to those who believe that we would have utopia if only government withdrew—for the Bihar government has long withdrawn.

On the way back we decide to avoid the Grand Trunk Road and make our way through *saal* forests and coal-dust-covered towns. In one such town we stop for tea. Next to the tea stall is a tiny store with a large board announcing '*Yeh ander ki baat hai*' ('This is an internal matter.') A peep into the shop reveals that it sells underwear and hot sauces. There is no time to inquire into the philosophy or marketing strategy behind this unusual bunching of products. As we continue on our journey, I decide I must return to Bihar, for this indeed is a land of enigmas.

37

Tango of Two Currencies:
Buenos Aires*

As our aircraft glides over Cuba and across the Caribbean Sea, the businessman in the seat across the aisle who has been holding forth on how the Third World has only itself to blame, switches to travel. 'Instead of Argentina you should have gone to Greece', he tells me, unmindful of the fact that I would miss the economics conference which is the sole purpose of my travel. 'The fish in Greece is better than anywhere else. Some of the fish soups are just heavenly.' He continues on the subject of fish for what seems like eternity. 'Just walk into any restaurant and say "fish" and you can't go wrong in Greece.'

'It was also the cradle of Western civilization,' I interrupt, emphasizing the 'also' in order not to offend his sense of priorities. I think he mis-hears 'the cradle' for he assures me that if it were crab I wanted, crab I would get. Fortunately, we hit turbulence and the theatre of the absurd comes to an end.

Around noon we are in Buenos Aires. This is the first time that I am in the southern hemisphere of the Western world. The sloping winter sun and the chill in the air in late August seems strange. In some areas the primary colours on house façades create an urban landscape of unmatched beauty, like nothing I have seen before. The only familiar sight is that of Meghna Reddy, with her deadpan good looks, on the cover of *National Geographic*, displayed seemingly on every magazine

*First published in *India Today*, 18 October 1999.

kiosk in the city. She looks overclothed though, amidst the medley of more daring Latino magazine covers.

With time one sees more signs of the familiar. The gentleman in the hotel lobby, whom I had taken for an Argentine, gives himself away when from his briefcase he takes out Pan Parag. On the way to San Isidro, to the villa of Victoria Occampo, an unusually cerebral travel agent rightly guesses that I am going there to see the villa where 'Tagore' had once lived.

There is a lot to see in Buenos Aires and I manage to see these between the conference sessions, and, I may as well admit now, some during. Sessions that I try not to miss are the ones on dollarization because Argentina is considering a daring experiment to give up its own currency, the peso, and adopt the US dollar. This will mean that Argentina will have no control over its monetary policy and be completely at the mercy of the US Fed. On the plus side, it will not have to worry about exchange-rate fluctuations and, in all likelihood, it will never again face the kind of hyperinflations that have plagued its economy in the past.

Whether or not dollarization is good for Argentina, what is impressive is the openness with which the subject is being debated by politicians and senior bureaucrats. I believe that currency unions will be increasingly common in the future and it is well known that several nations, especially in South America, are considering dollarization or common currency areas, but these discussions are being conducted behind closed doors.

In some ways, dollarization would be less dramatic for Argentina because since 1991 it has been under a Currency Board (CB), and so is halfway there already. Broadly speaking, a country is under a CB if it locks its currency into a completely fixed exchange rate *vis-à-vis* a major international currency and the Central Bank guarantees this by holding a large reserve of that international currency. In Argentina, one peso is pegged to one dollar. This is so constant that no one minds which currency you use. After a cab ride or eating in a restaurant, we paid in any combination of dollars and pesos and no questions were ever asked.

The CB is an old institution. It was created in 1849 by the British Empire for Mauritius. Subsequently it went out of use; but in recent times, as some countries have suffered huge inflation and exchange-rate volatility, governments have sometimes decided to forsake some of their monetary freedom in favour of the CB. The CB is not without its disadvantages and uncertainties. Over the past year or so, as other Latin American currencies have lost value, Argentinian exports have steadily shrunk, thereby creating unemployment and political instability. Under a CB Argentina cannot lower its exchange rate and give a boost to its exports.

Some people have speculated that this tango with the US dollar should be ended and the country should go back to the flexible exchange-rate system. Such anticipation can be self-fulfilling. One of the speakers from the Central Bank pointed out that while for small purchases one can pay with any currency in Argentina, if you want to buy a house the seller invariably insists on being paid in dollars. The reason is that people are afraid of a sudden abandonment of the CB and a drop in the value of the peso.

No one wants to be caught with large peso holdings in such an eventuality. One way to put an end to such speculation is to go for an even more dramatic move—to give up its currency altogether and use the US dollar for all transactions and holdings. This is exactly what Argentina is considering. If it does dollarize, it will be the first time that such a large nation will have voluntarily given up its own currency for another's, and it will be an experiment that will be keenly watched the world over.

38

A Vietnam Diary*

As soon as our flight from Delhi touches down in Bangkok there is pandemonium. Virtually all the Indian passengers are up, taking down their luggage and jostling to get to the door. In the Olympics, India wins no medals; our economy trails far behind that of most other nations; but when it comes to disembarking from aeroplanes, Indians have no peer. It is a pity that the International Olympic Association does not recognize this as a sport.

From Bangkok a short flight takes me and my family to Ho Chi Minh City (formerly Saigon). It may be a manifestation of my geographic infidelity, but Vietnam seems more fascinating than any other place I have seen.

The basic facts about Vietnam I knew well before my journey—that it has a per capita income of $370 per annum (significantly less than India's 450); that its economy is controlled by a large, Communist government; that it fought a devastating war with the world's most powerful nation from 1964 to 1975; that it won the war but at the terrible cost of 4 million civilian lives (10 per cent of its population).

But what we see refuses to square up with these facts. Nowhere in HCM City does one see the kind of poverty one encounters in Indian cities. There are beggars but they are better dressed and better nourished than their Indian counterparts. There is no animus (at least none that is visible) towards the large numbers of tourists, mainly from Europe and America. The dollar is as much a Vietnamese currency as the *dong*. The average quality of life is impressive. In the evening young

*First published in *India Today*, 3 September 2001.

couples ride their bikes to the bank of Saigon River in the fashionable
Dong Khoi area, to sit locked in embrace and watch barges. The women of Vietnam, all elfin charm, have the alluring quality of being
both liberated and demure (besides having the best posture in the
world). Clearly they feel secure in the streets for they are out late in the
evening, in their flowing *ao dais* or, more commonly, Western dresses.

Another big surprise is art. In Vietnam, the art shops are everywhere.
Most of the canvasses are copies of paintings of Western art. But they
go beyond the familiar Van Goghs and Picassos. Small Janpath-like
shops sell replicas of Fernando Botero, Tamara de Lempicka, Ed Hop-
per, the German expressionists and the Mexican muralists. The price
ranges from $5 to $50. There are also original paintings by Vietnamese
artists. I explore several galleries. For top-of-the-range works, prices go
up to $3000. I do not see paintings that measure up to the level of, say,
Anjolie Ela Menon, Dodiya, or the two Bhattacharyas—Bikash and
Sanjay—but what is surprising is the high *average* quality and the
amount of art being produced and sold.

The answer to the Vietnam puzzle unfolds only gradually, through
speaking to people in the streets and economists in the know, and by
travelling to the suburbs and beyond the cities.

One of the first clues to the puzzle is the realization that there are
no sprawling residential bungalows or dachas. And indeed a little
investigation confirms that there are few very-rich people here. Most
of the cars on the roads belong to the embassies and donor agencies.
The Vietnamese, overwhelmingly, use motorbikes and bicycles. Even
ministers and politburo members go to work on bikes. Hence, despite
the low per capita income of the nation, there is not as much poverty
as in other Third World countries—the cake is divided much more
equitably. Another factor that has fuelled Vietnam's cultural and
artistic achievements is its literacy rate. At a level of 95 per cent this is
not only way above India's 65 per cent, but is comparable to southern
Europe.

The economic policy that the Communist government has pursued
is notable for its pragmatism. In the late 1980s the government began

abandoning its overarching control of the economy. The reforms—the so-called *doi moi*—included greater openness to trade and foreign direct investment. This, coupled with the state's genuine commitment to equality, has given a great fillip to the economy, which has grown at rates as high as 9 per cent in recent years.

The economy's battle is by no means over. As it moves up the value chain in terms of trade and production (the Hanoi newspapers keep referring to India's software success as something that Vietnam could replicate) it is being forced to do more business with MNCs. The latter are seasoned in doing business, while, for that very reason, the Vietnamese are full of apprehension that they will be duped. This understandable hesitation can and does easily turn to bureaucratic delays, hampering business and efficiency.

The other problem is that its admirable economic egalitarianism is likely to come under strain. As the economy globalizes, the local people will sooner or later resent the wealth of 'outsiders', and many will strive to emulate them. This will unleash new energies but is bound to skew incomes and, unless there is skilful government intervention, may even exacerbate poverty.

With each passing day in Vietnam I begin to notice and understand the country's strange mixture of socialism and the free market. On our last day we visit the Temple of Literature in Hanoi, which is an eleventh-century institution of learning and instruction, dedicated mainly to Confucianism, now preserved as a museum. There, at the bookshop, amidst piles of books on Marx, Lenin, and Ho Chi Minh, sits a stack of some book in Vietnamese. It is prominently displayed, clearly in the knowledge that whoever sees it will want to buy it. The book, I realize on turning a copy over, is a life of Bill Gates.

39

South Africa: Zebra Country*

The country of Nelson Mandela, of Nadine Gordimer, of Steve Biko, of Desmond Tutu, and also of Gandhi. It was impossible not to feel excited as the aeroplane did a broad sweeping turn and lowered itself gently on to the tarmac. The airport at Johannesburg, or Joburg—as the locals call it, presumably to save breath—could have been anywhere in Europe. Men and women of European descent and clothing hurry along to catch flights or taxis, the boutiques overflow with expensive fashion products, and the aroma of good coffee wafts out of stylish cafes.

Upon arrival, another guest and I are driven to Glenburn Lodge, and the address sounds pleasingly exotic to my ears—Kromdraai Road, Muldersdrift. The drive takes nearly an hour. The roads, lined with the most magnificent jacaranda trees in bloom, are wide and smooth. One sees very few people on the streets and the houses, with red begonia, are well spaced with plenty of land surrounding each cluster. It is evident that, with 35 people per km^2 (India has 350), one shortage that South Africa does not have to contend with is land.

Glenburn Lodge is far removed from the bustle of Joburg. Its lodgings and conference rooms are interspersed with brooks and wilderness; and from one's window on a quiet afternoon one can see springboks grazing, and, on lucky days giraffes silhouetted against a clear blue sky. The chief organizer of the conference is a young South African economist of Gujarati descent, Haroon Bhorat. His idea is the clever one of

*First published in *Business Standard*, 11 December 2002.

holding the participants captive. It works well. With nowhere else to go, we pass an intense three days discussing the South African economy.

With a per capita income of $2900 per annum, South Africa is wealthier than most African countries but it is much poorer than Europe, where almost all nations have per capita incomes upward of $20,000. Yet during the conference, and travelling to parts of the city like Sandton, one could have been in Europe. The conference is full of Whites and a smattering of people of Indian origin. Where are the natives, I wonder. And if South Africa is so poor, why is that not evident? The answers emerge gradually, during the conference, and then all at once during my last day in Soweto.

Apartheid was abolished in 1994 but this remains a country of stunning disparities. Like the stripes of the zebra, South Africa has Blacks and Whites, but they rarely mingle. Unemployment stands at 36 per cent; life expectancy at birth is only 48 years (compared to India's 63), caused, in part, by the high incidence of AIDS. More importantly, the dispossessed are disproportionately Black Africans. Thus, for instance, an astonishing 44 per cent Blacks are unemployed, compared to 7 per cent Whites.

Why is this so? Why do wages not fall to clear the market, as textbook economics predict? Here, textbook economics fails because it does not make room for the fact that, when hiring labour, employers worry about how trustworthy the labourer will be. The usual way in which they try to ensure trustworthiness is to hire workers through contacts, that is, by asking others whom they trust (including their employees) for recommendations. If an anonymous worker walks up to an entrepreneur and offers to work for a lower wage than the prevailing rate, the entrepreneur will, typically, be disinclined to take him on for fear that he may turn out to be unreliable. When, thanks to a fractured history, society is as segregated as South Africa's, this becomes a serious problem. It is easy to have large sections of society not connected to the network of people who are active in industry and business, and so their unemployment does nothing to budge the market wage.

On my last day I have some free time and persuade Rashad Cassim, who heads a think-tank on Trade and Industrial Policy, to get me a taxi to take me to Soweto, the Black township where the revolt against apartheid began. Patrick, a large, lumbering African who drives his own taxi, is appointed to take me around. As we drive into Soweto it is clear why some parts of South Africa look like Europe: it is because other parts are exclusively Black. Soweto is a huge sprawling slum-like settlement. Not quite as poor and overcrowded as Indian slums, but, compared to some parts of Joburg, terribly unseemly. The atmosphere is gay, with roadsides full of little girls and boys, hopping and skipping, and idle young men and beautiful women chatting and laughing, seemingly with no care in the world. But it is impossible not to notice that beneath this veneer of peace there are scars of injustice that South Africa must attend to soon if it is not to get embroiled in political instability and debilitating dissent.

Patrick takes me to Mandela's original home—now a museum, the Regina Mundi Church—where an assembly of peaceful protesters with all escape blocked were teargassed and shot at, and the Hector Pieterson Museum. I had forgotten this name, Hector Pieterson, but as soon as I see his picture, dead at 13 in the arms of his friend and with his sister crying next to him, shot by riot police while marching in protest against apartheid, I remember that eternal image from 1976.

The most touching moment for me comes when Patrick agrees to show me what no tourist in Soweto gets to see, his home. As we approach there, slowly negotiating the curves in narrow lanes, people stare at me and wave at Patrick. His home is full of people. There are his sons and daughters from his first marriage. The boys are grown up but without jobs; they cannot find any—they do not know anyone who can introduce them to the 'connected people', the industrialists and entrepreneurs one sees in the restaurants in Sandton and at the airport. Then there is his girlfriend who has recently lost her job and so is spending a lot of time with him.

When Patrick was 5 years old his father left his mother in Zimbabwe and, along with Patrick, came away to South Africa. The memory of his mother faded but, after his divorce, feeling lonely, Patrick decided he had to find her. After a gruelling search he tracked her down in Zambia and brought her back with him. She came with her two grand-children from another marriage. And here was Patrick, generous be-yond measure, looking after all these dependants, whom he seemed to love to the point of distraction.

He and his extended family belong to the statistics of the excluded in this bewildering country. It is difficult to think of South Africa's eco-nomy divorced from its politics. It is a nation of indefinable charm and enormous prospects. But before these can be realized, policy-makers will have to work hard to build political institutions that can help the country outlive its tragic history. There are no longer legal barriers to the people of different races coming together to work, marry, and co-habit. But it will be long before Blacks and Whites truly manage to come together in the zebra country.

40

North Meets South: In and Around Bangalore*

I

Back in Bangalore after several years, I find that the city lives up to its avant-garde reputation. The large dotcom hoardings, the cyber cafes, the sleek restaurants offering cuisines ranging from Coorgi to French, and the pubs lining the road are impressive.

But equally impressive is the rapidity with which all this disappears as one drives out of the city. Within miles of cruising west the modern buildings give way to modest tenements. Another hour or two of driving and the landscape changes to open fields, with gigantic boulders, eucalyptus clusters, coconut groves, and banyan trees disfigured by the human quest for firewood. The simple huts and hovels of the poor are a reminder of the sameness of India—a sameness dominated, even now, by poverty.

Our first halt is at the Magadi Taluka headquarters, where the executive officer (EO) explains the development work going on in the region. He is currently involved in a housing subsidy scheme under which any poor villager can get a grant of Rs 20,000 for building a house. There are conditions, of course. The house must be built using labour-intensive technology; the original owner cannot sell the house; and the building must include a toilet, presumably to wean away residents from the lure of the fields. The EO is pained that villagers resist

*Based on 'North Meets South', *India Today*, 7 August 2000 (Section I); and *Mantram*, 2001 (Section II).

the toilets, and even after he persuades them, on occasion he has bumped into residents returning from the field, *lota* in hand.

The programme has its strengths, but the ban on selling the house is bad economics. It is rooted in the government's fear that the same people will corner the grants, build houses, and sell them. But, as in the case of Kolkata's Salt Lake, discussed earlier, the way to guard against this is to enforce the rule that only the very poor get the grant, and only once in a lifetime. If then the person prefers to sell the house, it must be because he considers it will make him better off. Why should the government stop a poor person from doing what makes him better off?

To try to prevent resale by legislating against it cuts down mobility; it has given rise to India's national institution, the 'power of attorney' sale and its attendant corruption. Indeed, the EO complains of 'loiterers' around government offices who have mastered the government's multifarious rules and take advantage of them.

For the next few hours we stop at several villages, visit schools, panchayat leaders, and social workers and talk to villagers. The trip's highlight is a rehabilitation centre for child labourers—Chigaru for girls and Ambara for boys. Here we converse with children and the workers looking after them. Natraj is 13 years old. For five years before he was brought to this Unicef-funded centre by social workers, he worked 8–9 hours a day in a silk factory, virtually as a bonded worker, because his parents had borrowed Rs 9000 from the factory owner for their daughter's marriage. He loves it here but lives in fear of his former employer, who threatens him every time he goes home.

At these rehab centres, with their cast of pan-Indian greats—Gandhi, Ambedkar, Tagore, Visvesvaraya, Vivekananda—on the walls, one meets social workers whose enthusiasm and commitment give hope. The way the children wrap themselves around Jayasheela, one of the girls looking after them at Chigaru, makes it plain how comfortable they feel in their 'home'.

One finds the same hope in the *anganwadi* centre, where children from ages 1 to 6 come for the day, get a nutritious meal, learn a little, and play. The children dance and recite and show us their paintings of churches, temples, and mosques, and tell us how all religions ought to be respected. In these days of dwindling secularism, it is heart-warming to see this kind of initiative among anganwadi volunteers.

What impresses me every time I travel in rural India is how, despite the distances and the poverty which restrict people from moving from one region to another, there is so much in common across the regions.

Three days later, near Hassan and Belur, on NH 48, we come across one more evidence of the mingling of cultures. One after another, there are restaurants offering 'Punjabi dhaba' food. Just beyond the dusty town of Channarayapatna, we decide to stop and try out one of these. Hotel King's Fort is made of red bricks and is uncharacteristically well designed. The cooks and the waiters are Kannadiga. The menu is North Indian and has everything, including butter chicken. The restaurant's command over the culinary arts is commendable. The only thing they still need to work on a little is their spellings: for the travel weary, the restaurant offers 'chicken Malia takka', 'mutton seakskabab', 'malie kufta', and, most intriguingly, 'Sweet Lassie—Rs 25'.

II

I happen to be in Bangalore when news comes of the latest *Human Development Report (HDR) 2001* declaring it 'one of the world's most dynamic technology hubs' and, by some measure, the fourth-highest-ranked city in this regard. There is understandable euphoria in the city, with some local magazines and newspapers clearly going overboard and forgetting that the UNDP, the organization that publishes the *HDR*, is located on earth. On the heels of this has come the announcement that the city will have a new airport, Bangalore International Airport, which will be better than any other in India. This is heartening because the gap between Indian airports and other Asian ones, such as Bangkok or Singapore's Changi, has grown steadily large.

But even if one ignores such hype, Bangalore's rising fortune is transparent even to the most unobservant observer. Information technology is the heart of it. One can see this not just from the number of famous institutes and colleges of learning that have sprung up in the city, but from the many not-famous ones that are thriving. On a recent drive to Nrittyagram (twenty miles west of the city) I realized that in Bangalore all you need to do now is think of a word X and start an institute called X Institute of Technology and you will have students knocking at your door.

Many years ago, on my way to the Delhi School of Economics, I would regularly, in Daryaganj, look out of my bus window and see a sign: 'Asian Institute of Technology'. Below it, in smaller font, in the manner of Nissim Ezekiel's Indian-English poems, it said 'Entrance from backside'. Amidst the clutter of shoulder-to-jowl houses this was a useful tip for the potential student. The institutes in Bangalore display no such modesty. Many have their own buildings, they advertise computer labs, and one invariably sees students bustling in and out.

It is arguable that America's Silicon Valley would not have taken off if not for the great universities of that region, most notably, Stanford, Berkeley, and Caltech. It may not be pure coincidence that Bangalore's corporate excellence is matched by its rise as India's number one city for science research and studies. Once one crosses the agricultural lands, ploughed up and rural, and enters the campus of the National Centre for Biological Sciences, one may as well be in a US academic campus. It is a young institute but is already known for its cutting-edge research and has leading figures from the world over as visitors.

Technology is just one aspect of Bangalore's new confidence. For a city to develop, it cannot be unmindful of culture and aesthetics. It is true that in the humanities and the social sciences Bangalore lags behind other Indian cities, and for better all-round development the state needs to invest more in these. But the arts are beginning to stir. Nrittyagram and next to it the Taj Hotel, Kuteeram—both founded as a single complex by the late Protima Bedi—are good examples of this. As a dance school, it seems to have fallen on hard times, with only the Odissi section now open and, somewhat short of students. But the whole structure, designed by the architect Gerard da Cunha, is an outstanding piece of art, drawing on India's folk traditions and art heritage. It is all built with cheap, local material, but the intellectual and aesthetic input that has gone into it is clearly very large. A sign of a nation's development is, I believe, its people learn the value of these inputs.

The high point of the new Bangalore is the headquarters of Infosys Technologies Limited on Hosur Road. The achievement of Infosys and its CEO, Narayana Murthy, has been written about extensively. We know about Infosys having created 400 dollar millionaires, its network of close to 10,000 workers[1] being spread over India, North America, and Europe, its clients being leading firms like Goldman Sachs, Cisco, Nestle, and DHL. To me what is most attractive about the vision behind Infosys is the combination of corporate excellence and basic human simplicity. At one of the coffee stalls inside the campus, young staffers move out to make way for their CEO, as Mr Murthy and I walk up for coffee. But Mr Murthy will have none of it. For lunch I am given a choice between the upmarket eating place associated with the boardroom and one of the large cafeterias where the young programmers eat. I opt for the latter, wondering if that will make Narayana Murthy uncomfortable. But he is completely at home in the cafeteria, eating amidst his employees. The place is spotlessly clean, the food is very good and simple.

In India, business is associated in the minds of most ordinary people with greed and the single-minded pursuit of lucre. That it can also be a pursuit of excellence, of social commitment and concern, and, most importantly, of creativity is what one learns at a place like this. If all businesses were run like this, India's attitude towards business would be different and it would have contributed to her economic progress.

One must not get an exaggerated sense of what has happened in Bangalore. It is still a tiny segment of the population that has benefited from the boom. Beyond the technology complexes on Hosur Road, the glitzy shops of MG Road, and the institutes of higher education,

---

[1] It is a testimony to the company's remarkable growth that the number of workers now (at the time of copy-editing this manuscript) is just short of 60,000.

Bangalore looks like any other city. The attention to detail that I encountered in the Infosys campus is certainly not yet the norm in the city.

One evening, in the Nagarbhavi area, feeling cavalier, I walked into a ramshackle restaurant and from among a wide selection of misspelled dishes I ordered the most intriguing, 'Fried pamphlet'. I was sufficiently hungry to risk eating a circular fried in batter. But I was lucky. The pomfret was delicious.

41

Muito Obrigado, Portugal*

'Is it expected to rain today?' I ask the liveried porter at our hotel. 'I' 'ope not, Sir', he replies. 'I also hope not. But *will* it rain today?' I persist, trying to find out the weather forecast. 'Sir, that is what I am telling you, I 'ope not.' I abandon my meteorological quest.

His hope turns out to be true. As we step out for our first day in Lisbon the weather is gorgeous, like the Delhi winters of my student days in the early 1970s, with blue skies and an invigorating nip in the air. Lisbon lies sparkling in the sun, like an old feudal mansion, jaded, gutted, overrun by crowded homes, but still undefeated and proud of its history. Castles jut out from hilltops and splendid marble statues with chipped edges adorn the piazzas.

Our first day is spent walking aimlessly in the city. Alfama, spread along the side of a hill, is a rundown old part of Lisbon, crisscrossed by narrow lanes. There one comes across old women leaning out of windows, chatting with their neighbours across the road, raising their voices freely to counter the sound of the breeze that coasts in from the Atlantic and the flutter of clothes drying on clotheslines flung across the lanes. The lanes give way in places to stairways, where there is a particularly steep slope to negotiate, and then, spectacularly, to the *miradours*—marble terraces, where the passerby can stop to view the ocean.

It was along this very sea that Vasco da Gama set out to discover India for Europe and raise Portugal from ignominy to a major

*First published in *India Today*, 7 May 2001.

European power. It was hunger for the gold and spices of the East and the urge to spread the word of God that propelled the Portuguese outwards, to Senegal, Sierra Leone, and, ultimately, India. In India they mastered the technique of controlling masses of natives, not by bringing in a large conquering army, but through an ingenious form of organization and managerial skill among a small number of 'ruling' Portuguese, thereby giving birth to the system of colonialism. The technique would soon be learnt by the British who would then outmanoeuvre the Portuguese.

One of India's continuing tragedies has been its failure to learn the importance of coordination and what may be called 'organizational capital'. When the 60,000-strong Indian army was defeated by Robert Clive's 3000 soldiers in 1757 in Plassey, the defeat could clearly not be put down to imbalance in numbers. Nor was it caused by an asymmetry of firepower or individual skills. According to historians, lack of co-ordination and loyalty made the Indian forces look not so much like a defending army as a rioting mob. It was essentially what in business schools today would be called an organizational failure. An English friend of mine once observed, after a visit to an Indian hospital, how he found the chasm between the immense talent of the doctors and the utter chaos of the hospital impossible to reconcile.

Our next stop is Porto, the world capital of the fortified wine, port. The street corners are full of little port shops where one can buy a bottle for anywhere between $5 and $500. The bottles of vintage port are dust-laden, the dust signalling their age, which can run into several decades. At the roadside alcohol shop in Patparganj, East Delhi, bottles manage to get the same dusty look within days—I wonder if the owner has thought of the export possibilities.

Porto reminds me of Calcutta, with its crowded streets, helpful people, and haphazard network of tram lines. One side of the city is marked by the river Douro and on the other side is the even more crowded suburb, Gaia.

We travel to other memorable towns: medieval Coimbra, with its stunningly beautiful university (and some stunning inhabitants thrown in for good measure); Evorra, with its Roman ruins and a city centre marked by a beautiful, forlorn square. In Evorra, just as I begin to feel that we have at last come to a place where the ubiquitous Indian has not reached, a lady in *salwar-kameez* walks up, looking completely at home. She is from Daman, she explains, sounding somewhat incomplete, for Daman never sounds right without 'and Diu'. She has been living in Evorra for many years now, running a small grocery shop with her husband, she explains in halting Hindi. She tells us little bits of her life in Evorra and, before that, in India. Pleased by this opportunity for nostalgia she breaks into the one language she is clearly comfortable in and thanks us profusely: 'Muito obrigado'.

On the last evening, after a late dinner, as we walk past the main railway station in Lisbon, the roads have become deserted. It is that time of the day when the plaza, with its few scattered remains of the day—a can, a single glove, a swirling newspaper—is a picture of desolation. A young, pleasing-looking African man folding up his pavement business of village crafts, stops on seeing us, smiles and breaks into, '*Main pal do pal ka shair hoon* . . .' He sings it perfectly—the complete song (without understanding a word, he later assures us), the lilting tune drifting into the emptying Praca Rossio. He is a refugee from Senegal, a fan of Hema Malini, saving money by selling wood and leather crafts from Senegal, because, he tells us, he wants to go to India, get married there, and live happily ever after.

42

Queuing in Kolkata and Delhi*

I

'The Registrar of Assurances, Government of West Bengal, Kolkata, Office of the Additional Registrar of Assurances III'. As I stand outside the office thus labelled, surveying the milling crowds and waiting for my turn, I have a sinking feeling that I am in a Kafka novel and will never be able to emerge from it.

I had sold a small property some time ago and the buyer asked me to accompany him and his lawyer to the Additional Registrar's Office to have the sale registered. I agreed, partly to be helpful and partly out of curiosity about how the bureaucracy works. That explains my predicament, though the thought of being here all day is beginning to make me regret the decision.

The building complex in Kolkata's office district, where the Additional Registrars' offices are situated, is interesting. There is an L-shaped building, twelve storeys high. On the open face of the L is another building, five-storeyed and crescent-shaped. These two buildings enclose a yard that looks like a truncated D. In that small yard someone has had the sense to plant leafy green trees—palm, and what to my botanically untrained eyes look like giant money-plants.

There are rows and rows of women sitting in the corridors of the crescent-shaped building, signing in people like me who are waiting to have a property transaction registered with the Offices of the Additional

*Based on 'Bureaucratic Musings', *Business Standard*, 9 April 2003 (Section I); and 'Queues and Capitalism', *BBC News Online*, 27 August 2004 (Section II).

Registrar III, and filling in ledgers while taking care not to have their elbows jogged by home buyers and registrars.

In the yard, mingling with the verdant plants, stand new home owners, sellers, merchants, chai-wallahs, property dealers, and lots and lots of lawyers in their black coats, creating the strange atmosphere of penguins in a tropical forest. Suddenly, a beggar walks into the yard. Carrying a trishul, locks tumbling down his forehead and back, wearing a yellow chador with black spots, he looks something between a godman and a leopard. The sight of the quasi-leopard causes commotion among the penguins, adding colour to the tropical forest.

When we are finally called, a clerk informs me that the entire power of attorney has to be retyped on 'boxed paper' before I sign. And he then goes off to take care of that. I wonder what 'boxed paper' refers to and am surprised to discover, when the clerk returns, that it refers to exactly that—sheets on which a grid of horizontal and vertical lines create little boxes. Curious, I ask him why it had to be done on *boxed* paper. He looks at me surprised and says 'because it is a government document' and smiles at the lawyer, who smiles back at him. I feel thoroughly foolish for not having figured this out myself.

A little later, the clerk shows up again and calls us all in. We furrow through the crowd to an office where a lady reads the sale agreement and initials every page. I ask her why she has to do this. I think she is deaf for there is absolutely no response from her. From the nail-biting of our lawyer, I figure the officer was checking the legalese of the document. We are then taken to the main person—I surmise the Additional Registrar III. Next to him is his assistant, with whom we have to interact; Additional Registrar III will merely sign the document finally. The assistant is a laconic man, who thrusts various sheets of paper marked with little crosses at me, each time with the single-word instruction 'Signature'. He then moves a pad of black ink to the centre of the table and says, 'Thumb', which is unnecessary because he catches my left thumb before I can do anything, presses it on the pad and guides it to other places to leave thumb impressions on the sale document and in his register.

Finally he says 'Wipe' and points to a piece of cloth lying on one corner of the table. The cloth is as black as the pad, having, no doubt, been used by scores of people before me. Not wanting to appear lily-livered I wipe my thumb with it, which emerges coal black from the encounter. I politely tell the assistant that they can save on ink if, half-way through each day, they put away the pad and begin using the cleaning cloth in its place. But I think he is deaf for there is absolutely no response from him.

I have to confess that, eventually, the experience turns out to be not as bad as I feared. Despite the Kafkaesque atmosphere, with minions going about their chores without knowing why they do what they do, and with no one seeming to be fully in charge, the whole process takes less than two hours and no one asks for a bribe. It may have just been my lucky day, or maybe the Kolkata administration has improved in recent times. Just possibly, palms have been greased by the buyer of my property in advance of our arrival at Additional Registrar III. I have not investigated this enough to know the answer.

Nevertheless, the point remains that we still have a great distance to go and must not slide into the complacence of thinking we're doing better than Myanmar and Sierra Leone. India needs to work relentlessly to cut bureaucracy, bureaucratic delays and transactions costs. There are extreme laissez-faire economists who argue for the removal of government from the domain of markets and exchange. But that is utterly naïve. As George Soros remarks in *On Globalization*, markets are extremely important but markets cannot run on their own; and government is needed not just for law and order but for 'the maintenance of the market mechanism itself'. This is the hard truth; there is no escape from government. We cannot banish it; we just have to make it work.

Many economists studying informal credit markets in India argue that the single-most important reason for formal bank credit not mak-ing enough inroads into rural areas is the absence of proper land regis-tration records. If a person cannot show government-certified legal documents for his land, he cannot use it as collateral for borrowing money from a bank and is forced to rely on informal rural networks. Hence, unless the registration of sales is done properly, which is the task of government, the credit market cannot function efficiently. This simple example illustrates well the intimate relation between government and market. It shows that if governance is good, the burden of development does not have to fall on the exchequer; the market can automatically take over much of the task.

India's government is so cumbersome and slow that there is room for great improvement here. This is the ironic reason why, even if the world goes into a slump, India can in principle continue to grow. It can do this by releasing resources caught in its bureaucratic black holes, which make India function much below its true capacity. But to release these resources requires a commitment, in the highest offices of government, to study the layers of bureaucracy that have developed over the years and then to take concrete steps to rationalize the system and make it efficient.

II

Some years ago, as I drove into the city from Calcutta airport, there was an initiative to make people stand in queues when waiting. I do not know if the initiative came from government or some citizens' group, but there were volunteers with loudspeakers urging anarchic gatherings of men and women at bus stops to 'stand in a line'. I wondered if these Samaritans knew that attempts to make the citizens of this great city stand in queues had started in earnest from the time of Robert Clive in the mid-eighteenth century. The British were roundly defeated.

The 'Indian queue' is indeed a fascinating subject for sociological analysis. Arriving in New Delhi in July 2004, my wife and I discovered that our Indian driving licences had expired. The last time I renewed my licence in Delhi, in 1989, there were jostling touts everywhere; and 'doctors' by the dozen accosted you, promising certificates for good eyesight for a fee and 'irrespective of your eye condition'—as a particularly kind 'ophthalmologist' assured me. Anybody curious about how a completely free market, with no trace of governance, works should have been there.

Now, more than a decade later, we mustered up courage and went to the Road Transport Office in Anand Vihar. The first sight was not reassuring. The sky was ablaze with a copper sun, though the weather office had forecast 'the possibility of rain', with the further, completely unnecessary, qualifier, 'in some areas'. There was a small courtyard, around which were barrack-like rooms with awnings cleverly made of asbestos to draw all the available sun and make the throngs in the courtyard look like characters in a Bosch painting.

However, I was glad to see that there were proper queues. We were directed to the ones at window 17A for 'ladies and senior citizens' and 17B for 'men'. My queue was long but there was never a dull moment for me: I was kept busy dodging the paunch of the man behind me. I was irked initially but reminded myself that many people pay to have their lumbars massaged. Moreover, one had to understand that the 'paunch to lumbar' queue (the analogue of what in the automotive world constitutes 'bumper to bumper' traffic) has evolved over the ages to keep at bay transgressors looking for breaks in the queue.

There is always interesting conversation to be overheard in queues. But in this case it quickly turned to moral philosophy. A man behind me noticed that my wife was in the adjacent, faster-moving queue, and remarked—'If your wife is there, it is lawful for you to join her in that queue', as if quoting from some ancient treatise.

Others behind me joined in, some going so far as to assert that it was incumbent on a man to be in a 'ladies' queue' whenever accompanied by a woman. As I was about to give in to the temptation of crossing over to 17A, a murmur of protest started up among the women and elderly behind my wife. They were of the view that I should be in 17B. One of them even wondered if my wife had not forfeited her right to be in 17A by virtue of having her husband in 17B. The wisdom I gained from this colloquium on rights and obligations was that individual rationality was alive and well in India.

In any case we were out of there in less than two hours with our re-newed licences, which seemed an improvement on my previous experience.

There has also been some improvement in the 'virtual queues' that were such a part of Indian life. When, after completing my studies in London, I returned to India in 1977, I joined two virtual queues. I applied for a telephone connection and for accommodation in Delhi University housing. There were long queues for both and I, partly out of sloth and partly out of not knowing otherwise, did nothing to hasten my turn.

It was impressive when six years later I got a letter from the telephone authorities, thanking me matter-of-factly for my application and telling me that my phone line had been sanctioned, and even more impressive when, in 1994, a few weeks after I had left India for a job in the US, a letter came from Delhi University informing me that an apartment was ready for my use.

One reason why queues are important to economics is that they provide an alternative to the price mechanism. Suppose an organization owns a limited number of some 'good'—seats to a concert, for instance. How does it allocate these to the large number of people wanting them? One way is to raise the price of the good to the point where the number of people still demanding the product is equal to the number of units available.

The other is to allow a queue to form. As the queue becomes longer, the cost of waiting will deter more and more people from wanting the good, and a point is eventually reached where demand equals supply. Many observers therefore consider prices and queues as alternatives.

But they miss out on one crucial difference. Both methods use 'cost' to curtail demand. In a price- or market-based system the cost borne by the buyer is, however, not a cost to society because it consists of a *transfer* of money from him to the seller; but in the queue-based system the cost is a loss to *society*, since the time spent in a queue is no one's gain.

This is the essence of why markets are considered efficient. Of course, one cannot be unmindful of the fact that markets can exacerbate poverty, and so we may have to design controls to prevent this. But the widespread resort to allocation by queuing that the bureaucracy tends to do is not in general a good idea.

43

Viewing Bengal from Bankura*

Dating back over 150 years, with heavy wooden doors, ceilings reaching into the skies, a sprawling verandah overlooking a yard with ancient banyan trees, the Circuit House in Bankura is a curious mixture of the Raj and independent India. The latter adorns the wall in the form of portraits of artists like Ramkinkar Baij and Jamini Roy, and the bookshelves, where tomes left behind unwittingly by visiting bureaucrats (*Do-it-Yourself Plumbing and Heating*, *The Economic Development of India* by Brian Davey) rub shoulders with those that may not be there quite as purposelessly, for, read carefully, they could just win the CPM a few more adherents among the vulnerable: *Das Capital*, three volumes, and the collected works of V.I. Lenin.

My visit to Bankura and, just before that, to the Sunderbans had nothing to do with tourism. It was driven by curiosity. On most indices of development, Bengal is trailing. Its rank, on India's interstate scorecard, has slid not just in terms of per capita income but even on social indices such as literacy, morbidity, and the progress of higher education. Talk to a random person in Kolkata and he will tell you the disaster that the CPM government has been for the state. How then does one explain the CPM's electoral popularity and unwavering rural support? It is this conundrum that compelled me to cut into my Kolkata vacation and travel.

Bankura's terracotta horses, elephants, and other artifacts are known the world over. But hardly anyone knows of Panchmura, one of the

*First published in *The Telegraph*, 14 January 2004.

primary villages in which these are crafted. After spending a while talking to the artisans who produce these works, we drove to the village of Taldangra. Here we spent a long time talking to villagers and, in particular, to the *pradhan*, Sagar Goswami, the *upa-pradhan*, Sandhya Mondal, and several members of the *gram panchayat*. During this conversation and also from talking to various people in the block development officer (BDO)'s office in Dhokra, one thing that became clear was the left-front government's policy of inclusiveness in rural areas. The attempt has been to reach out to all communities and caste groups. Ordinary Muslims, poor Hindus, the Scheduled Castes and adivasis that we spoke to told us how panchayat members came to their homes, ate with them, visited them during their festivities and rarely discriminated on grounds of religion and caste.

One of the panchayat members we talked to, Ajit Basuli, was a peasant farmer. Well versed in global politics, he argued with me about intellectual property rights and international labour laws. While he clearly took the party line on most matters, it was impossible not to be impressed by his personal simplicity and commitment to the poor, irrespective of their religion or caste. He has learned the language of the Santhals, written a play in that language, and spoke passionately about the importance of mankind's common human identity. A part of this may well be politics, but I also know that not all politicians speak like this. This kind of behaviour must have helped keep the winds of fascism from the state.

It has been remarked, and I am sure that there is truth in this, that there is discrimination against those who are not members of the CPM. This is deplorable of course, but not as bad as discrimination against people for some *innate* characteristic of theirs, such as race or religion. Faced with *party*-based discrimination, people can at least pretend to be sympathetic to the party. Indeed this is happening in rural Bengal; far more people claim to be Communists than are Communists or have a clue about what Communism is.

One notable quality of the left-front administration that I could see in the Sunderbans and in Bankura District is its commitment to the poor and its relatively open decision-making process. The commitment to the poor one would expect from a left-wing party. What is surprising is the democratic openness, especially since the world's most important Communist nations failed so miserably in this regard. Here, people seem to have a voice in the projects that are undertaken. And, further, this is what has curbed runaway corruption and helped prop support for the left front.

The left front's symbols are visible in rural Bengal in a way unimaginable in Calcutta. The Communist Party's official newspaper, *Ganashakti*, is easier to get hold of than the *Ananda Bazar Patrika*. Its pages are pasted on public boards for people to read. The symbols and slogans of the party leave little space on mud walls for locally favourite films like *Boumaar Bonobaash*. This propaganda blitz is also testimony to the organization and reach of the party and the panchayat. No other party in India has this kind of rural organization.

This is what makes Bengal's overall poor performance a tragedy. With such well-developed grassroots organization, and so many committed party workers, why has the state failed economically? The answer is simple: commitment by itself is not good enough. A group of people—whether they be social workers or political activists—genuinely interested in helping the poor can do some good, true, but in *overall* effect they cannot match the benefits that can come from a bunch of entrepreneurs and industrialists who may have no interest in poverty removal but who set up factories and firms to maximize their profits. The heightened demand for labour that comes from a vibrant industry, and the consequent (unintended but inevitable) increase in the bargaining power of labourers, can rarely be matched by merely providing direct financial and rhetorical support to workers, no matter how earnest the support.

It is the failure to understand this principle that explains Bengal's trailing economy; and this is what distinguishes India's and China's Communists. The Chinese figured this out in the 1970s. They realized that the laws of economics are like the laws of nature; they have to be understood from the observation of facts and the use of reason. Ideology may help shape our values and objectives but it has absolutely no role in understanding the link between policies and their effects. In the world as it stands today, if a particular country or region wants to prosper it needs to attract industrialists, multinationals, and entrepreneurs.

This realization does not come easily to a political party, left or right, when it is not just moored but mired in a fixed ideology. Such moorings usually lead to a reflexive tendency to blindly defend a position rather than check it out against facts. This emerges clearly from Eric Hobsbawm's autobiography, which is also a magisterial, if personal, history of twentieth-century Communism. Writing about his fellow Communist, the charismatic Rajni Palme Dutt, he observes: '[The] night he spent in my house in Cambridge . . . had left me with a lasting admiration for his acute mind and a lasting conviction that he was not interested in truth, but used his intellect exclusively to justify and explicate the line of the moment.' I believe that China's 'adaptation' of Communism came from its good fortune of having a few creative leaders who realized the plain truth and had the gumption to carry the cadres with them.

I do not know if there are such leaders here. But, given the organizational advantage that the left-front government in West Bengal currently has, and the relatively greater honesty of its leaders, if it can break away from its ideological shackles and change its industrial policy, it can, I have no doubt, be one of the fastest growing regions of the world.

44

Loitering in Lahore*

It is welcome news that flights are resuming between India and Pakistan, and a pity this did not happen a few months earlier. I had to first fly for nearly four hours to Dubai, and then back three hours to Lahore.

As I gathered my bags in my Delhi apartment to leave for the airport, I must confess to a slight feeling of nervousness mixed with excitement. I was going to Lahore to give a lecture on globalization. An American economist who knows Pakistan well told me not to be too excited about the lecture because only half my audience would be professional economists; the other half a combination of Taliban without beards and CIA agents with.

Lahore International Airport at 2 a.m. does nothing to alleviate one's misgivings. Rundown, with cavernous hallways, the clanking sound of large, rusty luggage trolleys, and a slight medicinal aroma of detergents, it has the air of a police station. The immigration officer takes my passport and the special papers that Indians entering Pakistan are meant to carry, and looks puzzled. She has never 'handled an Indian case' and leans over to a colleague. They confer, send for the supervisor, and then in a short while I am out of the airport.

Pearl Continental Hotel, in the heart of the city, is all colonial splendour. When I check in at 4 a.m., a wedding party has just broken up. Young Pakistani men with jelled hair and smart outfits, and beautiful women, several in saris and with henna on their hands, mill around, chatting, laughing and generally having a good time.

*First published in *Business Standard*, 7 May 2003.

At 10 in the morning the phone rings and I wake up with a start. It is a student from Lahore University of Management Science, phoning to ask if, as I had told the organizers of the conference by email, I still wanted to explore the city. The morning sun is strong, the air bracing and soon I am out with some student escorts and visiting economists to see Lahore. The next three days, in between conference sessions, before dinner banquets and late at night, I spend time in the alleyways of old Lahore, at the kebab and tea stalls on Gawal Mandi, looking at art in the more notorious Heera Mandi, and the colonial Mall Road.

As so much Indian writing testifies, Lahore was once a hub of culture; it was a cosmopolitan city of many religions and people. But successive rounds of military dictatorship and a steady rise in religious fundamentalism, especially after 9/11, has meant that Lahore's free-floating style and cultural activism has had a setback. It has not been driven out, but reduced to subversion. Hunting contemporary art I discover a vibrant world that survives only by not drawing too much attention to itself. The best example of this is the art of Iqbal Hussain. Hussain gained prominence when his one-man exhibition in Lahore's Alhamra Arts Council was cancelled hours before the opening ceremony because of his obsession with fallen women and women without *dupattas* (scarves). But his obsession is not difficult to understand. He was born in 1950 in the ghettos of Heera Mandi—the red light district of Lahore, named after Heera Singh, a favourite of the nineteenth-century Maharaja of Lahore. His mother was a 'professional', he never knew his father. He is a painter with consummate skill for capturing human pathos; and with his interest in the underworld and the defeated, his art is reminiscent of Lautrec and Hodler. There are other artists of breathtaking intensity—Colin David, Saeed Akhtar, Ghulam Rasul, and Shaheed Jalal. And, talking of the Lahore School, one cannot but mention B.C. Sanyal, who was one of the most important founding members of that school, though he later left for India.

I did not manage to meet Iqbal Hussain but ended up meeting all kinds of artists and people from various walks of life. Everywhere I went, even when I was introduced as 'an Indian, who lives in America', a 'Hindu', all I got was affection and warmth. Shopkeepers in the old Anarkali Bazaar told me about relatives in India, a cobbler polishing my shoes asked if cobblers could get visas to America. There were tensions indeed in our conversation when the subject of Kashmir came up. But anger was reserved for only one topic: Iraq.

Modern women, cursing the fundamentalists for having 'driven us into our homes', mullahs with their traditional robes, peddlars with little knowledge of the world beyond, all seemed united on one matter. The US had no *moral* reason to attack Iraq and then to decide what a 'democratic' Iraq must choose. The most chilling argument I heard was from an old man selling books in the bazaar: the lesson for Pakistan is clear. It should develop its nuclear weapons and missiles quickly, while good relations with the US last, because possessing a large amount of weaponry and delivery systems, as China and maybe North Korea do, is to be safe. Iraq's mistake was that it did not have enough weapons.

I was much taken by the charms of Lahore and its people. But I was also left with some sadness. Thanks to the fear factor—much of it exaggerated—that makes foreigners and people of other religions scarce, Lahore—and I am sure this holds for Pakistan as a whole—has become very homogeneous in terms of ethnicity, religion, and language. Landing in Delhi and seeing, once again, Western hippies with rucksacks, and Hindus, Muslims, and Christians, and listening to a babble of languages, I felt grateful that India has remained such an open society.

Till a few years ago Pakistan had a higher per capita income than India. But no longer is that true. The pressures of fundamentalism, causing the tendency to build protective walls and have a closed society, are beginning to leave their scars on the economy. I do not think the common person wants this—the people I interacted with certainly did not. But the confluence of history, global developments, which are beyond Pakistan's control, and the machinations of a small number of religious extremists is taking Pakistan inexorably and against its own wishes towards this predicament.

Seeing this made me realize what a pity it would be if Hindu extremists got their way and put an end to the openness and diversity that is the hallmark of India. What is tragic about Hindu fundamentalists is that, while proclaiming pride in India, they act in a way which reveals a sense of rivalry *vis-à-vis* the very groups they criticize. Consider the common Hindu nationalist's argument: since Pakistan is an Islamic state, why should India not be a Hindu one? What this misses out on is that, to opt for theocracy in India *because* Pakistan is theocratic, is to mimic Pakistan. It needs greater self-confidence to say that, no matter what Pakistan does, we will stay with our openness and diversity.

45

Thinking about Currencies in Kathmandu*

One of the first signs that greets arriving passengers at Kathmandu's Tribhuvan Airport instructs them to 'first clear immigration before you pass out'. On a recent trip to Nepal I fully appreciated the airport authority's concern. Thanks to the bumpy flight over the Himalayas, one does feel somewhat light in the head as one conducts oneself through the rites of entering the country.

I took to Nepal quickly. It is beautiful; the people lack intrigue; the artwork on building façades and *thangkas* is exquisite. Besides, there is much to occupy an economist's attention—the haggling in the bazaars, the attitude to money and work among auto-drivers and roadside entrepreneurs, the stratagems and irrationalities in gambling parlours, and, most remarkably, the economy's ability to effortlessly switch between two currencies. Buy a yak-bone sculpture, have a meal at Rum Doodles (highly recommended), or take a taxi. Everywhere you have the choice of paying in Nepalese or Indian rupees.

This is a textbook case of 'currency substitution' or 'dollarization', where one economy accepts another's currency for its day-to-day transactions. This need have nothing to do with the dollar—though it often does. For instance, Panama has no national currency of significance. It runs on American money. It is true that it saves on running a central monetary authority, but the policy makes Panama vulnerable

*First published in *India Today*, 6 October 1997.

to the actions of the American Fed. In times of crisis, the US is able to hold its economy to ransom, as Ronald Reagan did quite mercilessly during his showdown with General Manuel Noriega.

Less extreme cases of currency substitution happen all the time, as in Nepal. India has, on the other hand, overdone its phobia of other currencies. This has protected us from international crisis but it has also contributed to keeping our exports low and economy poor. In a modern economy, one should be able to move from one currency to another with ease. Hence, the recent talk of moving to a convertible rupee is welcome.

But there are few subjects on which so much is written with so little understanding. The best way to grasp the idea is to consider the extreme case. We would say that the rupee is 'fully convertible' if Indian law permitted individuals to freely exchange rupees with other currencies and hold any financial or other assets they wished in any location. This full convertibility can be broken up into two categories. If in a nation people are allowed to move from one currency to another for the purpose of buying goods and services, then we say that the nation has 'current account convertibility'. If people are allowed to change currency in order to buy capital assets, such as bonds, shares, and property, then the nation has 'capital account convertibility' (CAC). Thus, if India had CAC, a company (Indian or foreign) owning shares in India would have the freedom to sell the shares, change the rupees into yen, and move the money out of India.

What is disturbing is the confidence with which people take up positions in favour of or against CAC. In truth, this is one area where there is a preponderance of uncertainty. The advantages of CAC are many. Suppose interest rates in Singapore become very high. Americans, Europeans, and the Japanese will immediately divert some of their savings to Singapore and profit. But Indians cannot, thanks to our not having CAC.

Yet CAC has its risks. As exchange rates and interest rates fluctuate, there can be large, sudden outflows of foreign exchange. Till the rupee establishes itself globally as a reasonably hard currency, such outflows can affect the economy adversely. In addition, once people are allowed to hold non-rupee assets, there will be some of the same costs associated with dollarization that are seen in Nepal. There is, for instance, the cost of 'seignorage'—of giving up real goods and services to acquire foreign currency.

Despite these risks, we need to move gradually towards CAC; what is ideal for India is near-CAC rather than full-CAC. The more pressing problem is that we do not still have current account convertibility, despite official claims to the contrary. Walk into a bureau of exchange in, say, Delhi and ask them to change Rs 1000 into pounds. You will typically be given a booklet of rules, an A2 form, and asked for proof that you are taking the pounds for legitimate purposes (and there are very few of those). The government justifies this, saying it has to ensure you will not invest the pounds in an English bank or in some other illegal activity.

Every country has restrictions on what you can buy. But if the check is executed at the place of exchange, then, in the name of monitoring, the government will end up thwarting current account convertibility. Japan does not allow its citizens to buy drugs but it does not try to ensure this by setting up checks at bank counters. Instead, it punishes a person caught with drugs.

India needs to move towards greater currency convertibility. This could cause a depreciation of the rupee but there is little to be gained by keeping the rupee value high by artificially preventing people from buying other currencies. Moreover, such depreciation can give our exports a much-needed boost.

Index

('t' indicates table; 'n' indicates footnote)

Lightning Source UK Ltd.
Milton Keynes UK
08 January 2010

148282UK00001B/47/P